LETTERS TO W. B. YEATS

LETTERS
TO
W. B. YEATS

VOLUME I

edited by

RICHARD J. FINNERAN

GEORGE MILLS HARPER

WILLIAM M. MURPHY

with the assistance of
Alan B. Himber

Columbia University Press
New York   1977

Selection and editorial matter copyright © 1977 Richard J. Finneran,
George Mills Harper and William M. Murphy
All rights reserved

Published in Great Britain in 1977 by THE MACMILLAN PRESS LTD

Printed in Great Britain

Library of Congress Cataloging in Publication Data
Main entry under title:

Letters to W. B. Yeats.

Includes index.
1. Yeats, William Butler, 1865—1939 — Correspond-
ence. 2 Poets, Irish — 20th century — Correspond-
ence. I. Yeats, William Butler, 1865—1939.
II. Finneran, Richard J. III. Harper, George
Mills. IV. Murphy, William Michael, 1916—
PR5906.A63   1977   821'.8 [B]   77—5645
ISBN 0-231-04424-0 (v. 1)
      0-231-04425-9 (v. 2)

TO BOBBIE HARPER

Contents

Preface

A considerable portion of Yeats's busy life was spent in carrying on a voluminous correspondence with friends, admirers, publishers, fellow students of occult orders, Irish nationalists, members of his family, et al. And he no doubt received far more letters than he wrote. Because he was aware of his own importance in literary and political circles Yeats began preserving letters while he was still a young man. He frequently noted across the top of the first page that many of them were 'answered', and he sometimes indicated what they were to be filed under. At some stage, probably after marriage, he began keeping the letters in large brown manila envelopes with names and headings written across the flaps. Although hundreds of letters were thus preserved, there is reason to believe that many more — in the main those that he received away from home — are now lost. The extent of these lost letters is suggested by the number of Yeats's letters, usually in answer, preserved in the papers of several of his correspondents —for example, W. T. Horton and W. F. Stead. Yeats's failure to preserve these letters represents a serious loss to literary, social, and political history.

Of course, the selections in these volumes are only a small portion of the total number of letters to Yeats preserved in the library of Senator Michael B. Yeats, the New York Public Library, the Berg Collection, and some few other collections. We wrote letters of enquiry to the chief libraries of Ireland, Great Britain, and America, but did not attempt an exhaustive search. Although we have consciously selected letters from a considerable number of people writing over a broad chronological span (1886–1939), our chief criteria were, first, to represent the range of Yeats's interests and, second, to imply through letters from artists, writers, and critics the development of Yeats's aesthetic. Unfortunately, for a variety of reasons, we have been unable to include letters from numerous writers and friends: from Eliot, Joyce, Synge, O'Casey, and Lady Gregory, because comprehensive editions of their letters are published or in progress; from Pound, chiefly because all but a few and those not the best have been published.

Although it is our intent and hope that this collection should consist entirely of letters never before published *in toto*, we are aware that some few may already be in print. We are also aware that passages from a sizeable number of them have been quoted in books and periodicals which we have not cited. Because we have attempted to include as many letters as possible we have kept the headnotes succinct, and we have avoided identifying well-known names and titles referred to 'in the letters as well as the sources of many brief quotations in our notes.

In order to keep the editorial apparatus to a minimum, we have adopted the following policies: because misspellings, ungrammatical constructions, and the absence of standard punctuation marks often project the character of the writer, we have, with few exceptions, avoided the use of *sic*; we have occasionally corrected misspellings of common words, titles, and names (especially if they appear in typed letters and if they are spelled correctly elsewhere in the same letters); in some few instances we have supplied paragraph indention, chiefly when we could not be certain of the author's intention; finally, we have used brackets very sparingly, chiefly to supply words necessary for clarity rather than to suggest uncertainty with transcription, though some few words have defied our best efforts.

We have used the following abbreviations in the headnotes: *L* for *The Letters of W. B. Yeats*, ed. Allan Wade (New York: The Macmillan Co., 1955) and SPR for The Society for Psychical Research.

Acknowledgements

Like most scholarly works relying on many sources of information and assistance, this edition of letters represents a communal effort. Indeed, it would not have been possible without the approval, co-operation, and hospitality of Miss Anne Yeats and of Senator Michael B. Yeats and family. We are grateful also for the assistance of Dr Patrick Henchy, Director of the National Library of Ireland, and Dr Lola Szladits, Curator of the Berg Collection, New York Public Library. We are indebted to several other libraries for supplying copies of letters: those of the University of Chicago (Harriet Monroe), the University of Kansas (T. W. Rolleston and A. E. F. Horniman), the University of Missouri (William Rothenstein), the New York Public (John Quinn), the Bodleian, Oxford (Robert Bridges), and Yale University (F. P. Sturm and William Sharp). We are grateful to Dr Ian Fletcher, University of Reading, for copies of letters from Frank J. Fay; and to Dr John Kelly, co-editor of the projected comprehensive edition of Yeats's letters, for assistance with names and addresses of executors.

The editors and publishers also wish to thank the following copyright-holders for permission to publish the letters from the people named in parentheses: Miss Pegeen Mair (Sara Allgood); Lady Anne Lytton and the Fitzwilliam Museum (Wilfred Scawen Blunt); Roger Lancelyn Green (Gordon Bottomley); Lord Bridges (Robert Bridges); Dr William H. Button, Jr (William H. Button); Miss Collins and A. P. Watt & Son (G. K. Chesterton); Mrs Austin Clarke (Austin Clarke); Emmet M. Greene (Padraic Colum); James B. Conant; Smt. Rukimi Devi Arundale (James Cousins); H. Edward Robert Craig (Edward Gordon Craig); the Society of Authors as the literary representative of the Estate of the late Walter de la Mare; Carl Dolmetsch (Arnold Dolmetsch); Mrs Dolly L. Robinson (Edward Dowden); Dame Marie Rambert (Ashley Dukes); Mrs Geraldine Anderson (Edmund Dulac); G. W. Paget (Florence Farr Emery); the Society of Authors as the literary representative of the Estate of the late St John Ervine; Stephen Fay (Frank Fay); The Hon. Mrs Basil Feilding (Everard Feilding); Mme Janice Biala (Ford Madox Ford); the Society of Authors as the literary representive of the Estate of the late E. M. Forster; David Garnett (Edward Garnett); Richard Garnett (Richard Garnett); Patrick Campbell (Lord Glenavy); Oliver

D. Gogarty (Oliver St John Gogarty); Miss Jennifer Gosse (Edmund Gosse); A. P. Watt & Son (Robert Graves); Mrs T. G. Moorhead (Stephen Gwynn); Dr A. R. B. Haldane and the National Library of Scotland (Lord Haldane); Dr Edgar M. Ross (Frank Harris); Public Trustee Office, London (Annie E. F. Horniman); Miss P. H. K. G. Hull (Eleanor Hull); Executor & Trustee Department, Allied Irish Banks Ltd (Douglas Hyde); Laura (Riding) Jackson; Anne Wyndham Lewis (Wyndham Lewis); Nicholas C. Lindsay (Vachel Lindsay); The Hon. Clayre Ridley (Sir Edwin Lutyens); Michael Maclagan (Sir Eric Maclagan); Ethel Mannin; T. M. Farmiloe, Macmillan (Thomas Mark); the Society of Authors as the literary representative of the Estate of the late John Masefield; Mrs Elizabeth Ryan and Mrs Margaret Farrington (Thomas McGreevy); John C. Moberly (Charlotte Anne Elizabeth Moberly); Mrs Marguerite Foster Fetcher (Harriet Monroe); J. C. Medley (George Moore); Miss Riette Sturge Moore and D. C. Sturge Moore (T. Sturge Moore); Mrs Julian Vinogradoff (Ottoline Morrell); Alexander Murray (Gilbert Murray); Dr Michael Solomons (Seumas O'Sullivan); Lady Elizabeth Pelham, now Lady Elizabeth Beazley; Jay Michael Barrie, Executor, Estate of Gerald Heard (Horace Plunkett); J. W. R. Purser (Louis C. Purser); Dr Thomas F. Conroy (John Quinn); The Hon. Mrs P. D. Gill (Elizabeth Radcliffe); Miss V. van Straubenzee (Margaret Radcliffe); Mrs Dolly L. Robinson (Lennox Robinson); Mrs Honor Drysdale (T. W. Rolleston); Mrs Lisa Rossi (Mario M. Rossi); Sir John Rothenstein (Sir William Rothenstein); Diarmuid Russell (George W. Russell); Miss Jemina Pitman (J.S. Sargent); Omar S. Pound (Olivia Shakespear); Noel F. Sharp (William and Elizabeth Sharp); by permission of the Trustees of the Will of Mrs Bernard Shaw (Charlotte F. Shaw); the Society of Authors as the literary representative of the Estate of the late G. B. Shaw; Mrs Sylvia Strong (L. A. G. Strong); Maxwell Sturm (Franklin Pearce Sturm); P. C. Gupta (Rabindranath Tagore); Miss Pamela Hinkson (Katharine Tynan Hinkson); Miss Sybil Waite (Arthur Edward Waite); Geoffrey Nigel Watkins (John M. Watkins); Michael B. Yeats (Elizabeth Corbet Yeats, Jack B. Yeats, John Butler Yeats, and Susan Mary Yeats).

The editors and publishers have made every effort, but have failed, to trace the other copyright-holders concerned, and would be happy to make necessary arrangements at the first opportunity. We wish also to recognize our unacknowledged debt to hundreds of editors and authors whose books have supplied countless factual details.

Finally, the editors are indebted to several agencies and foundations for financial assistance without which the research for these volumes would have been much more difficult: to Professor Finneran a Grant-in-Aid from the American Council of Learned Societies (1973–4) and a Grant for Postdoctoral Research from the American Philosophical Society (1976); to Professor Harper for two grants for research support (1973–5) from the Graduate School of Florida State University and a Fellowship from the National Endowment for the Humanities (1976–7); to Professor Murphy a Fellowship from the American Council of Learned Societies (1968) and two grants from The American Philosophical Society (1968, 1975).

List of Correspondents

The Letters

From JACK B. YEATS

Sligo, Ireland
MS Yeats   [*ca.* 1886]

[John Butler Yeats, Jr (usually known as Jack B.) was a distinguished painter and the author of numerous pixieish plays, novels, and poems. *Mosada* was published in *The Dublin University Review* (June 1886) and also in a separate offprint the same year. Both he and W. B. liked Uncle George Pollexfen. Like most of Jack's letters this one is illustrated with pen sketches.]

My dear Willy

If you have a copy of the *Mosada* or any other thing that has been published you ought to send it to Uncle George.

The sketch at the top is supposed to illustrate an extract from a novel called Bill Sticker the Gorey. Bill has captured a man of war and when he enters the cabin he says to the steward, "Quail." The steward being a punster asks if grouse wouldn't do to which Bill replies, "You shall die the fit death for all jokers. You shall be (c;h)oked." So ended the relentless joker.

Bear and for bear.

Hoping all are well, I remain

Your loving brer
JACK

From EDWARD DOWDEN

Dublin
MS National Library of Ireland   28 January 1889

[The novel in progress was probably *John Sherman*. Ellen Terry, famous London actress, played the lead in A. C. Calmour's *The Amber Heart* (opened at Lyceum on 21 June 1887). Bram Stoker was touring manager and secretary for Sir Henry Irving, distinguished Shakespearean actor. Dr John Todhunter's review appeared in *The Academy* on 30 March 1889. Although Morris was "greatly pleased with *Oisin*", his promised review in *Commonweal* never appeared. Sir Edward Burne-Jones was a well-known Pre-Raphaelite painter. William Watson, prominent poet of the nineties, was knighted in 1917.]

My dear Yeats,

It gave me great pleasure to get your volume of poems, & to get it from yourself, & to see it a fact accomplished, & last to read it from cover to cover. I do not think there is a page in it which has not its own beauty, & there is also a kind of unity in the whole book, which perhaps it might have lost if you had added larger poems of more recent date. A great many were already familiar to me, & I think it is a good sign of your quality that I remembered them so well. I decidedly think the "Wanderings of Oisin" the best thing in the volume, but I wish you had made the book a little larger so as to include the whole of the "Island of Statues." Fragments are very provoking & somewhat illegitimate things. (Except when Time is the sculptor of the torso.) I do not expect to get from you as good Fairy poetry in any future volume. You will I suppose advance rather in the direction of the poetry of human romance and passion. Someone, I forget who, told me that you are writing a novel. What I should like you to do would be to write a poetical play specially for Ellen Terry—something infinitely better than "The Amber Heart" in which she was so graceful last year. It is probable that through Bram Stoker you could get anything fairly considered. The field for the poetical drama seems virtually open at present. For Ellen Terry it should not be tragic & it should end happily.

I am glad that Todhunter is to review your book in "The Academy." But you must not be surprised or greatly care if the public only shows a liking within certain narrow limits for such a poem as your *Oisin*. I hope you will send a copy to William Morris who ought to like it if Socialism has not perverted his imagination, & you ought to send one to Burne Jones.

I have no notion of where Watson is at present. He was in London, but went to Southport before Christmas, & I haven't heard from him since. When I learn his whereabouts I will let you know.

In a few cases my ear is offended by neighbouring rhymes which have too much in common e g : p 3 *shell* & *fell* near *rill* & *still*, & on p 2 the final *d* in stee*d* so*d* mea*d* sho*d*. I am glad to prove my critical value by alleging a fault, which you could probably prove a merit.

Remember me most kindly to your father & believe me

Sincerely yours

E. DOWDEN

From J. T. NETTLESHIP

London

MS Yeats   2 April 1889

[A painter and a friend of Yeats's father, he is referring to *The Wanderings of Oisin* (Jan 1889). On 10 April Yeats wrote to Katharine Tynan: "I enclose a letter from Nettleship which please keep safe, as I value it much" (*L* 121). Nettleship is speaking of the "2nd and 3rd parts" of the title poem and of Yeats's brother Jack.]

My dear Yeats

There can be no doubt that the title poem of your book is a new birth in poetry; it has come at the right time, because it had to come; criticism of it would be futile, because it is a real creation which must stand or fall by its own nature, and not by any outside supports or blows. That is the way I speak of it to myself, and I may as well say it to you —

I revel in the whole of it, myself, its whole framework as well as its smallest detail of phrasing; another man may pass it by or hate it, but I should have felt the same had I never heard your name.

I suppose you think the 2d & 3d parts stronger than the first, and it reads as if there had been a pause in you after the first part was written, there is a difference in tissue; am I right.

The whole book is a revelation to me, a new thing in the gift of speech, but I won't talk anymore in detail about it just now, being rather tired; will you come and see me again sometime when you are at the Museum or in the neighbourhood?

Please give my love to your father and my best remembrances to your mother and your sisters and Jack and

Believe me yours gratefully always

J. T. NETTLESHIP

From LIONEL JOHNSON

London

MS Yeats   26 October 1892

[Yeats had apparently asked for review copies of books for libraries to be established in the country districts of Ireland. *The Countess Kathleen and Various Legends and Lyrics* had been published in September; Johnson's very favourable review appeared in *The Academy* (1 Oct 1892), the "notice of the Countess" in *Saturday Review* (22 Oct). Nora Vynne was the editor of *Woman and Progress*. Edwin J. Ellis and Yeats were preparing their three-volume edition of *The Works of William Blake* (1893).]

My dear Yeats,

I am afraid, I have no books just at present to part with: I have done little reviewing of late, and have already got rid of my last batch of unnecessary books. And I fear that I know of no reviewer sufficiently patriotic, and not too poverty-stricken, to be of any use. But I will put the wants of Ireland in mind, both as regards myself and others. Would a paragraph in some of the literary papers be of any service?

I am delighted to know that you are pleased with my review: though those abominable misprints still grieve me. The Saturday Review had a very good notice of the Countess. The Rhymers have been meeting, with some good results in the way of rhyme: but do come back, and put some new life into us. Sligo must have inspired you sufficiently by this time. Miss Vynne has sent me Narcissus: I go to see her on Monday. Ellis has talked to me about my Blake notes, to my perfect satisfaction.

> Yours ever,
> LIONEL JOHNSON

From EDWARD GARNETT

MS Yeats

London
18 November 1892

[Garnett was a reader for T. Fisher Unwin, which had agreed to publish the "New Irish Library", a series of books for the Irish Literary Society planned by Yeats and Rolleston. When Duffy, whose ideas differed greatly from Yeats's (see *L* 215), was made general editor of the scheme, Yeats was greatly upset. His letter to *The Freeman's Journal* appeared on 6 September.]

Private & Confidential./ Dont quote any of my remarks here to your set. Please consider this as entirely a friendly letter.

My dear Yeats,

I want you to read this letter *dispassionately* & consider what it contains without any preconceived ideas.

Last night Unwin visited me to meet Rolleston & discuss the Irish Literary Schemes.

I came away, as I went, with the firm ideas of trying to reconcile your differences with Duffy, & at the same time of getting what *you* want done accomplished.

Now my dear fellow I'm not going to preach anything at all, but

I do ask you to examine what the differences *are* between your view & the rival schemes & see whether it is for the good of the idea *you* are working for that you & your party should be *irreconcileable.*

By dint of taking an open part I drew from Rolleston a very clear & definite account of the way things have worked up to their present state.

I understand exactly your point of view. Your letter to the Freeman's Journal shows that you are afraid of "Duffy's Irish Literary Society" not being at all *representative* of the best men or the best books.

I also take for granted that you are ready to sink your *personal* feelings, & not to let any petty pride, or any feeling that you have not been treated fairly & squarely by Rolleston & Duffy come in the way of the things you want being carried through.

It seems to me absurd that Duffy should want to boss a National affair, but why not let him have the *figureheadship* so long as he isn't really *Dictator?*

You will say that he *will* make himself *Dictator* & take all the credit to himself.

Well I know you well enough to know that *you* dont want the credit & honour & glory — you want the eternal things. And as to the *Dictatorship* I am sure *that the thing could be worked practically to the issue of all the books that your party wants published being published.*

The fact is the whole issue of the split lies between you & Rolleston. If you & he would join hands (you representing the Parnellite party, & Rolleston the London Irish Literary Society) you would find that you & he are practically of the same mind about the books & that *your own ideas would be carried through.*

Now dont imagine that I'm trying to square you, & that Rolleston & his set influence me in the least. My sympathies are all with you & the party you represent: it is only because I have the sense to see this is the eleventh hour when differences, *that are not vital,* can be adjusted that I take the trouble to write this letter. Is it not a pity that all sections should not be united on the broad ground of *Irish Literature,* & that you make this thing *National* instead of *partisan?* I tell you plainly that I believe the two separate Series will be a great mistake, & end in failure & bitterness.

Why not drop personal feeling, quiet the hornet's nest on your side, come over here *first,* & see whether you cannot make a practical agreement?

Rolleston didn't commission me to write a word of this Christian (!) letter, but I can see that the letter he told me you had written him has wounded him & that he would [be] glad to be friends. You must remember that unless you are *definitely* agreed to split & bring your rival scheme out promptly, everything you say in writing or *print* makes it still more difficult for your party *to have its way* or to work in any way *except against Duffy*.

Unwin is definitely casting in his lot with the Duffy set, & no English publisher would take up the rival scheme I'm pretty sure — so what's the use of you writing to Rolleston saying they have stolen your ideas, your plan of publishing & all the rest?

You may say "its true." Well, never mind if it is; dont be personal, but come over here & you'll find that if you say to Rolleston "here are the half dozen or dozen books I want published," they *will* be published. Dont let loose the dogs of war against a Duffy Dictatorship when it could be turned into a Duffy Figureheadship.

Enough. I'm sick of preaching. Just analyse your position first, that's the advice of a disinterested outsider.

Yours
EDWARD GARNETT

I also recognize that formal Committees on both sides will only embroil matters more. Let Duffy be the English Monarch, & you & Rolleston the joint Prime Ministers.

It's always on one or two men who *work* for a thing that the issue depends. Now Rolleston & you are the prime movers, & the question depends on *your* good feeling.

From EDWARD GARNETT

London
MS Yeats   [18 November 1892]

[Yeats had proposed a committee of five distinguished men to work with Duffy.]

I have just got your letter. From what I heard last night there are only two courses open to you — one is to start your rival Series at once — the other is to put your Side's demand into definite shape, & *to come behind the scenes to present them to Rolleston*. Duffy wont bow to the decision of any Committee publicly — but privately you could arrange with Rolleston to carry your ideas into facts.

E G

Committees are such a nuisance — they will fetter you, instead of your representing them singly.

From C. CARTER BLAKE

London
MS Yeats   31 January 1894

[A member of the Golden Dawn, Blake refers to Yeats's *The Celtic Twilight* (1893) and to Alfred T. Story's *William Blake* (1893). Story states that Blake came from "the same family" as Admiral Robert Blake.]

Dear Yeats,
    Story's book is not worth a damn, & the story of Blake being related to Admiral B. of Bridgewater is a cock-&-bull. I am sorry I cannot write with my own hand.

Yrs. fraternally,
C. CARTER BLAKE

P.S. Your book is excellent.

From ALTHEA GYLES

[London]
MS Yeats   [probably 1895]

[E. J. Oldmeadow was editor of *The Dome*. "The Offering of Pan" appeared in *The Commonwealth* (June 1896). Lady Colin Campbell did a portrait of Gyles. Sir Vincent Caillard was an author and musician. Gyles quotes the first two lines of "Sympathy", which Yeats chose for Brooke and Rolleston's *A Treasury of Irish Poetry in the English Tongue* (1900).]

My dear Mr. Yeats
    I have just received your telegram asking for the meaning of "Noah's" Raven! I told you nearly all I know in that letter I sent you (Did you get the tracing?) it is really but the vaguest idea I once had as part of a romance of the world under the sea. I first did a study

for the "Romance of the Red Sea," with the Queen enthroned on Pharoas chariot. But I suppose that this mermaid tempted the Raven with the ring that had belonged to his Master, a Magician, (or perhaps the Magician turned *himself* into the Raven?) (but perhaps Mr Oldmeadow would think that if this latter were the case Jehovah would not have let him into the Ark.) — Pray do not try Mr Oldmeadow any further. I have been very angry with him about my "Rose" but I can not help seeing how good he has been all through, he has taken such a lot of trouble & is really wonderful for a parson — You will see the hands of the other sea people have on the treasures of the Mighty of the Earth. I do not think there was any genuine emotion or romantic passion in the sea before they beheld the Rose. (*This* is the rose of the world.) It caused entire revolution! Perhaps it was lucky for Mr Oldmeadows feelings I did not choose a later period for illustration. I have written some things about them which I will show you sometime.

It is not dreadful about the Rose of God? I suppose Mr Oldmeadow told you he rejected it on the grounds — Oh I cant go into it now, but it's supposed to ruin the Dome to print it. You hate the only three other finished ones I have. I dont know that he'd like "Pan" *or* "Lilith" but I have another study (if I can get it back in time) it too is deeply religious.

It is the study of two figures for a drawing of Pan & his Nymphs stoning the image of the Star of Bethlehem seen in the waters at their feet. The Real Star they did not see.

There is another too I might just get. Write a few words about the Star one that can be left out if not wanted. If they use *the other* I will wire particulars.

Lady Colin's portrait is *quite* a success it is in quite flat colour yellow black & grey, the face & head white.

You have the knight, do please speak of the hearts of the bulbs. I needn't explain they are the symbols of resurrection. People are given to calling this drawing morbid which annoys me. It is a pity about the rose as it is the best bit of *fine* work I have yet done. Sir Vincent Caillard saw it today & wishes to buy it but I have not yet quite settled what to do with it. He would be a good person to have it because any time I wanted it again I could get at it.

Do write to me & give me an idea of what you are saying & tell me if you got the tracings. Lady C. has an idea about the Studio taking the Rose drawing. She is much interested now in my verses & says I had much better not let the Rose poem go without the picture as Mr. O doesnt much value it. I mean to substitute

> The colour gladdens all your heart
> You call it "Heaven," dear — but I etc

Do remember that you liked it. I might send him another for a choice. I hope he will take one as bad luck stares me in the face.

I cannot help scraps of bad writing and no paper. I am nearly *dead*.

No news of my Uncle. If I get the money from him I intend to work most hard at writing beautiful ideas have come to me.

It is a pity about the 4th drawing. Do write if there is time to Mr Oldmeadow & urge him to take a drawing in the place of the rose but it must reach him before 1 on Saturday next.

This is all I think

Yours
ALTHEA G.

Im so pleased you like the drawing.

From PAMELA CARDEN BULLOCK

MS Yeats

[London]
3 January 1895

[Mrs Bullock ("Shemeber") held the office of Sub-cancellarius in the Golden Dawn at this time. "Care and Very Honoured Brother" is a standard form of address in the Golden Dawn. She instructs Yeats that the sign of Leo rules the Element of Fire (summer) and Taurus that of Earth (spring). The Course of Zelator in the Order reverses the Course of Seasons. Sapientia, etc. is the Order motto of Florence Farr Emery, Non Omnis Moriar that of William Wynn Westcott, both friends of Yeats.]

Care et V. H. Frater,

Of course you know that in the consecration of the Lotus Wand you hold the Wand by the Band of the particular Sign you are invoking. In other consecrations and invocations, hold it by the Band of the Sign ruling the Element in question, as ♌ for △, ♉ for ▽, and so on. Also you should think intently on the Element you are invoking, and feel that you are tracing the Pentagram in solid △, or ▽ as the case may be. I have just been particularly told this by our V. H. Soror Sapientia Sapienti dono data, Theoricus.

B. The Magician in operating, should stand in and face towards the quarter whose Element he is invoking, with his back to the Altar or Table.

C. In the case of charging or consecrating a Symbol, you should first invoke round the room, as above and then, standing W of the Altar, face E., and describe the necessary invoking Symbol over the object to be charged.

D. Should you wish to banish the Forces from a consecrated Symbol, you would, of course, proceed in the same way, but if your desire is to charge a Telesma or other object, your first work after full consecration would be to wrap it in silk to preserve its influences pure, to put it in a safe place, then you may, if you like, banish the Forces you have invoked round the room, taking care to make no banishing Symbol at this point, over the newly charged object. An alternative method is to face E., and say aloud:—"In the Great Name of Strength through Sacrifice, Jeheshua Jehovascha, I now license all Spirits to depart that may have been retained by this Ceremony, excepting only such as I have bound to the consecration of this Telesma (or other object.) Depart ye therefore, such other Spirits as may be retained here; depart ye in peace unto your habitations. May the blessing of (here use appropriate Divine Name) rest upon ye. Be there peace between me and ye, and be ye ready to come when ye are called."

You will find this a potent formula in such a case, & may hear the rush of the departing Forces, and this also obviates the danger of de-consecrating your newly charged Symbol.

E. In performing the Supreme Ritual of the Pentagram, you may make the appropriate Equilibrating Pentagram in each quarter if you like before each Elemental Pentagram, but it is not absolutely necessary. The positions I previously described to you, viz: — from N.W., perform equilibration of Actives towards S.E., and from S.E., perform Equilibration of Passives towards N.W., is the usual method employed here. A third alternative would, of course, be to perform these Spirit Pentagrams all round the room first, in each quarter, and this, making a Circle of the Spirit round your room, would, I should think, considerably strengthen your position, though I have never tried it. I will do so, however, at my earliest opportunity, and see what effect it has, different from the ordinary method.

F. With reference to the Fire Wand enclosing a magnetized rod, our G.H. Frater Non Omnis Moriar, usually keeps a stock here, which he sells to the members. At the present moment we are out of them,

but some are on order. When they come in, I will send you one if
you wish it, but if you prefer it, you can, of course, have one made
yourself. The usual size is about six inches.

    I must apologize for the untidiness of this letter, but I have not
time to copy it all out before the next post. Therefore kindly pardon
this.

        With kindest fraternal greetings for the New Year from us both,

I am

Yours fraternally

SHEMEBER.

From EDMUND GOSSE

London

17 October 1895

Ms Yeats

[Gosse refers to *Poems* (1895).]

Dear Mr. Yeats

    It is very kind of you to send me this beautiful edition of your
poems. (I was going to write "complete," but may it be long indeed
before your enrichment of English literature ceases!) I find that you
have put almost all the pieces I love & know best into the section
called "The Rose." I have no words too strong (& yet I am not fond
of flinging words about) to say how I delight in these penetrating,
poignant lyrics of yours. You are indeed, what one dares so seldom
say, a poet, and may you long continue to write as well as you do
now, and better — each book better — is the sincere wish & prayer of

Yours most faithfully

EDMUND GOSSE

I am now going to read "The Rose" aloud to my wife & my
daughter: but they know most of it.

From PAMELA CARDEN BULLOCK

[London]

30 November 1895

MS Yeats

[The sixth step in the "Progress of a member through the Zelator
Sub-Grade of the 5=6 Grade of Adeptus Minor" was to "Receive
Ritual D and make Lotus Wand and consecrate it". The next step

was to "Receive Rituals E and F and make Rosecross and consecrate it". Yeats passed D on 15 June 1895 and E 1 (the first of two parts) on 22 June. L.O. ("Levavi Oculos") was Percy W. Bullock, Shemeber's husband.]

Care et V. H. Frater,

Thank you for Book "D", received this morning. I am sending you registered by this post Book "E".

A. The correct way to spell the word is שׁ‎7ק‎ה‎.

B. There is no reason at all why you should not make your Lotus Wand as soon as you like. The mere making of a Magical Implement fixes the Symbols more firmly in your atmosphere. Also it would be as well to have it ready for inspection in case you should be able to come over earlier than you at present anticipate.

C. 18 inches is a very convenient length to make the wand, that being large enough for dignity but not too large to use with ease. Some members, however, make them of only a foot in length, but I, personally, prefer the longer one as providing a larger basis for the Forces.

D. Your surmise respecting the positions of the initial and final 7ה‎א‎ is correct. The first is placed at the right side of the apex of the erect triangle, and the latter at the left of the apex of the inverted triangle, of course, looking from you.

It is not necessary to put the English words round the Hexagram, as you asked me in your last letter.

With kindest regards from L.O., and myself,

I am
Yours fraternally
SHEMEBER.

From PAMELA CARDEN BULLOCK

[London]
28 December 1895

MS Yeats

[She refers to the symbols of the four elements (▽ earth, ▽ water, △ air, and △ fire) and the sun (☉). LUX symbolized "the Light of the Cross", Malkuth is the tenth sephira on the Cabbalistic Tree of Life; "it represents everything that we can apprehend with our physical senses". S.S.D.D. is Florence Farr Emery, S.A. is W. W. Westcott.]

Care et V. H. Frater,

I have been chary of posting Order letters or Rituals during the Christmas press as so many things are delayed or go astray, but now that the holiday time is practically over, I proceed to answer your letters.

With reference to making the Circle of the Room, this means a circumambulation with a sword in the right hand. Any sharp pointed instrument will do until you have your Consecrated Sword, but it is very necessary to make a clean circle first in this manner before proceeding to perform a Ceremony, as in this manner evil influences are kept at bay and the forces you subsequently invoke are drawn into your Circle as a vortex, and all danger of dispersion is obviated. This is, therefore, a very important point and one much dwelt upon by all practical magicians. First make a complete Circle of the room or that part in which you intend to work, and then proceed to your Invocation. The performance of the Lesser Banishing Ritual clears the room, and the Circle renders the clearance permanent during your working, so that your invoked Forces may be as pure and unadulterated as possible.

For the Invocations of Forces of the Pentagram and Hexagram, either use your unconsecrated Lotus Wand, or a sharp pointed instrument as before suggested. A sharp pen-knife may be used with advantage if you have no dagger available.

I should use the Divine Names and Tablet Names as given in the Rituals of the Outer in opening ceremonies. You cannot charge a general Symbol too thoroughly. It is not necessary to hold the Elements from the Altar in your left hand though you can do so if you like. I should not. I have just read your last letter again and should certainly consecrate Lotus Wand and Rose Cross first of all, as you then have efficient weapons. S.A. has lately officially nominated me Sub-Registrar, but of course in all matters of uncertainty I appeal to him as my Chief before making statements. With reference to purification and consecration by Water and Fire, it is preferable to use Incense for the latter as in this manner all four Elements are pressed into the service. Salt is sprinkled into the Water, giving ▽ and ▽, the two passive Elements for purification, and Incense, *which is lighted from the Lamp*, unites △ and △, the two active Elements for consecration.

In the Greater Invoking Ritual of the Pentagram, having made the Kabalistic Cross, proceed with the ☉ to the N.W., of Altar, facing S.E., and perform Equilibration of Actives. Then proceed to S.E., face N.W., and perform Equilibration of Passives, then to E., and proceed as you know, with △, △, ▽, ▽, Lux Signs in East, etc.

I have read your Consecration Ceremony carefully and having taken the liberty of making sundry suggestions of it and also in this letter.

Do not scruple to command my services at any time. If I have not sufficiently answered your questions, I shall be most happy to go into the matter more fully.

Now to descend to Malkuth. I must thank you most heartily both for L.O., and myself for your kind gift of the turkey which arrived at a most opportune moment, just as L.O., was going to get one. We had a very festive Christmas shared by our V. H. Soror S.S.D.D.

Pray accept out best wishes for a prosperous and happy New Year, in the course of which I hope we may have many opportunities of meeting. With kindest regards and best thanks from us both,

> I am
> Yours fraternally
> SHEMEBER.

From WILLIAM THOMAS HORTON

MS Yeats

Brighton
28 March 1896

[Drawings by Horton appeared in the April 1896 *Savoy*, as well as in the issues for August, October, and November; the *Savoy* was edited by Arthur Symons. "The Rose" series is in *Poems* (1895); Horton quotes the first line of "To the Rose upon the Rood of Time". D. B., Dr Edward W. Berridge (Resurgam), was respected as an astrologer by his fellow members of the Golden Dawn. Isis was the Egyptian goddess of fertility, and Ptah the shaper of the world. *The* meeting is a reference to Horton's initiation into the Golden Dawn on 21 March. Annie E. F. Horniman (Fortiter Et Recte) joined the Golden Dawn in January 1890.]

My dear Yeats

I must write & thank you most warmly for laying my drawings before Symons who has very kindly chosen 3 for the forthcoming "Savoy."

The reading of your Poetry has been a great delight to me, many things I have felt come into your Poems. "The Rose" series especially appeals to me, in fact I have tried to render my feelings by a face, it is just an idea, a sketch for "Red Rose, proud Rose, sad Rose of all my days!" (Symons has seen it & likes it, I am happy to say). I feel this right thro' & thro' every part of my being. I for one am grateful for such a poem. "Red Rose, proud Rose, sad Rose of all my days." It keeps on returning — it'll never leave me — I am glad of it.

I had been reading your Poems last Tuesday when there came over me a feeling of majestic, mighty power, strength, justice, wisdom & calmness which I tried to depict by a face. I seemed to get into an Egyptian sphere & as I worked in my inward ear came the word *M e n — K a — r a* several times. After finishing the drawing I looked thro' a list of Egyptian kings & found *Men-Kau-Ra* 4th dynasty (B.C. 3633–3600) renowned for his virtues & justice. Most likely I had read this name before, but at the time I was decidedly not thinking about him. (Ramses II) [word indecipherable] would have been the most likely name, seeing he was supposed to be one of my Spirits in the old days of Spiritism). Ysty I find that he is sometimes called "Man-*Kau*-ra" at others & more often "Man-*Ka*-ra." This is most singular, especially the *Ka*. Happening to write to D. B. I mentioned it to him & he tells me the influence he thinks good but I must remain *positive*. On Wedy I did *Isis* & felt a pleasurable inclination to burn incense while & after drawing her. I then looked up the signs of the Zodiac. On Thursday I did Ptah the "Supreme Artist".

Quite Egyptian you see — the feeling & the time is very pleasant & gentle yet mighty in Power, certainly no constraint. I can do it or leave it.

I remember what you told me about the "Priestess of Isis". This Egyptian phase coming immediately after *the* meeting I thought you might care to hear of it. Is it possible to be thus occultly, as it were, initiated into the Mysteries little by little — I have *not* received any papers from the G.D.

I can't help thinking you right about my star being Venus & *not* Virgo as suggested by Miss H. I have always been in love with some girl ever since I was a child. Always some girl that I idealised, put on a pinnacle & tried to keep myself pure for *her* sake. If it was not one girl it was another. I can't help thinking that if I had not married young & also had a very strong spiritual bent, I might have given full sway to the Venus proclivities. But more of this when we meet. I shall be looking forward to my horoscope at your leisure.

Now, my dear Yeats, for Heaven's sake don't feel that it is necessary to write me in answer to this — altho' I need hardly say how delighted I should be for your opinion. I have only written thinking it may interest you & above all to offer you my deepest & heartiest thanks. With warmest wishes

Believe me

Yours very sincerely & fraternally

WILLIAM T. HORTON

P.S. I shall not be in Town till Friday week (Ap. 10th) when I hope to see Mr Symons at Fountain Court at 2 p.m.

From WILLIAM THOMAS HORTON

Brighton

MS Yeats   29 April 1896

[The Brotherhood of the New Life was founded by Thomas Lake Harris, American spiritualist and prolific author. Dr C. M. Berridge (Respiro) was the author of twelve pamphlets about Harris's Brotherhood. In a note to Horton (dated 3 March 1896) Yeats referred to two of Harris's books: *God's Breath in Man and in Humane Society* and *The Arcana of Christianity*.]

My dear Yeats,

It is with extreme regret that I have to tell you that I cannot proceed any further with the G.D.

Personally I find it extremely antagonistic in 3 ways — (1) As a follower of Jesus Christ, (2) as a Brother of the New Life (3) as an artist. Harris' message to me was "————If he—she can hold themselves up to the Divine One-Twain alone, and not become involved in the nature-play through spiritism, and other detractors, he—she will some day become a great artist."

The G.D. has been undoubtedly a *detractor* for several days now I have not done any good work.

Believe me my dear Yeats that it is not without much cogitation that I have come to this conclusion, but I am fully convinced that for me *the only* safe path is Jesus Christ & He *alone*.

From what I have seen of you I feel sure that this decision will in no way affect the warmth of your feelings towards me. The only thing I am worrying about is that you should have had the trouble of initiating me, but how could I know of this antagonism until I had joined & experienced it.

Am looking forward to seeing you at 2 p.m. on Friday week (May 8th) when perhaps you will be able to let me take away some of the Harris books as I shall be seeing somebody about the 16th & want them for reference.

With warmest wishes

Yours very sincerely,
WILLIAM T. HORTON

P.S. Have written to Respiro

From WILLIAM THOMAS HORTON

Brighton
MS Yeats   1 May 1896

[Horton refers to a spiritual doctrine of Harris, who claimed to be united in "counterpartal marriage to Queen Lily of the Conjugial [sic] Angels". Edward Maitland's *The New Gospel of Interpretation* (1891) and other books concerned with esoteric Christianity were known to Yeats. MacGregor Mathers dedicated *The Kabbalah Unveiled* (1887) to Anna Kingsford and Maitland, co-authors of *The Perfect Way* (1882).]

My dear Yeats

Your letter has made me very happy especially that where you say my present action in no way affects our friendship. As it happens you do not know my views on Christ. Altho' I believe in Him as having lived & suffered on earth & risen & is God, I believe that He dwells within each one of us in some more fully than in others. It is this Inner Christ that I am following. This to my mind is the counterpartal path & as the highest love of men & women is for the opposite sex, it is but right that the holiest & highest Love (God is Love) should take the form of one of the opposite sex.

Christ immanent as woman in man, and man in woman.

It is in faithfulness to the Christ *within* me that I have given up the G.D. which imparts knowledge from the *outer*. I believe that by following Christ & Christ alone it is possible to reach unto *all* knowledge. Thus Harris thro' doing so has passed thro' all the secret knowledge of the G.D. Theosophy etc. & has attained a higher plane than either of these. Also the Christ will lead to what books to read, people to know or shun etc. Every minute I feel that I have obeyed Christ in doing as I have done but that for some reason it was necessary for me to glance at the G.D. just as I had to glance at Spiritualism, Atheism, Orthodox religion (I was brought up as Ch. of England), Maitland etc. At the present I find Harris contains the highest teaching and blends sympathetically with the Christ within. So far I feel that I have entered the right sphere & influences. Day by day I feel greater spiritual strength & less of the emotional. Do you know I am surprised at your remaining in the G.D., you a student of Blake.

The G.D. to my mind, lays itself out to only cultivate what Blake deprecates & that is the Intellect alone while it crushes that that Blake upheld the Feminine or Feeling. Now Harris like Blake upholds the Union of both in Equality. However I feel convinced that in the present day the Intellect only has been cultivated & that, at the expense of the Intuitional. I believe that this accounts greatly for the stationary state of Art. Now you see Art has but little, if anything, to do with the Intellect — I mean the dry, matter of fact, collecting of divers knowledge Intellect. The more a man *knows* the worse Artist — I refer to Poets as well as Painters & Musicians — he becomes. Forgive my saying so, my dear Yeats, but I verily believe it would be better for you to have nothing to do with the G.D., but to rely on the Inner Christ alone.

In Spiritual matters all knowledge from the *outside* is tainted by magnetisms etc. The *Christ within* will teach all that is necessary and what is especially to be noted *The right thing at the right time.* Having Christ within — what on earth! is the use of the G.D. or any other socy. unless for selfish ends such as the man you told me of who by the G.D. increases *his* vitality, or merely for the sake of knowing or out of necessity as a hobby or a pastime.

But more of this I hope when we meet at 2, next Friday. (Today I have not come up to Town.) I only wanted you to know that as to the Inner Christ I out-Herod, Herod.

Of course I don't expect you to write an answer to this, it was very kind of you to write so long a letter as you did.

With warmest wishes
Yrs very sincerely
WILLIAM T. HORTON

Strange you should mention Boehme I have often wanted to read some of him. The little I have seen of him has interested me. Now you mention him I shall make it a point of looking him up, also the Kabalah Unveiled.

From WILLIAM THOMAS HORTON

                                                    Brighton
MS Yeats   6 May 1896

[In his letter of 5 May Yeats had told Horton that "even Miss Horniman is not so purely intellective as you think", also that she was philanthropic (*L* 262). "Rosa Alchemica" was published in *The Savoy* (April 1896); see *Mythologies*, 285 for the passage quoted. The arch-natural beings and the counterpart are terms used by Thomas Lake Harris to describe spiritual forces. B.N.L. is the Brotherhood of the New Life.]

My dear Yeats

I shall be delighted to be with you at 11.30 this Friday & partake of a cup of tea as I generally do when I come up to Town.

This morning I had a vision of you, as I was lying in bed & just before your letter came. I give it as it came & I know you'll take it in the right spirit & as it came to me.

I think you'll find that my visions are not very different to yours.

You see I am a sure one for individuality. I have a perfect passion for it & also that every man must work out his own individuality in his own way. I am quite as strong as Blake on this. I quite agree with you about the Intellect clearing away the rubbish from the mouth of the sybil's cave & that it is not the sybil.

But I most emphatically and strenuously deny the right of any man or Society telling me that the sybil's cave is still uncleared or on the other hand that it is cleared. The only judgment I bow to and acknowledge is the Voice of Christ speaking within me. If I err or if I do not, at all events I am true to myself — my higher self.

I rejoice to hear what you tell me of Miss H. Far be it from me to *harbour* any ill feeling towards her, I make it a rule of *nursing* no ill feelings against anyone — how easy to misunderstand one another while still we see most things reversed thro' our earthly eyes — but at the same time *there* is such a thing as antipathy & sympathy, the which do not blend. To the best of my ability I try to love everybody & it is not always easy.

Am looking forward to the exchange of views.

With warmest wishes

Yours very sincerely

WILLIAM T. HORTON

I have much enjoyed Rosa Alchemica. There are many lovely things in it & the whole thing appeals very strongly to me.

"but the divine powers would only appear in beautiful shapes, which are but, as it were, shapes trembling out of existence, folding up into a timeless ecstasy, drifting with half shut eyes into a sleepy stillness."

I remember you telling me this — it is exquisite & true. Often have I seen these lovely beings & vainly attempted to picture them — however some day I hope to succeed. They are so indistinct that on paper they appear to a great extent formless. I shall have to try chalks some day.

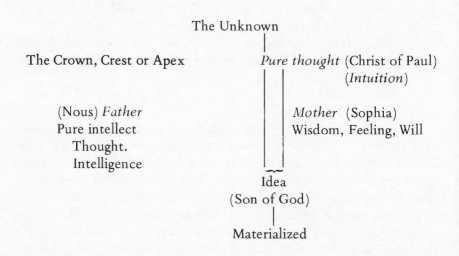

I made above as an easy way of remembering something I read in a book called "Healing by Faith" by W. F. Grant.

By the bye I have never found my intuition lead me wrong.

Take the G.D.; my intuition (Christ within) told me not to join but earthly sense & logic said join. The Voice was not very strong about it & doubtless, as I have said, I joined for some reason or other

& having done the required work the Voice spoke with strength & command to withdraw myself.

I mean to follow the Voice more closely in future as I have had several encounters with horrible serpents etc. I call on Christ in spirit & behold immediately there flashes from over my right side a mighty figure in glittering armour, with drawn sword, that kills the serpent etc. or puts it to flight.

In fact I feel that, in the Spiritual, on guard by me, ever stands this armed figure to keep all hurt from me as I go on my way.

I feel sometimes that it is one of the arch-natural beings.

The counterpart to guide, the guardian to defend & both Christ in different aspects & forming part of the Christ within, the Christ as incarnate in Jesus, and Christ by whom all things are & in whom all things rest, move & have their being.

As to emotional religion I now belong to no sect or church & never go to church or rarely as I find it affects me. This is again following the intuitions.

While I think of it, do you know that it is spiritually extremely dangerous to actively oppose Harris. He is extremely forgiving & of himself thinks nothing, but of course he is in touch with extra-ordinary forces & these are the Arch-Natural beings.

This is all strictly between you & me. Another cause of my leaving is Miss H. to whom I feel strangely & most virulently opposed & antagonistic. She is my bete noire. I hope you have not shown her any of Harris' books.

Somehow I fell that she is not content to passively ignore Harris & the B.N.L. but she is actively engaged in opposing both him & all Powers that to her mind are not in harmony with NOUS & NOUS *alone*. She had better take care & beware. The Arch Natural beings are not to be trifled with. Of course you must take this for what it is worth but this is how I feel inclined to write you.

Vision.

It is night.
Yeats — naked and gaunt, with long black dishevelled hair falling partly over the face of a deathly whiteness, with eyes that flame yet have within them depths of unutterable sadness.

He is wearily going on his way following many lights that dance in front and at side of him.

Behind follows with outstretched arms a lovely girl in long trailing white garments, weeping.

Within Yeats, a knocking is heard & a Voice "My son, my son, open thou unto me & I will give thee Light."

From DOUGLAS HYDE

Frenchpark [Ireland]

MS Yeats   7 May 1896

[George W. Russell (AE) was contemplating "a book containing a declaration of our principles" on the order of *Literary Ideals in Ireland* (1899). The "slight essay" Hyde suggests was first published in Irish and included in *Ideals in Ireland* (1901) as "What Ireland Is Asking For". Professor James E. H. Murphy was appointed to the Chair Hyde desired. Hyde's Gaelic pseudonym is *An Craoibhín Aoibhinn* ("Pleasant Little Branch").]

My dear Yeats

Just a line to thank you for yours, and to ask what the book is which you speak of. You want an abstract in half a dozen lines of my article for the book of essays, do you mean the book Russell is contemplating? If so I was going to do a slight essay on the damage done to the Irish race by the neglect and abolition of all hereditary & instinctive Gaelic traits in his modern development & education — something like that any how.

I was "mad" about Mr Murphy getting the Chair of Irish in Trinity. It is a proselytizing institution & the money therefore contributed by the "Irish Society", a proselytizing institution. They w^{d} not have me at any price & I fancy the worse the man was the better pleased they were, so that no attention c^{d} be drawn to Gaelic studies by him. Yet I had the most excellent letters from the great Gaelic scholars etc.

Yours ever
AN CRAOIBHÍN

From RICHARD GARNETT

London

MS Yeats   24 May [probably 1896]

[The keeper of Printed Books at the British Museum, Garnett made numerous translations from Greek, German, Italian, Spanish and Portuguese, and was the author of *William Blake*, which Yeats reviewed in *The Bookman* (April 1896).]

My dear Yeats,

On looking carefully in to your horoscope, I find that Mars was just entering 12 Leo. If, as seems very likely, the Ascendant to his apparition in the zodiac occasioned your attack of scarlet fever, and this took place at the age of seven years and six months, you would be born under Capricorn, but if at seven or a little more, still under Aquarius. Can you ascertain the exact period?

I hope that my translations have found their way to you.

Yours very sincerely,
R. GARNETT

From GEORGE W. RUSSELL

MS Yeats

Dublin
November 1896

[William Larminie, collector and translator of *West Irish Tales and Romances* (1893), contributed to *Literary Ideals in Ireland*; Lionel Johnson and Douglas Hyde did not. Professor Patrick Geddes established a publishing firm in Edinburgh "to revive the Celtic influence in art and literature". William Sharp was first the manager of the firm, then literary adviser; he used the pseudonym of Fiona Macleod.]

Dear W. B. Yeats,

I have just had a letter from Larminie whom I have interviewed. He suggests one of two subjects:

    (1) Material for literature in Ireland
    (2) The Celts as legend-makers

He inclines to the first, but says probably the second would be of wider interest as it would include Scotch & Welsh. What do you think? I suppose it is always best to let a man work on what he feels most inclined to do. I think also a possible subject though perhaps a little far from the general scheme of the book would be an essay on an old Irish mystic Duns Scotus whose works he is translating. Perhaps as you think the appeal ought to be made to the Gael generally some one of the Scots might be asked to fill OGradys place. How about Fiona Macleod? Still I am of opinion it is best to speak to the Ireland of today as much as possible. I will anyhow, and if we do that in any really high sense we will also speak to the Gael wherever located. Please give me your advice. And if any arrangement can be come to with Geddes, let me know the estimated length for each essay, a limit either way. I think also as all are versemakers, we might interpolate between the essays poems on such themes as inspire our various souls. This would tend to give a more poetical & beautiful character to the book. I know Larminie would do this. I would, and so I think would Johnson and Hyde. I wish we could make up our full seven — Could you try the black art or white as the case may be, on S[tandish] OG[rady]!?

Yours
GEORGE RUSSELL

From GEORGE W. RUSSELL

Dublin
[December 1896]

MS Yeats

[Johnston was a contemporary and old friend of Yeats and Russell. He contributed articles to various American magazines (including *Harper's, New York Times Book Review*, and *Atlantic Monthly*) after he and his wife (Madame Blavatsky's niece) moved to New York in October 1896. Standish O'Grady was a barrister, journalist, and editor, noted chiefly for his *History of Ireland*. Thomas William Rolleston, disciple of John O'Leary, classical scholar, and editor of the *Dublin University Review*, helped found the Rhymers' Club in 1891. William Kirkpatrick Magee, essayist and editor, used the pseudonym John Eglinton. Eglinton contributed to *Literary Ideals in Ireland*, but O'Grady did not; the volume was published not by Geddes but by T. Fisher Unwin in London and the *Daily Express* in Dublin.]

Dear Willie,

I enclose letter received from Charlie Johnston. He is writing a series of illustrated articles in [an] American magazine upon modern Irish writers, you, OGrady, Hyde, myself & others. He wants to interest the Irish millions in America, who are not readers, in the latest developments and the Celtic renaissance. All this is in line with our plans and we ought to help him in every way. Even as a mere matter of business it ought to appeal to you. My publisher has sent over almost twenty pounds in royalties within the last year or so, and I know that if you and OGrady who make an appeal to a much wider public were properly place[d] in the American market, it would result in much monies, a thing which the spirit despises but which the lower man accepts with a sneaking gratitude, as it is by this he lives. Do what you can at once to help out this laudable purpose. He is making a presentation of modern Irish Books with autographs of authors to the library of the New York police force who are Irish almost to a man, and one of the most powerful influences over there in all matters concerned with Ireland. I do not know where you are now, London or Paris. If in London move the Literary Society there to see the true inwardness of this. It is in fact "throwing a sprat to catch a whale." Johnston is communicating with OGrady, Hyde, Rolleston, and others on this. Back of it all lies our hopes. Johnston has become a fervent Celt. It will do him much good, and us also, as his articles are very popular in U.S.A. in the best magazine[s] there like the Arena and are much quoted. He leaves New York in March for further west, so this thing ought to be carried through at once. Also dear Willie Yeats I conjure you as you love Ireland and the Gods, do not let the Spring pass without *one* book at least being in the hands of a publisher. I have finished my contribution. Hyde I know had part of his done last autumn and I am writing to him about this and other things. Magee can finish his on a weeks notice. Do what you can Willie, we have a splendid chance which *must not* be let pass. What Emerson did for America by his declaration of intellectual independence we can do here with even more effect. The Gods are filling the country with fire; we must do our share. If you I and the others do not you will find others inspired to your shame. Dont delay my dear old friend, for the sake of this dreamy beautiful land of ours, act as only those can who are fired by long dreaming. Be like one of those swift doers of deeds the heroes of ancient Eri, and let us strike our blow. Work up Lionel Johnson or let him drop out if he wont fall into line. You, OGrady, Magee and myself will bring the new spirit and perhaps Hyde. Anyhow now is our time. We must have Geddes. A London publisher would be no good.

> Write me as soon as possible.
> Ever yours
> GEO. W. RUSSELL

From ROBERT BRIDGES

MS Bridges

Yattendon, Newbury
10 December 1896

[Bridges is replying to *L* 268. The postscript concerns the final line of "Fergus [not Cuchulain] and the Druid", which read "Lay hidden in the small slate-coloured bag!" in *The Countess Kathleen* (1892). In *Poems* (1895) Yeats changed "bag!" to "thing!"; in his copy of *Poems* Bridges noted "(bag) 1st edit. better". Yeats was always uncertain about the line, retaining "thing!" until 1908, reverting to "bag!" from 1912 to 1924, trying "thing!" again in 1925, using "thing?" in 1927 and 1929, and finally settling on "thing!" in 1933.]

Dear Sir

Your letter is as great a surprise as it is a pleasure to me this morning — and as you date from a hotel I answer by return. When I wrote to you I purposely wrote such a letter as you could answer or not — for nothing is more tedious than admiration from people with whom one does not feel in sympathy — and had I said as much as I felt about your poetry you would have been constrained to thank me. As it was I was reconciling myself to the idea that you didn't care whether I liked your poetry or not. As a matter of fact I can read very little poetry so called — and your book is a great exception. It has given me a great deal of delight, and I find magnificent things and very beautiful things in it. And it is most pleasant to me to hear that you have cared for my verse: and will therefore welcome my admiration for your work.

I hope when spring comes that you will consent to pay us a visit here. The country is pretty enough, tho' as you date your preface from Sligo I must not boast — still I feel safe from comparison because all is so different here.

I wonder what you are doing in Paris, and whether French farce delights you. I do not like Paris in the winter, but they have become more musical than they were when I used to be there.

I ought to say that your letter to me is unsigned — from which I hope I may conclude that you are in the middle of some piece of work which has got hold of you — I can not make a mistake however in recognising in it the answer to the only letter which I have written in the required sense.

Thank you very much for promising to send me your forthcoming book. I shd greedily buy anything of yours on the strength of the poems.

> Believe me,
> Yours sincerely,
> ROBERT BRIDGES

I should like to write to you some day about your poems, or better talk with you. — I think you have hit off one form (and really a new one as you do it) perfectly — in Cuchulin and the bag of dreams. By the way let *bag* stand in last line — why did you alter it? But I liked most of your alterations — I saw the 2 editions.

From MRS MACGREGOR MATHERS

Paris

MS Yeats   16 March 1897

[Mina (later Moina) Bergson Mathers, famous clairvoyant, was a close friend of Yeats for many years. She probably refers to Edmund Bailly, editor of *Isis Moderne* (pub. Oct 1896-Mar 1897). In 1890, two years after founding (with Stanislas de Guaita) the Cabalistic Order of the Rosy Cross, Josephin Pêladan (called Le Sar) formed a splinter group known as the Order of the Rosy Cross, the Temple, and the Grail. Yeats kept the records of visionary explorations he and friends in the Golden Dawn had experienced. S.R.M.D. stands for *'S Rioghail* Mo *Dhream* ("Royal is my tribe"), one of Mathers's mottoes in the Golden Dawn. *Vestigia Nulla Retrorsum* ("No traces behind") was the Order motto of Mrs Mathers.]

Care Frater,

Bailly, the editor, 11 Rue de la Chaussee d'Antin, Paris, has just been here, & is very anxious to communicate with you on the Celtic Religious movement.

He says that there is the commencement here of a great enthusiasm in that direction (I suppose principally among the literary & artistic men) & he is thinking of making his new magazine "Isis" an organ for the "cause". He thinks that there are people over here who would help in every way including giving monetary assistance —

If you should write to him, do you not think that it would be well to impress on him that nothing can be done until the most important part of the affair be accomplished — that of resurrecting the Gods, & the ceremonies etc — "S R M D" is going to work at this but as you know, it may be a long & difficult business, & not a thing to be hurried at all —

Anything of the mind got up without the solid basis of Truth we will not have to do with, neither will you, of course. — People like Bailly (rather journalistic & superficial) would start an Order at once & it would become a regular "Sar Peladan" over again.

He says that the whole nearly of the french press are ready to help in this matter.

Well, all this seems splendid but rather premature. While presently nothing could be better.

Perhaps I was indiscreet in telling him when I first saw him on returning to Paris, of your account of the visions of Celtic "Forms" "seen" by some of your friends — This has interested him so much, that he would so much like you to write to him about them —

Would you object to his publishing an account of the same in his paper?

If you feel so disposed therefore, will you write to him on these subjects? (in English of course)

He will greatly value your opinion as presenting the Irish side —: & please, please! do not forget to say that we & you & all insist on getting at the absolutely correct symbolism before starting on the more external side of the question —

We did not see Geddes in Edinburgh as he was away — Are you corresponding always with "Fiona MacCleod" —? "SR" would write to you but is very much occupied —

Yours fraternally
VESTIGIA

From ROBERT BRIDGES

Yattendon, Newbury

MS Bridges   30 March 1897

[Bridges refers to *The Secret Rose* and to the lyric in "The Rose of Shadow", later included in *The Wind Among the Reeds* as "The Heart of the Woman". Though Yeats later revived him, Michael Robartes dies in "Rosa Alchemica", the final story in *The Secret Rose*. For Yeats's reply, see L 268.]

My dear Yeats

We enjoyed your visit very much and I hope that you will think of Yattendon as a place where you might some day run down for a weeks country air and retirement in the summer.

You left your dress shoes behind you. I sent them off by parcel post today. I hope that they have reached you safely.

I have read most of the book and come to a great deal that I like very much, but it is so unlike anything that I know that I have not formed any judgement of it and shall not till I have reread it all carefully. I do not know whether you wd care to have it criticized. This is of course merely a practical question, as to whether you imagine I might chance to say something which wd be of use to you. If you wish for criticism will you let me know.

Today has been lovely. I wish Sunday had been like it. We took the children out into the woods, and gathered firecones. You did not see any of our woods, or rather forests: which I now much regret as they are our chief attraction.

By the way I liked some of the lyrics in the Secret Rose, especially "O what to me the little room". I hope that you will take care of your body and that the saints or goddesses will preserve you from too much of the Rosa Alchemica. I am glad that Michael Robartes is dead.

My wife joins in kindest regards.

> believe me
> yours very sincerely
> R BRIDGES

From GEORGE W. RUSSELL

Dublin

MS Yeats   [June 1897]

[AE married Violet North in June 1898. Paul Gregan dedicated his collection of poems *Sunset Town* (1901) "To my dear friend AE". The pamphlet was *The Future of Ireland and the Awakening of the Fires*, already published as "The Awakening of the Fires" in *The Irish Theosophist* (Jan and Feb 1897). George R. S. Mead was a prominent writer and editor of occult literature and a member of the Theosophical Society while Yeats belonged. Angus Óg was the Irish god of love. *The Earth Breath* was published by John Lane in September 1897.]

Dear Willie

Many thanks for your letter especially for that part which refers to Miss North. It will encourage her. She and Paul Gregan are the most promising of my literary neophytes, but I have three more who may do as well or better. I tell them everything I know and am mainly concerned with giving them ideas and impressing on them the value of the more subjective as contrasted with the reasoning and pictorial ideas. I nag at them over commonplace phrases in a way which would do credit to you. I get my holidays on 19th July and am going either to Sligo or Bundoran. Please tell me if you know of any place in Sligo or near it where it would be possible to get two bedrooms and a sitting room for a week. Miss North is coming with me to hunt the astral splendours. If you were thereabouts it would be very pleasant. Miss North will only be able to stay a week but I may remain a full fortnight or may go elsewhere in the same district. The pamphlet will be ready in about ten days when the next I.T. is out.

(Private) The Celtic adept whom I am inclined to regard as the genius of the renaissance in its literary and intellectual aspects lives in a little whitewashed cottage. I feel convinced it is in Donegal or Sligo. There is a great log of a tree with the bark still on it a few feet before the door. It is on a gentle slope. He is middleaged, has a grey golden beard and hair, (more golden than grey) face very delicate and absorbed. Eyes have a curious golden fire in them, broad forehead. It seems the spiritual archetype of a face like George Mead's but much more subtle. He ought to be in your sphere from dream touchings. He has been seen by four or five; three saw in cottage and two the log before door. *Don't spread this about.* Through him ray the lights of Angus. If I see that cottage I will go in on any excuse I can get. There are other places there which swim before me — very mystical.

By the way about my book. I gave it to Lane last December on condition it would be published in the Spring. I have reason to believe that Lane is purposely delaying it to Autumn while pretending to hurry it up. I cannot come to any other conclusion. If he wrote frankly and said it would be better in the Autumn, I would not mind but I feel something underhand about him. I am going to write him an ultimatum, that he has the book out by a fixed date or I withdraw it. Also I would like to know from you, is it usual to have a written agreement between author and publisher? He has broken so many promises (intentionally I think) that I can't trust him. I would like to know your opinion of Lane as a publisher (to be kept Private of course). I get a bad psychometric impression.

                                                              GEORGE RUSSELL

From GEORGE W. RUSSELL

                                                    Dublin
MS Yeats   9 August 1897

["Your man" was probably one of the people living near Coole Park from whom Yeats was collecting material for a series of articles on

Irish folklore and the supernatural and for the expanded edition of *The Celtic Twilight* (1902). The poem was included in an essay on "The Fountains of Youth" (*Irish Theosophist*, 15 Sep 1897) and revised as "The Well of All Healing" in *The Divine Vision* (1904.]

Dear Willie,

    I am very much interested in your man. It confirms my theory that the peasant seers call faery what I believe to be the memorial images of the ancient mystics with their crowns and initiation robes. I am busy but will scribble down one or two auras for you and send them off tomorrow if I can get time. By the way one of our folk had an intensely interesting vision of an old initiation. A figure appeared to him offering a cup to drink. He said, he does not know why, "not that, give me the white stone" and the figure produced a diamond of wonderful light and then he brought him from Ireland to Egypt where he was laid in a sarcophagus with mighty fire forms about him. I had intended going to the mountain for Bove Derg but it has been too wet. I will get time sometime. I am going to New Grange next Sunday I hope, and will recover something. Miss North is again at Rosses with another member and writes that she is getting things about Knocknarea and also the caves at Benbulben. I have not seen O'Grady yet but will look him up at the end of the month when he should be back from Skerries. I tried to make something out of the "Well at Ballykeele" but would not care for anyone who knew the well to see it. I don't know the well.

> There's a cure for all things in the well at Ballykeele
> Where the scarlet cressets oerhang from the rowan trees:
> There's a joy breath blowing from the land of Youth I feel,
> And Earth with its heart at ease.
>
> Many and many a sunbright maiden saw the enchanted
>   land·
> With star-faces glimmer up from the Druid wave:
> Many and many a pain of love was soothed by a faery
>   hand
> Or lost in the love it gave.
>
> When the quiet with a ring of pearl shall wed the earth,
> And the scarlet berries burn dark by the stars in the pool
> Oh, its lost and deep I'll be in the joy breath and the
>   mirth,
> My heart in the star-heart cool.

If its a real well it ought to feel like that, and if it has not the rowans above someone ought to plant them for the purposes of poetry. I plant them there astrally anyhow. Please give greeting on my behalf to Lady Gregory.

Yours
GEO W RUSSELL

From SAMUEL LIDDELL MACGREGOR MATHERS

Paris

MS Yeats   28 March 1898

[Mathers was a founding chief of and the moving force behind the Isis-Urania Temple (London) of the Hermetic Order of the Golden Dawn, into which Yeats was initiated on 7 March 1890. Mathers was assisting with information about and rituals for the Celtic Mysteries, a religious order which Yeats hoped to establish.]

Dear Yeats.

You will think I have been a long time over the Celtic matter, but I have had so much else on my hands. I have however almost finished a Ritual of Initiation for the commencing Grade.

Can you tell me anything of Toth Rury & Cleena beyond their being the Deities of the 3 Royal Waves? Rury is apparently Rudraige Son of Partholon whence I should imagine that Toth & Cleena belong to the Partholon cycle. If you can, please let me know at once. Also do you think Ethleen the mother of Lu is the same as Kathleen? And do you think that the Keithoir of Fiona MacLeod is the same as the ancient Goddess Cessair. Keithoir is called by Fiona the God of the Green World.

I am certain that you are in error in attributing the Hazel trees to the Tree of Life. They are the Tree of Knowledge of Good & Evil, I am persuaded.

In great haste; yours fraternally & sincerely,
MACGREGOR

From SAMUEL LIDDELL MACGREGOR MATHERS

Paris

MS Yeats   6 April 1898

[Mathers refers to John Rhys's *Lectures on the Origin and Growth of Religion as Illustrated by Celtic Heathendom* (1886) and *The Voyage of Bran* (1895, 1897), edited by Kuno Meyer and Alfred Nutt. Yeats's review article on *The Voyage*, "Celtic Beliefs About the Soul", appeared in *The Bookman* (Sep 1898).]

C. et V. H. Fra.,

Just a line to thank you so much for sending me the Hibbert Lectures & the voyage of Bran; they are of the very greatest use; though as usual many wrong parallels are drawn e.g. between Manaanan and Helios. —

> With every kind wish;
> Yours in haste,
> S.R.M.D.

The date you mention will, I think, suit us all right.

From WILLIAM SHARP

MS Yale University Library

Dover
30 April 1898

[Miss M. is Fiona Macleod. Yeats was in Paris, perhaps on the invitation of MacGregor Mathers, for "a great Celtic gathering". "My art-work" is perhaps a reference to drawings for *Ulad of the Dreams* being made by Mrs Mathers. Irish mythical history records two battles of Moytura, one in County Mayo, the other in County Sligo. Marie Henri d'Arbois de Jubainville was the author of *Cours de Littérature celtic* (12 vols., 1883–1902).]

My dear Yeats

I was just about to write to you when your note came, to tell you that a sudden & serious collapse in health not only will prevent Miss M. from coming to Paris, but will probably end in her having to go to some remote Baths for 2 months for special treatment. This *may* prove unnecessary: I trust so. Meanwhile it has materially affected immediate plans. As for myself I partly for this and partly because of being myself (*as you will understand*) seriously indisposed in the same way, I am unable to go to Paris either, & have had to cancel my art-work &c. I shall now be at above address for a week or more to come.

No I do not recall the new Revue Celtique address — but think it is in the Rue Bonaparte. *Parts cannot be had separately — as it is by yearly subsc*[ription]. Your easiest plan wd. be to borrow the

Moytura part either from Jubainville or from Douglas Hyde, who, I know, takes the R.C. or you could easily copy what you want at the Bibliotheque Nationale. Send me a pc to say you have rec'd this.

[unsigned]

From WILLIAM SHARP

                                                            Dover
MS Yale University Library   5 May 1898

[One purpose of Fiona Macleod's proposed visit to Paris was "to see visions" with Yeats, Maud Gonne, and the Matherses (see *L* 298). Macleod's "Children of the Dark Star" was published in *The Dome* for May 1898, as was Yeats's "Aedh hears the cry of the Sedge", "Aedh Laments the Loss of Love", and "Aedh thinks of those who have spoken Evil of his Beloved".]

My dear Yeats

In strict privacy, my friend Miss Macleod is here just now. She was on her way to Paris, but as I told you was suddenly taken too unwell. She was sleeping when your letter came, but I left the enclosure for her at her bedside – & if she wakes before the post goes she will doubtless give you a message through me, unless she feels up to writing herself. If well enough, she leaves here on Saturday morning – but to go north again.

You ask me if I were in any unusual state on either May 1st or 2nd. I do not remember anything on Sunday 1st beyond a singular depression, and a curious sense of unreality for a time, as though I were really elsewhere. But on Monday 2nd, late, I suffered in a way I can't explain, owing to what seemed to me an unaccountable preoccupation of Miss M.

All this is very private – but I trust you.

Her father was tall, fine-looking, with a rather singular concentrated expression. The Macleod tartan is dark (dark green & dark blue almost black). I don't quite understand why you ask. I forgot to add that F.M. herself at times sees a startling likeness between me & her father, though I am taller & bigger & fairer than he was. There are, however, many similarities in nature, &c., and also in the accident of baptismal name.

In case you do not get it, I ordered to be sent to you in Paris (at her & my simultaneous suggestion) a copy of *The Dome*. Perhaps you will care for the story there. Your own poems there are very lovely.

I am afraid I must now go and post this: but

P.S. Have just time to say that Miss M had awaked, & is feeling much better. She cannot write at the moment however — but asks me to say that she has read your letter. In reply, she asks me to write as follows: —

"I *have* been going though an intense emotional crisis. One less poignant period was on the evening or night of the 1st, but far more so, & poignantly on the 2nd. But of this, being private, I cannot speak further. I was, on both occasions (though differently & for different reasons) undergoing tragic feeling. I am at present at a perilous physical & spiritual crisis. I can say no more. The one who shares my life & self is here. It is as crucial for him. I will talk over your letter to *us* — for to *us* it is, though you send it to me. Are you sure it was not Will whom you felt or saw? If I, then I must only"

P.S. Hurriedly adding this at the P O to say that my friend's neuralgia was too severe to talk any more. The subject too was exciting her. She will show me your letter when I get back.

Note *this* time today. *About* 3 p.m. today Thursday she went through (& I too) a wave of *intense* tragic emotion — and last night, between 10 and 12 or later, we nearly *lost* each other in a very strange way. Something I did by the will was too potent, & for a time severed some unconscious links (we were apart at the time: I thought she was sleeping) — & we both suffered in consequence. But I think the extreme crisis of tragic psychic emotion is over.

God grant it.

[unsigned]

From KATHARINE TYNAN HINKSON

London

MS Yeats 13 May 1898

[Although *The Wind Among the Reeds* was not published until April 1899, Yeats had announced his intention of publishing a volume with that title in an interview in *The Irish Theosophist* for 15 November 1893. Hinkson's *The Wind in the Trees* was published in 1898.]

My dear Willie —

I am sorry for the clashing of titles. I will tell you how it happened, and am glad of the opportunity. I had sent in the book without a title; & Grant Richards wrote to me for one. I sent him a list avowing my preference for "Country Airs." At the end of the letter I said — "Only for W. B. Yeats's "Wind Among the Reeds," "The Wind in the Trees" mightn't be a bad title." I heard nothing from him till my husband called there some time after & found that they had selected "The Wind in the Trees." I wrote & asked them not to use that title — on my own account, for every reviewer will say, "Mrs Hinkson's "Wind in the Trees" comes *longs intervalles* after Mr Yeats's "Wind Among the Reeds." But Grant Richards wrote that the title-page was designed & printed, & no alteration was possible.

The injury will be entirely to me & my book. You know I have never placed my verse on the same plane as yours, and I am sure to suffer from the similarity of names.

But I am glad to let you know that I tried to prevent it.

Ever yours
K.H.

From "FIONA MACLEOD" (WILLIAM SHARP)

Midlothian, Scotland
MS Yeats   28 June 1898

[Sharp's essay on *The Shadowy Waters* and *The Wind Among the Reeds*, "The Later Work of Mr. Yeats", was published in *The North American Review* (Sep 1902). Yeats's "Le Mouvement Celtique" (about Fiona Macleod) appeared in *L'Irlande Libre* (Apr 1898), "Irish Fairy Land" in *The Outlook* (Apr 1898), "The Broken Gates of Death" in the *Fortnightly Review* (Apr 1898), and "The Celtic Element in Literature" in *Cosmopolis* (June 1898), which also contained Sharp's "The Wayfarer". A long passage and a postscript of several lines has been blotted out, evidently by Sharp.]

My dear Mr. Yeats

I am very glad to get the letter duly forwarded to me, and to hear from you again. As you know, there is no living writer with whom I find myself so absolutely in rapport as with you. I am eagerly hoping for more beautiful work from you again in prose and verse, soon. How often I have meant to write to you about your lovely opening pages of "The Shadowy Waters", which I do hope you will complete soon, and about the alas still unpublished lyrics "The Wind in the Reeds." I was deeply interested in your Folk-lore articles — but it is new imaginative work that I most long to see. I dread for you a too great preoccupation in other interests — and the consequent inevitable dispersal of energy, and the insatiable avarice of the hours and days of our brief time. I was glad to hear that you liked "Children of the Dark Star" and "The Wayfarer."

I have been told that long ago one of the subtlest and strangest minds of his time — a man of Celtic ancestry on one side and of Norse on the other — was so profoundly influenced by the kindred nature and spirit of a woman whom he loved, a Celt of the Celts, that, having in a sense accidentally discovered the mystery of absolute mental and spiritual union of two impassioned and kindred natures the flame of anguish that had been his in a far back day was in him, so that besides a strange and far reaching ancestral memory, he remembered anew and acutely every last clue and significance of his boyhood and early life, spent mostly among the shepherds and fishers of the Hebrides and Gaelic Highlands. His was the genius, the ancestral memory, the creative power — *she* was the flame — she, too, being also a visionary, and with unusual and all but lost old wisdom of the Gael. Without her, he would have been lost to the Beauty which was his impassioned quest: with her, as a flame to his slumbering flame, he became what he was. The outer life of each was singular, beyond that of any man or woman I have heard of: how much stranger that of their spiritual union. A profound and resolute silence lay upon the man, save when he knew the flame of the woman "through whom he saw Beauty," and his soul quickened. She gave him all she could, and without her he could not be what he was, and he needed her vision to help his own, and her dream, and her thought, and her life, till hers and his ceased to be hers and his and merged into one, and became a spirit of shaping power born of them both.

How does that strike you as a subject for a tale, a book? It would be a strange one. Does it seem to you impossible? It does not seem so to me.

Your friend and comrade
FIONA MACLEOD

From T. W. ROLLESTON

                                            Dublin
MS Kansas University Library   1 July 1898

[To *A Treasury of Irish Poetry*, not published until December 1900, Yeats contributed several of his poems and sketches about Lionel Johnson, AE, Nora Hopper, and Althea Gyles. Versions of the first three notes were printed in the Dublin *Daily Express* (27 Aug, 3 and 24 Sep 1898); a long essay on Gyles appeared in *The Dome* (Dec 1898). Lionel Johnson did not contribute the brief note on Doulgas Hyde to the anthology. Rolleston's best-known poem, "The Grave of Rury", is about Ruraidh O'Conchobhar, last High King of Ireland. Rolleston compares lines one and four of "To Virgil" to lines fifteen and sixteen of his own poem. Yeats's new volume was *The Wind Among the Reeds* (Apr 1899).]

My dear Yeats,
        I am glad you can do A. E., Johnson and Miss Hopper. I will look after the biographical bit to be inserted as in Ward's Engl. Poets, before each essay, & in different type. So don't trouble yourself about that at all, except in so far as you want to do it in connection with criticism.
        You can print your essays later on as you desire. It is very important to bring out the book this year and as early in autumn as may be – and there will be very much to do even after all matter is in – so please keep the undertaking in your mind – I shall ask Johnson to do Hyde.
        You may remember writing to me about The Grave of Rury – & saying you object to the long second & fourth lines in the stanza. It is the same metre as Tennysons *Ode to Virgil* –

        Roman Virgil, thou that singest
        Wars and filial faith and Dido's pyre –

        Stone by stone the stately Abbey
        Falls & fades in passionless decay –

The movement is so different – never no doubt the defect in my metre – that one hardly perceives them to be the same, but they are. I never met with the metre elsewhere.
        When is your new volume of poems coming out?
                                            Yrs sincerely
                                            T. W. ROLLESTON

From GEORGE MOORE

London

MS National Library of Ireland   13 October 1898

[The "trial revised edition" of *Evelyn Innes* (May 1898) was made by pasting revisions into copies of the second, revised edition (Aug 1898). Yeats, who was writing *The Speckled Bird*, was the model for Ulick Dean. Gabriel Fauré was a French composer. Martyn's *The Heather Field and Maeve* with an introduction by Moore was published in January 1899.]

My dear Yeats.

At last I have finished "Evelyn Innes" and I much want to send you the revised edition; my revised edition exists only in an edition of 12 copies. The revisions will have considerable interest for you, I think — You are now writing a novel and from a technical point of view they will interest you. I really think I have improved the book, all the revised passages concern Ulick Dean who is now no longer a scrappy copy of a brilliant original. I shall receive my little edition early next week and wish to send you a copy at once. Will you please to write me a line saying where I am to send it.

I was at the Leeds festival and there I met Faure. I half read half told him the story of your Countess Cathleen. He thought your play most beautiful and I gave him my copy so that he might have a word for word translation made of it. The play is finer even than I thought it was. I liked it better on the second reading and I shall have an opportunity of saying how much I admire it in my preface to Martyn's plays which by the way I shall begin tomorrow. I am your best advertizer, in all the houses I frequent I cry: I am not the bard. There is one greater than I, the latchet of whose shoe I am not worthy to tie.

When is your new book The Wind among the Reeds to be published? I look forward to seeing you — I hear you are coming back at the end of the month.

As ever

GEORGE MOORE

From GEORGE MOORE

London

MS National Library of Ireland   28 October 1898

[Moore refers to the last three pages of Chapter 14 and to the farewell letter in Chapter 32.]

My dear Yeats,

I send you my revised Evelyn. You will find Ulick Dean rewritten *everywhere*. I wish you would compare page 184 to the end of the chapter with the original. Chapter 22 is entirely rewritten and in the intention of converting an episode into a symbol. Ulicks farewell letter did not satisfy me — I have written another — if the second does not satisfy you you must write a letter for Ulick yourself. I have finished the preface for Martyns play. You figure in it conspicuously and I think in a way that will please you. Write to me I beg you about the revised text.

As ever
GEORGE MOORE

From MRS MACGREGOR MATHERS

                                                        Paris
MS Yeats   31 October 1898

[Fiona Macleod's story "Ulad of the Dreams" is divided into three sections, the first of which is "The Melancholy of Ulad". Alfred T. Nutt was editor of *Folk-lore Journal* and manager of his father's publishing firm for which Yeats had done some copying in the Bodleian and the British Museum. "F.M." is Fiona Macleod. Henry D. Davray's translation of "Rosa Alchemica" appeared in *Le Mercure de France* (Oct 1898). "The Awakening of Angus Og" is included in volume five of *The Works of "Fiona Macleod"* (1910). Edwin J. Ellis assisted Yeats with *The Works of William Blake* (1893). Mathers's translation of *The Book of the Sacred Magic of Abra-Melin the Mage*, subsidized by F. L. Gardner, a friend of Yeats, was published in 1898.]

Dear Fra. Yeats,

Did you get my card asking where to send "Ulad"? I do not gather from your letter just received if you have — Anyhow I will forward four copies to you at Sligo —. & will you be so kind as to send *three* to Fiona Macleod as she desired. Presently if you like I will send you more if you think they (music & sketch) will interest certain people — I wonder if "Nutt" could do anything with some copies, but probably you will know what to suggest. I will send the story of Tristesse d'Ulad, which is coming out in November as soon as it arrives here — to you. The colour sketch is well reproduced although done in rather a cheap process —. I was sad to see how much of the original "feeling" it had lost notwithstanding — I am trying various experiments with colour now which I will shew you presently, I hope —

As to the music of Ulad, as far as I have heard it, I like it *much* but it is so difficult to play (& to understand from the *popular* point of view) that perhaps few will care for it — I think you will, & it is I am sure very true in its correspondence to the idea — of F. M.

Bailly is very much interested in all you & the other "Celts" write, & he wants me so much to go on translating & illustrating etc. with him. He tells me that your Rosa Alchemica is just translated — The thing I would like to try of yours is "Land of Heart's Desire" or "Countess Kathleen" — of the latter one might do fragments — Also I want to do if not yet done — "Awakening of Angus Ogue" of Fiona M's — but we will ask her when we send her "Ulad". There is no hurry — & she might then criticize the translation of the latter if she knows french well — — I am much puzzled occasionally over some of the sentences.

We are working *frantically*. Am so glad that you are working at the Celtic revival. With some frenchmen, as I think I told you, we are endeavouring to restore The Mysteries (Egyptian). At last one sees the practibility & possibility of all the things that we have so desired — We have not seen Miss Gonne since you left, but I am writing to her today. E. Ellis & his wife come sometimes. I like him very much —

Shall be glad to have my drawings but do not bother if they are not easily to be got at —

Yes! Is not Abramelin fine? There is any amount of *real* magic in it. Very dangerous book however! — Mind what you are about (with its material formulas).

Every kind wish from us both ys —

M. BERGSON M. MACGREGOR

From GEORGE W. RUSSELL

Dublin

MS Yeats   7 November 1898

[AE refers to Eglinton's "Mr. Yeats and Popular Poetry" (Dublin *Daily Express*, 5 Nov), which was a response to Yeats's "Mr. John Eglinton and Spiritual Art" (Dublin *Daily Express*, 29 Oct). AE's reply was "Literary Ideals in Ireland" (Dublin *Daily Express*, 12 Nov). These and other articles were collected as *Literary Ideals in Ireland* (1899).]

My dear Yeats,

    I agree with you John Eglintons reply is weak. Do not trouble
to reply this week. I have just since receiving your letter written
something defining I think your own position and mine, and if you
think after reading it in the Express that anything further need be
said or if Eglinton again replies you can join in. I take him to task
over his dictum about ancient legends and show they have a value of
symbolic power from long use which the images & shows of the
day have not, and I also answer his question˙about the liberation of
the arts from life and give what I believe to be your meaning when
you say the poetic passion is not in nature. I think it is a good
definition of the mystical position and perhaps it may be as well
until it appears that you should not write anything which by taking
up a different line of defence might point to a difference of opinion
between us two which does not exist in these things. I think the
discussion will do good. I have carefully incited Magee to answer
you because I think that nothing better can be written than a serious
discussion on these primary questions of art in Ireland. It will draw
attention through reiteration to our aims and will acquaint people
with the fact that a new school of thinkers is arising in Ireland in a
way that no book could do just now. When does your book come
out?

Yours ever,
GEORGE W. RUSSELL

From GEORGE MOORE

London

MS National Library of Ireland   24 November [1898]

[Yeats's suggestions were incorporated in the third edition of *Evelyn
Innes* (1901). Moore did not review *The Wind Among the Reeds*.
Edward Martyn was not finally satisfied of the orthodoxy of *The
Countess Cathleen* until it was approved by two churchmen.]

My dear Yeats,

    I received your wonderful letter last night. You are the only one
I can depend upon for an essential criticism — I should say for a
constructive criticism. You have put your critical finger on what I
know to be the weak spot. I knew that Ulick Dean was a litter of
disparate elements waiting to be moulded or knit together. These
disparate elements wanted a centre of gravity. I have found an

exellent place for this centre of gravity and have written the passage you suggest in your letter and have sent it to the printer. I have sent him the other alterations. I have suppressed the last two paragraphs of the letter and have made up the deficiency, very ingeniously I think, from your letter. Your letter is most complete and I had little more to do than to arrange it for the narrative. I am most grateful to you for your assistance, but I will suggest that you do not take any one into your confidence regarding this little collaboration. To do so would merely give occasion for some vain merriment and would prevent the beauty of the present creation from being seen. I am willing to take the credit for work which I have not done without assistance so that the few who are capable of seeing may see its beauty. I long to show you the new text: for I think I have made very dexterous use of the material. I cannot tell you of the impatience with which I am waiting for your new book of verse. I shall try to write about it in the Chronicle. You will be pleased with my remarks about the Countess Cathleen in the introduction. Martyn thought there was something paradoxical in the idea of a woman selling her soul so that she might buy the salvation of the souls of others. I have explained this seeming paradox. I said to Martyn "I know that Yeats is right but I cannot tell you why he is right today, but I will tomorrow or next day"; and I did. I want you now to finish "Shadowy Waters" and then to write "Grania." To fully realize yourself you must produce more. The question arises can you produce more. I think you can. If you don't your genius will not perish, it will result in a small gem of great beauty, not a jewel of the first magnitude like Shelley but equally pure in quality. I hope however that you will abandon politics as Wagner did and that you will realize as he did that his mission was not politics but art. I have much to say to you and long to see you. When will you be in London?

Always yours
GEORGE MOORE

From NORA HOPPER

MS Yeats

London
4 January 1899

[She refers to poems later included in her *Songs of the Morning* (1900). Yeats's essay on "The Poems and Stories of Miss Nora Hopper" (Dublin *Daily Express*, 24 Sep 1898) concentrates on her *Ballads in Prose* (1894) and *Under Quicken Boughs* (1896).]

Dear Mr Yeats,

I am so glad you liked the *Angus Oge* poems. The *bees* are of my own seeing: and *clad* is the word not *shod*. I must get them to send me a copy or two; I have not seen the Express. I wish they would put me on their free list. Are you writing a book on Angus and his kin, or an article.

I am busy thinking out a vivid dream I have had of a weaving goddess, — my dream found her & left her nameless — who has two looms, the web on one is brown and the warp of it is death: the other is green and life is its woof. Who is she, I wonder? I dreamed of her in a dark place, her looms & herself lighted only by the glow of her flowing hair — honey-coloured.

Very sincerely yours
NORA HOPPER

From GEORGE POLLEXFEN

Sligo
MS Yeats   24 February 1899

[Uncle George had "hopes" that the money was to be spent on marriage to Maud Gonne, whom Yeats had seen while in Paris to consult with her and MacGregor Mathers about the Celtic Mysteries. Mary Battle, Pollexfen's servant, was gifted with "second sight". Yeats recorded several "Visions of Old Irish Mythology" which he and Festina Lente (i.e., Pollexfen) had experienced in December 1898. Pollexfen was an accomplished astrologer. As a member of the Order of the Golden Dawn, he inquires whether or not Yeats plans to attend the General Meeting at the Isis-Urania Temple in March. Archer's criticism of *The Countess Cathleen* and Moore's reply appeared in the *Daily Chronicle* in January (see *L* 308 for Yeats's response). Yeats's "High Crosses of Ireland" (Dublin *Daily Express*, 28 Jan 1899) was signed "Rosicrux".]

Enclosure

My dear Willy

I have your letter and herewith I enclose the cheque for £7 you require the loan of.

I was in hopes you would have required more and for another purpose but suppose affairs did not culminate favorably.

When I told Mary some time back that you had gone to France she said you were in great form at present (i e then) but added that some thing that *you and I* had in mind would not come off this time: I made no remark or reply to this, but wondered whether her prognostication might refer to the Celtic Rite or to another matter more immediately to do with your going to Paris.

Last Tuesday week she told me that looking out of the kitchen window during the day she saw the sky become very dark and a funeral procession pass across it. She said I might hear of the death of the Queen or the Holy Father (the pope) because it was like a Royal Funeral the black cloths on the Houses were down to the ground &c. that was Tuesday and on Friday came the death of the President of France.

I am pleased to learn that MacGregors vision & mine agree as to Aengus. It should give me some measure of confidence again.

I have not done much at vision since as for the past 3 weeks or months I have had a very bad head getting worse at night and depressed, so that I have not been able to concentrate on any subject. I had to see Land this week about it and he says he will put me right that it is chiefly *Liver* a good deal out of order &c.

I saw some of the same figures dimly when I tried. I saw the Jester of Angus last kneeling on one knee at the edge of the lake or pool which stretches along under the hill on which the rustling trees are and he seemed to be pulling on the water little boats made out of the flaggens in which he had placed in each a Bumble Bee, which was buzzing away as it sailed forth in its tiny craft, a *very light* air barely rippled the water from the land.

I do wish my poor head would clear up there are so many *interesting* things I want to work at just now in Astrology and which I am unable to tackle for some time past.

Yours sincerely
GEO. W. POLLEXFEN

Do you think you will be in London at the time of the Equinox end of March?

I have heard several people mention the Moore and Archer letters in Daily Chronicle and the correspondence in the Express of course I recognized Rosicrux also.

From EDWARD MARTYN

                                          Tillyra Castle, Co. Galway
MS National Library of Ireland   23 March 1899

[Martyn was concerned about the unorthodoxy of Yeats's *The Countess Cathleen*. This letter is in answer to Yeats's letter of 22 March in which he suggested submitting "the matter to an arbitrator, Dr. Barry, Dr. Delaney, Dr. Vaughan, Father Finlay or any other competent and cultured theologian" (*L* 316). Yeats received affirmative letters from Father Finlay, a novelist, editor, and Professor of Political Economy in University College Dublin, and Father Barry, a theologian and man of letters. Martyn hesitantly accepted their judgement.]

My dear Yeats

I have just received your letter & one from George Moore. I am only too anxious to be able conscientiously to join in this movement.

I do not know anything about Dr. Delaney. Do you mean F^r Delaney the Jesuit? I suppose you mean by Dr. Vaughan the Cardinal. If they be as I surmise, I am quite willing to abide by their decision or that of Dr. Barry or Father Finlay. Anything that they pass I am satisfied to accept. So you may submit The Countess Cathleen to any one of them you like. The best man I should say would be Father Finlay who knows Ireland well. I was informed by a high authority who must be nameless, that the play has many passages most objectionable to Catholics & in my reading of it before I consulted him I thought so too. However if you are prepared to alter the work so that it satisfies any of these theologians I am satisfied. I have submitted it already; do you do so now. There is not the least doubt but that you will have to rewrite considerably — so send a copy at once to either of the theologians you mentioned. Father Finlay I should prefer; and let me see his reply & the passages he marks to come out.

I assure you I should have never made this fuss unless, I had very good authority at my back. *I was dreadfully mistaken & wrong not to have spoken of this at first* — but now I feel I am only doing right.

                                          Yrs sincerely
                                          EDWARD MARTYN

From EDWARD MARTYN

Dublin

MS National Library of Ireland 28 March 1899

[T. P. Gill was editor of the Dublin *Daily Express* at this time. George Coffey was Keeper of Antiquities in the Irish National Museum. Dr Gerald Molloy was a distinguished theologian and biblical historian.]

My dear Yeats

I received your letter together with enclosure of Dr. Barry the tone of which I need not say was pleasing to me. However I must tell you that the chief objection was not the central idea of selling her soul to the Devil in order to save other souls because the whole play is so mythical & undefined, but the fact that there are several passages of an uncatholic & heretical nature that would over here create a scandal especially if the work was promoted & championed by a person like myself who everyone knows to be a Catholic. This is the whole difficulty. Gill told me on Sunday that he was going to Father Finlay with the work. I have not heard from him since. I am quite prepared to abide with what he says should come out and what I should do. Dr. Barry does not seem to have realised that it is *my* difficulty & not *yours*. I have just written to him. By the way it was *Coffey himself* that told me about Dr. Molloy having left out a passage in the reading of the work. I shall keep Dr. Barry's letter safe & return it when required.

Yrs truly

EDWARD MARTYN

I think 8/- is considered much too high over here. 5/- was even considered doubtful.

From EDWARD MARTYN

Dublin

MS National Library of Ireland 31 March 1899

[Martyn's "valued friend" was Most Rev. John Healy, distinguished ecclesiastical historian and Archbishop of Tuam.]

My dear Yeats

I received this morning from Moore a most offensive letter which I will not stand. He attacks my valued friend Dr. Healy in a manner that disgusts me. Now he is quite mistaken about that prelate. I never directly or indirectly consulted Dr. Healy about The Countess Cathleen. He knows nothing whatever about this row. So you had all better be careful about mentioning his name in connection with it. It was another person altogether.

Now as to myself after Moore's words – I shall pay either to you, him, or Lady Gregory the sum of £130 in aid of the Irish Literary Theatre, (£100 my guarantee & £30 that of my late mother) withdraw my play, & leave the Irish Literary theatre altogether. I do not wish to be mixed up in the concern any more. I have had too much trouble in various ways and can not stand any more.

Yrs as ever
EDWARD MARTYN

From MRS MACGREGOR MATHERS

MS Yeats

Paris
29 May 1899

[She probably refers to the production of *The Countess Cathleen* in Dublin on 8 May. The *Bodinière* was a small Paris theatre which could be rented for a single performance, as Cladel apparently intended. Yeats and other members of the Golden Dawn conducted visionary Celtic explorations at the Well of Connla in December 1897. Much concerned with Egyptology, the Matherses kept a statue of Isis in their drawing-room in Paris.]

Dear Fra Yeats,

First of all, our sincere congratulations on your success. Our report was from one or two persons – as we have seen no papers of late. Have you yet those lines for The Land of Hearts Desire? – Two girls (the daughters of Leon Cladel the novelist) are much interested, & would like to act it at the Bodinière Theatre to begin with – I said I would ask you, & also for the added lines, but I am of opinion that after all this delay, it should not be acted until people return in the Autumn as the season ends at the finish of June (in Paris), & I doubt

if the play could be ready before then. However, would you let me
have the amendment, & one might have a rehearsal to see if the
actors are of the right kind?

I am so sorry it could not have been done when you were over
here — Bailly was suddenly called away, & I was plunged in
"Egypt" — am still for that matter. We have been much delighted to
meet William Sharp, who was over here. It is impossible to say how
much we liked him — We felt greatly in sympathy — He is a very
remarkable being I think — in every respect, & so strangely psychic
— After leaving Connla for ages, I have redone him, & the maiden on
Usna, as well as some other designs of a Celtic nature — But most are
unfinished at present on account of the many distractions in other
directions — I am praying for a day when I can really concentrate on
some art work. It is terrible to have to do such, simply in odd
moments.

With every good wish

Your fraternally ever
VESTIGIA

Have just received "The Dominion of Dreams" — & am much looking
forward to it.

From WILLIAM SHARP

London

MS Yale University Library   June 1899

[According to Mrs Sharp, the strain of Sharp's split personality had
led to "a severe nervous collapse" in 1898. Yeats reviewed *The
Dominion of Dreams* in *The Bookman* (July 1899). *Dark Rosaleen*
may have been intended as part of a series of plays on Celtic
mythology to be entitled collectively *The Theatre of the Soul*. Only
The House of Usna and *The Immortal Hour* were published. *Silence
Farm* (1897) was a realistic novel based upon "a tragic tale of the
Lowlands". The reference to "the strain of double life" suggests that
Yeats was aware of the identity of Fiona Macleod.]

My dear Yeats

Serious illness (in France I had to have a doctor) has still left me
so down, mentally & bodily, that I find myself unable to do anything

just now involving deep concentration or spiritual intensity. Therefore the rite waits. But I feel something moving within me. (I do not
think what you sent can stand, i.e. can do more than spiritually
indicate a direction: I'll explain later).

I am very eager to hear what you think of "The Dominion of
Dreams." If ever a book was born out of spiritual stress & suffering,
out of *the depths*, this book was: as I think Miss Macleod herself has
written to you.*

*Shall you be writing about it anywhere?

It is probable that after "The King of Ireland's Son", Miss M's
next play will be a short modern play of a deep & moving human
interest, called "Dark Rosaleen" (meaning Ireland herself). Today or
in a day or so Grant Richards should send you a copy of a new book
by myself "Silence Farm". I think you will find it the best & most
satisfying thing that has appeared under my name. (G. R. & his
reader seem to have a very high opinion, & very high hopes of it,
indeed.) If, perchance, you sh^d be able to say anything about it
anywhere I should be grateful. But this is just as you can, & feel
inclined. In any case I want you to have the book. I would send you
an advance copy with my inscription — but I find that the last of the
very few I have has my inscription to Lady Gregory — but G. R. will
have had my instructions by this. I'm sending Lady Gregory's to her.

We leave our flat about 20th July. Shall you be in town before
then?

Then we go to Ireland but I don't know where yet, probably to
the Mourne Mountains coast.

I doubt if I'll ever live in London again. It is not likely. I do not
know that I am overwhelmingly anxious to live anywhere. I think
you know enough of me to know how profoundly I feel the strain of
life — the strain of double life. Still, there is much to be done yet.
But for that . . . .

> Your friend
> WILLIAM SHARP

From ROBERT BRIDGES

MS Bridges

Yattendon, Newbury
30 June 1899

[Yeats's "Mr. Moore, Mr. Archer and the Literary Theatre" (*Daily
Chronicle*, 30 Jan 1889) took issue with some remarks by the drama
critic William Archer. In "The Theatre" (*The Dome*, Apr 1889)

Yeats had praised Bridges' *The Return of Ulysses* (1890). *The Feast of Bacchus* was published in 1889, *The Wind Among the Reeds* in April 1899. In fact, Yeats had written to Bridges twice in 1897 from 18 Woburn Buildings, London. The second volume of Bridges' *Poetical Works* was published on 1 November 1899. Bridges refers to the theological controversies surrounding the first performance of *The Countess Cathleen* on 8 May 1899.]

My dear Yeats

   I was very glad to get a line from you, and to hear something of your theatre. I take a great interest in it, but don't of course hear much down here. I was fortunate one day, being on the railway, & buying a "Chronicle" to hit on your letter on the Drama, aimed at some conventional critic. I liked it extremely, and it seemed unanswerable. I hope that your Dublin plays will be a yearly thing, and that they will pay their expences. As for London, it is hopeless at present — it is all scenery and low 'fun', with some fashionable rant. I expect it was never much better, but the conventions just now are the deadliest dreariness. Thanks for attending to "Ulysses" — I don't expect (or really wish) to see a play of mine on the stage, but I feel confident that when the "Feast of Bacchus" gets there, it will stay. Still that is not much in your line.

   A thousand thanks for "The Wind among the Reeds." I shall value extremely a copy with your inscription, but you do me wrong in imagining that I am not among your buyers. I got the book as soon as it came out. How then did I not write to congratulate you and thank you for it? I don't know where to write to you, and that uncertainty always prevents me from writing a letter. It's like talking to a man who may not be in the room. If you will send me an address whence letters are always forwarded to you I will trouble you from time to time with my praises & salutations. It happens that you have never written to me twice from the same place. Now it is Galway.

   This is a good place except in winter. Spring and autumn are not bad, and I hope that you may come in autumn. We are free of all hat and coat conventions, and you wd find it quiet here, and easy to work: and could stay on as you liked.

   The new poems delighted me. There are things I don't understand — but that is all the better. I am very glad that you have got so much recognition, it is really very lucky, tho' I don't suppose

you can have a very large sale. Still enough to pay a little I expect.
To publish at a loss is most depressing.

I have a new volume of "Collected Works" (a sad sign of age)
coming out in October. 1/3 of the book will be more or less new, &
hoping there may be some among the new poems that you will like I
will send you a copy if I know where to send it.

Accept, as the French say, the tribute of my lofty and
unimpaired esteem

Yours sincerely
ROBERT BRIDGES

I am glad the Papists went for you! They are very cheeky just now.

From WILLIAM SHARP

MS Yale University Library

London
[June—July 1899]

[Sharp apparently refers to one of the rituals Yeats was writing for
the Celtic Mysteries. Sharp's play was produced by the Stage Society
at the Globe Theatre and published in *The National Review* (July
1900) as "The House of Usna", perhaps because "The King of
Ireland's Son" was also the title of one of Nora Hopper's poems
quoted in "Dalvan", a story in *Ballads in Prose* (1894), which also
contains "The Wind Among the Reeds". Kilkeel, Annalong, and
Newcastle are coastal towns south of Belfast.]

My dear Yeats
    I have read and carefully considered the rite — but I think it
calls for something more definite in visionary insight and significance — for spiritual recasting, so to say. And as you well know, all
work of this kind — as all imaginative work — is truly alive only when
it has died into the mind and been born again. The mystery of
dissolution is the common mean of growth. Resurrection is the test
of any spiritual idea — as of the spiritual life itself, of art, and of any
final expression of the inward life.
    I cannot say when this rebirth will be: but when it comes I will
write to you, if the result seems to me to be of any worth, any
significance: as I hope it will be. The sole stream of inward thought
that can help is moving that way.
    I have been ill — and seriously — but am now better, though I
have to be careful still. All our plans for Scandinavia in the autumn
are now over — partly for the now impracticable expense, partly by

doctor's order, who says I must have hill & sea air native to me — Scotland or Ireland.

So about the end of July my wife and I intend to go to Ireland. It will probably be to the east coast, Mourne Mountains coast, as we must live cheaply & simply. Will you be eastward at all? Surely Tara-land, Ulidia, must have strong appeal to you? I would be glad go west of course, but we cannot afford it, as it would involve going about & living in hotels. We think of Kilkeel or Annalong or Newcastle.

I hope you like "The Dominion of Dreams". Miss Macleod has received two or three very strange & moving letters from strangers, as well as others. The book of course can appeal to few, — that is, much of it. But, I hope, it will sink deep.

If you are at any time announcing, or speaking of the play of Miss Macleod for acting next year, do not now speak of it as "The Tanist." Either that name will be relinquished, or used later for another play. Of *course if thought advisable* it can be retained — for the acting play — but in its literary & published form it will be called *"The King of Ireland's Son."* You will be interested to hear, if Miss Macleod has not already told you, that this play will be finished soon, relatively. I think it will not disappoint you.

Are you to be at Gort (or Tillyra) in August? I hope you are happily at work. What are you doing? I envy you in the West. My heart is always there. And you are amid green and beautiful things. There is no nostalgia like that of the green way.

Yours
W.S.

My most cordial remembrances & regards to Lady Gregory. London is prostratingly hot. You are well out of it.

From ALTHEA GYLES

MS Yeats   [London]
                                              [probably summer 1899]

[Miss Gyles probably refers to the productions of Yeats's *The Countess Cathleen* and Martyn's *The Heather Field* on 8 and 9 May 1899. Stephen Gwynn was a prolific writer and active member of the Irish Parliamentary Party. Yeats wrote to Lady Gregory in November 1899 about Miss Gyles's liaison with the "immoral" Smithers. He published *The Harlot's House* with her illustrations, probably in 1904. The Coopers and the Gore-Booths were landed families,

friends of Yeats, in County Sligo. Several drafts of Miss Gyles's
unfinished play are now in the Library of Reading University. Four
of the "short things" she speaks of are preserved in the Yeats papers.
Matt is probably Elkin Mathews, the London publisher. A. H. Bullen
had given Yeats an advance on his unfinished novel *The Speckled
Bird*, for which he arranged to substitute *Ideas of Good and Evil* in
December 1901. Rev. Matthew Russell's *Idylls of Killowen* was
published in 1899.]

My dear Mr Yeats
    I meant to write to you long ago and congratulate you on your
success with the Celtic Theatre — I hope it really was as successful as
I heard — & then again to answer your other letter but I have been &
am still so busy. Of course I will do the book plate with much
pleasure but you will have to wait a bit as I must finish this job &
then get poor Sir Vincents & Stephen Gwynns brothers done any
way if not before at the same time.
    I am doing a book for Smithers it is by Oscar Wilde & is called
"The Harlot's House." It is most interesting & I am supposed to be
doing it very well. Its chiefly shadows on a blind. I hope the drawings
wont shock Mr Symons. He wont see them in a crude state but
modified by Mr Smithers!
    People are being horrid to me about it so please listen to
this dont say anything to any of my personal acquaintances about it
such as the Coopers or Gore Booths etc if you chance to come across
them. They can do what they like when the book comes out but I
cannot endure any more lectures on the subject this hot weather &
they are most impertinent. Nothing will alter my determination to
do it. I have two most excellent motives & I cannot have my best
moods destroyed for no object. Mr Colin is horribly shocked. Dear
Lady Colin of course sympathises.
    Smithers is being *awfully nice* both about the work itself &
paying & now at last I shall be able to start with the proceeds; it will
be finished by August & I mean to return to the country & write the
play & do my own beloved pictures.
    I have no more of the little play done but when I have I will
send it to you to show Mr Symons — please thank him from me in
advance. I have "a few words" for both you & him which are that it
is very wrong to slander so *excellent* a person as Mr Smithers.
    I think the best design you can have for the book plate would
be a simple square filled with the "dust of the Dead."

I should not take more than 3 months to do this.

I have written a good many short things chiefly about Angus & the Red Hound.

I sent him the one you know & a new one & another about his prayer of a girl for her lover who was an outlaw.

Matt offered me a book, but he pays too little & Constable was quite pleased with my work & said would I suggest a book to them that I would like to do. I have one I have wanted for years to do but I dont think theyd do it so I shall suggest it to Smithers after this. I told them I wanted to do a Maeterlinck but they said George Allen published him so much. They have that wonderful man Hyde working for them.

I think you behave *disgracefully* to old Bullen, he is going to give me your novel cover to do — when its finished of course, but *pray dont hurry*, he is a dear old thing. I took a fit of virtue & went down & offered to work off my debt & he was so nice & Im sad to say didnt take me at my word. I was only virtuous because the Dr croaked about my having got consumption from my patient.

Now my cough is nearly gone I work for Smithers. Im still doctored about twice a week & I really do believe that the medicine I have makes me work: would you like the prescription? Something any way is making me work which seems miraculous. I did a cover for Father Russell's "Idylls of Killowen" it had to be shamrocks. Ive asked for her specimens so I may send you one — but I suppose you will see it. Seriously what do you think about your book plate being the original design for the poster I was so shamefully treated about.

Write soon.

Yours
ALTHEA GYLES

Dont forget not to talk about my book to people I know before it comes out if they come & lecture me I shall quarrel with them & I prefer them to quarrel with me after.

Let me know before you send any of the enclosed [?] Couldnt I get one of them in somewhere with a picture.

From STANDISH O'GRADY

[Kilkenny]

MS Yeats   16 July [1899]

[O'Grady is probably alluding to the libel suit as a result of which he lost the *Kilkenny Moderator* in 1899.]

Dear Yeats.

I look to you to do *all you can* to help me in this matter. There
is involved in it my rescue from a condition of the most degrading
slavery, into the particulars of which I dont care to enter.

You must imagine me a free man, a man who has done his
country some service, & who has a stroke of work in him yet living in
a condition of vile slavery & making this attempt to escape from it.

You must write to everyone you know enclosing this circular &
make them subscribe for at least a quarter & that will only cost them
1s–7½d no great price to pay for the rescue of an enslaved man. If
they join for a quarter they will go on for I shall give them a very
good penny-worth for their penny.

I remain

Yours sincerely
STANDISH O'GRADY

Now dont be lazy & dilatory in this matter but help me *all you can.*

From WILLIAM THOMAS HORTON

Brighton
MS Yeats   22 July 1899

[Horton produced "Seven Fine Chalk Drawings" for a de luxe
edition of Poe's *The Raven* and *The Pit and the Pendulum,* published
by Leonard Smithers in 1899. Horton's *A Book of Images*, with an
"Introduction" by Yeats, was published by the Unicorn Press in
1898. Several of Horton's drawings appeared in *The Pick-Me-Up*,
1897–9. H. Rider Haggard, the author of many popular romances,
had collaborated with Andrew Lang on *The World's Desire* (1891).
Horton designed the cover for George Egerton's translation (1899) of
Hamsun's *Hunger.* Horton's satiric "portrait and criticism" of Yeats
standing on an occult book and surrounded by volumes of "his
poetry and mysticism" appeared in *The Academy* for 8 July. Robert
Ross, good friend of Oscar Wilde, was a writer and art critic. E. J.
Oldmeadow was editor of *The Dome* and managing director of the
Unicorn Press. Horton quotes from Blake's essay on "A Vision of the
Last Judgment". Yeats's *The Shadowy Waters* was published in
December, the first part of his essay on "The Philosophy of Shelley's
Poetry" in *The Dome* (July 1900). Horton designed the cover for
Unwin's "Popular Edition" of George Moore's *Evelyn Innes* (1901),

the first edition of which was dedicated to Symons and Yeats (pictured as Ulick Dean in the novel). Horton suggests that Yeats had told Moore about the Brotherhood of the New Life, which was founded by Thomas Lake Harris.]

My dear Yeats

I am very glad to have received a note from you, and hope you will let me know when you are back in Town again.

I hope you'll accept the "Poe" I send herewith. I hate design on cover, but Smithers would have one on cover & there it is.

I have another set for Vol. 2 of Poe if Vol 1 pays & *perhaps* another Book of Images with drawings in Black Chalk — a bigger thing than the Unicorn B. of Images.

I am just now busy on decorative landscapes (black & white) and hope to get them accepted as heads & tail pieces to some book or another.

Then "Pick-me-up" has some line work of mine coming out shortly.

One is to appear in the Bank Holiday number. I intended it for "Orphee aux enfers" but suggested it might be called "The Poet Laureate," this I am afraid would be libelous. The Editor may add a few lines. I'll send you a copy when it appears.

The amusing thing about "P-me-up" is that thro a "Vision of Cresey, hatred etc" (you may remember it, a gigantic druid face appearing above a Town) Rider Haggard wrote & invited me to lunch to meet his wife & Andrew Lang. Of course I accepted & was much edified especially when your name cropped up — but of this, more when we meet.

My cover design to Knut Hamsun's "Hunger" seems to have created a little attention. It was in "The Academy" of June 17. You may have seen it as well as the portrait of yourself in "The Academy" of a fortnight ago (July 8th.)

Some, like Smithers, [words indecipherable] Robert Ross etc speak highly of my chalks, others, like Oldmeadow, prefer my B. & white landscapes.

You must remember the Poe chalks are merely an introduction to this style — I have done several since then which shew improvement. It is these and the decorative landscapes I hope to show you later on when we meet.

I seem — no, *not* I seem, I *am* walking with two angels, one of Power, Strength, Sadness, Mystery; the other Clearness, Warmth,

Joy & Rest. One is the Moon, the other the Sun. I see them both as glorious Woman shapes. One in robes of blackness with a dazzling white face & deep, oh! so deep, large soft black eyes, gazing sorrowfully out beneath black horizontal brows [words indecipherable] glitters the crescent of the moon, dazzling white on a black ground. The other form is nude save for thin transparent drapery that floats around her. Her hair of red gold enwraps her as a veil. She is ever dancing, singing & laughing. Her eyes are of a nearly blue black colour & around her glows the sun. She is all health, joy & happiness.

One thing they have in common, they bid me to leave earthly things.

These together form one glorious Being, sympathetic to all joy & sorrow. Is this Being one of Blake's "Images of wonder, which always entreat him to leave mortal things"?

However, these things must not be written — you understand. I am looking forward to "The Shadowy Waters" & your essay on Shelley. I think I have told you Keats & Shelley & Coleridge are the poets who appeal to me, especially Keats & Shelley. So anything about either I eagerly devour. Because of you I read Evelyn Innes. I know the exigencies of the story required, *perhaps*, your becoming the lover (No. 2). I should have preferred your remaining pure, serene, clear as crystal, hard as diamond, & make the Priest the lover. Perhaps he becomes Lover No. 3. I was especially struck at the mention of mystics who thro' chastity attain to knowledge of the bride of Eternity. You must have mentioned the B.N.L. to G.M. Of course I know this teaching is not exactly new & has always been groped after where spiritual love replaces the sickened & dead earthly ditto.

Please drop me a p.c. to say "Poe" reached you safely,

> Your's sincerely
> W. T. HORTON.

From GEORGE W. RUSSELL

                                                      Dublin
MS Yeats   4 September 1899

[AE drew a circular figure with lines extending out to suggest the rays with "mingled gold and silver", both important in alchemical symbolism. H.P.B. is Helena Petrovna Blavatsky, founder of the Theosophical Society in 1875. The poem about Connla's Well was probably "The Nuts of Knowledge", included in *The Nuts of Knowledge* (1904). W. P Coyne's letter appeared in the *Daily Express* (2 Sep). Horace Curzon Plunkett was currently a Unionist M.P. for south County Dublin.]

My dear Yeats,

I have been so busy since I came back that I have had no chance of thinking about the symbols. But I think that the true symbol is the form in the brooch of the figure we saw over the stream. See what you can get from it. I think I remember somewhere H.P.B. saying this represented the first dualism (in its cosmic sense) and in the human sense it ought correspondingly to represent the last division before spiritual unity. Tell Lady Gregory that I expect her sketches will be framed and set by tomorrow, so they told me in the shop. I will go round to see if they are all right before they are sent off. I promised you a sketch of Knocknarea from the third Ross. What am I to do with it? Will I keep it until you come up, or have it mounted and sent down to you, or to Woburn Buildings? Mounted sketches are awkward to carry. I would like to hear from you how The Shadowy Waters is progressing. I have been so far moved by the west and my stay there that I made a vigorous effort to get on with a mystical poem about Connlas Well which I have had in mind for a long time. If I do much of it, I will send it in to you for criticism. I suppose you do not consider it necessary to answer Coynes letter in the Saturday Express. I am off to Co. Waterford by the end of this week and the serene course of Druidic meditation is broken into by the necessity of preparing speeches. Tell Lady Gregory that Plunkett is now able to hobble about a little and he will probably be in Ireland at the beginning of next month. I have no news. I was up in the mountains on Sunday and the bells were going at a great rate. I think something must be up in Tirnanoge, perhaps its final incarnation in the visible Ireland. Kind regards to Lady Gregory.

Yours ever
GEORGE RUSSELL

From "FIONA MACLEOD" (WILLIAM SHARP)

Midlothian, Scotland

TS Yale University Library 16 September 1899

[*The Sin-Eater and Other Tales* was first published in 1895, *The Washer of the Ford and Other Moralities* in 1896. Appearing first in the *Fortnightly Review* (Nov and Dec 1899), "The Divine Adventure" was revised and included in *The Divine Adventure: Iona: By Sundown Shores* (1900). Yeats referred to "Honey of the Wild Bees" in his review of *The Dominion of Dreams* (*Bookman*, July 1899).]

My dear Mr Yeats

I am at present like one of these equinoctial leaves which are whirling before me as I write, now this way and now that: for I am, just now, addressless, and drift between East and West, with round-the-compass eddies, including a flying visit of a day or two in a yacht from Cantyre to the north Antrim coast. Thus it is that your welcome note of the 3rd was delayed in reaching me. You, I suppose, are still at your friend's in Galway.

I am very interested in what you write about the "Dominion of Dreams," and shall examine with closest attention all your suggestions. The book has already been in great part revised by my friend. In a few textual changes in "Dalua" he has in one notable instance followed your suggestion, that about the too literary "lamentable elder voices." The order is slightly changed, too: for "The House of Sand and Foam" is to be withdrawn, and a piece called "The Winds of the Spirit" substituted: and "Lost" is to come after "Dalua" and precede "The Yellow Moonrock".

You will like to know what I most care for myself. From a standpoint of literary art *per se* I think the best work is that wherein the barbaric (the old Gaelic or Celto-Scandinavian) note occurs. My three favourite tales in this kind are "The Sad Queen" in the *"Dominion of Dreams,"* "The Laughter of Scathach" in *The Washer of the Ford*, and "The Harping of Cravetheen" in *The Sin-Eater*. In art, I think "Dalua," and "The Sad Queen," and "Enya of the Dark Eyes," the best [in] the *Dominion of Dreams*. Temperamentally, those which appeal to me most are those with the play of mysterious psychic force in them — as in "Alasdair the Proud," "Children of the Dark Star," "Enya of the Dark Eyes," and, in earlier tales, 'Cravetheen' and "The Dan-nan-Ron," and the Iona tales. Those others which are full of the individual note of suffering and other emotion I find it very difficult to judge. Of one thing only I am convinced, as is my friend (an opinion shared with the rare few whose judgment really means much), that there is nothing in the *Dominion of Dreams* or elsewhere in these writings under my name to stand beside "The Distant Country." Nothing else has made so deep and vital an impression both on men and women — and possibly it may be true what a very subtle and powerful mind has written about it, that it is the deepest and most searching utterance on the mystery of passion which has appeared in our time. It is indeed the core of *all* these writings — and will outlast them all.

Of course I am speaking for myself only. As for my friend, his heart is in the ancient world and his mind for ever questing in the domain of the spirit. I think he cares little for anything but through the *remembering* imagination to recall and interpret, and through the formative and penetrative imagination to discover certain mysteries of psychological and spiritual life. (Apropos, I wish you very much to read, when it appears in the "Fortnightly Review" — probably either in October or in November — the spiritual 'essay' called "The Divine Adventure" — an imaginative effort to reach the same vital problems of spiritual life along the separate, yet inevitably inter-related, lines of the Body, the Will (Mind or Intellect), and the Soul.)

And this brings me to a point about which I must again write to you — I say 'again,' for once last summer I wrote to you, trying so far as practicable in a strange and complex matter to be explicit. Let me add that I write to you, as before, trusting to you honourably to destroy this letter.

You are both right and wrong in your diagnosis of the passive and expressional factors. (As a generalisation, I think what you say is right: but here, as so often elsewhere, the puzzling exception invalidates the idea of invariability.)

Again I must tell you that all the formative and expressional as well as nearly all the visionary power is my friend's. In a sense only his is the passive part: but it is the allegory of the match, the wind, and the torch. Everything is in the torch in readiness, and, as you know, there is nothing in itself in the match. But there is the mysterious latency of fire between them: — the little touch of silent igneous potency at the end of the match. Well, the match comes to the torch, or the torch to the match — and, in what these symbolise, one adds spiritual affinity as a factor — and all at once flame is born. The torch says all is due to the match. The match knows that the flame is not hers, but lies in that mystery of thitherto unawakened love, suddenly brought into being by contact. But beyond both is the wind, the spiritual air. Out of the unseen world it fans the flame. In that mysterious air, both the match and the torch hear strange voices. But the match is now part of the torch, lost in him, lost in that flame. Her small still voice speaks in the mind and spirit of the torch, sometimes guiding, sometimes inspiring, out of the deep mysterious intimacies of love and passion. That which is born of both, the flame, is subject to neither — but is the property of the torch. The air which came at the union of both is sometimes called Memory, sometimes Art, sometimes Genius, sometimes Imagination, sometimes Life, sometimes the Spirit. It is all.

But, before that flame, people wonder and admire. Most wonder only at the torch. A few look for the match beyond the torch, and, finding her, are apt to attribute to her that which is not her's, save as a spiritual dynamic agent. Now and then that match may also have *in petto* the qualities of the torch — particularly memory and vision: and so can stimulate and amplify the imaginative life of the torch. But the torch is at once the passive, the formative, the mnemonic and the artistically and imaginatively creative force. He knows that in one sense he would be flameless — or at least without that ideal blend of the white flame and the red — without the match: and he knows that the flame is the offspring of both, and that the wind has many airs in it, and that one of the most potent of these under-airs is that which blows from the life and mind and soul of the 'match' — but in his heart he knows that, to all others, he and he alone is the flame, his alone both the visionary, the formative, and the expressional.

Do you understand? Read — copy what you will, as apart from me — and destroy this.

Of late the 'match' is more than ever simply a hidden flame in the mind of the 'torch'. When I add that the match never saw or heard a line of "Honey of the Wild Bees" (which you admire so much) till after written, you will understand better.

Please send me a note by return to say that you have received this — and destroyed it — and if you understand: but as my address is uncertain, send it in an *outer envelope* addressed simply,

William Sharp Esq, Murrayfield, Midlothian.
Where it will safely reach me.

I have no time now to write you about the plays. Two are typed: the third, and chief, is not yet finished. When all are revised and ready, you can see them. "The Immortal Hour" (the shortest — practically a 1 act play in time,) is in verse.

Sincerely yours
FIONA MACLEOD

P.S. I think you could have a proof-set of "The Divine Adventure" in your case.
P.S. As this is such a long letter I have typed it.

From GEORGE W. RUSSELL

Dublin

MS Yeats   19 September 1899

[Thomas Bird Mosher of Portland, Maine, made a business of pirating foreign publications, but he did not publish "The Island of Statues". Selections from the work appeared in the "Celtic Christmas" number of *The Irish Homestead* (Dec 1899), doubtless at AE's urging. AE's poem was "The Feast of Age", included in *The Divine Vision*, which begins "See where the light streams over Connla's fountain". Ballina is in County Mayo.]

My dear Yeats,

You remember my once telling you I would pirate the Island of Statues if you did not reprint it here. You said you did not mind as it would probably be done some day or other. I wrote to Mosher my pirate in U.S.A. who asked me to get a copy for him. I hunted but could not find one and so it lay over. I have succeeded in laying my hands on the old magazine now, and I wish to know seriously would you be very angry if I arranged with Mosher to pirate it. If you would not object, I would write a preface for it saying that it was early work &c and that though your mature judgement rejected it it was too good to lose in the opinion of friends. Of course Mosher may not take it when he sees it, but I think he would be very glad to fulfil the law of his being which is distinctly piratical. I of course will tell Mosher that I am the culprit and you are not in it. Please tell me what you think. But I want to have a nicely printed copy of the Island of Statues for myself so badly that I really think I will send the copy I have borrowed to him whether you like it or not. I would like to see your sketches in pastels. My poem on Fountain is progressing but I am afraid I am wading beyond my depth. Miss Gonne looks well and will write you from Ballina where she could see you as soon as she finds what arrangements are made for her.

Your ever,
GEO. W. RUSSELL

P.S. I saw Sharp last night on his way to England. No particular news of him. Mrs. Sharp with him.

From ANDREW LANG

                                                           London
MS Yeats   10 October [1899]

[Edward Clodd was Vice President of the Folk-Lore Society.]

My dear Sir
    I have asked Mr Clodd to forward this catechism of Folklore. In
Ireland lately, at Lissadell, I got a lot of Fairies from Micky Og, but
he had no Second Sight, he did not seem aware of it. In Luchaher,
Apping, and Glencoe, I found second sight very common, but fairies
hardly seem to be active, though common enough as traditions of
what used to be. It would much oblige me if you could kindly let me
know whether this disproportion of second sight to fairies is the rule
in Ireland, and whether they still divine in blade bones of sheep, as in
the highlands. Micky Og knew nothing of crystal gazing. Elf shots are
medicinal in both countries. Please excuse this scientific curiosity,
and permit me to express the pleasure which I have had in reading your
papers on Irish traditions and usages.
        Believe me

                                                    Faithfully yours
                                                    A. LANG

From ANDREW LANG

                                                           London
MS Yeats   ✿   25 October [1899]

[Lang had read papers before the SPR and contributed articles to its
journals, but did not become a member until 1906 (President in
1911). Yeats and Lady Gregory collected many stories about Biddy
Early (some considered her a healer, some a witch), and she figures
prominently in Yeats's "Ireland Bewitched" (*The Contemporary
Review*, Sep 1899). Glencoe is a mountain village in the west of
Scotland.]

My dear Sir
    It was very good of you to write when unwell. What you say
further corroborates my opinion, as the phenomena you describe are
rather omens than the clear visions of distant persons and events later
fulfilled, that we call second sight. In the slang of the S.P.R. second

sight covers "premonitions," (audible and visible) and "veridical hallucinations," in general. Of course this kind of thing has always been going on, and in the Highlands is very common. Your Glencoe seer is regularly called in to find bodies of the drowned. He told me what he could, but it had to be interpreted from the Gaelic. The Caledonian Medical society lately published a number of tales in their journal. What puzzles me is why this kind of thing should be so rare in Ireland, where most conditions are the same as in the Highlands, where Catholics and Protestants are equally second sighted, and well educated ministers cannot escape the gift themselves. Biddy seems to be a kind of crystal gazer, in the Highlands they use a blade-bone of a sheep for the purpose. I am sorry you don't publish your own experiences, I don't care what people believe, and have just got a good case of second sight (English) from the East End.

We leave for St. Andrews in a fortnight, where (I don't know why) half the population can scry in glass balls.

Believe me

Sincerely yours
A. LANG

From MICHAEL DAVITT

Dalkey, Co. Dublin

MS Yeats   4 November 1899

[Yeats and Maud Gonne strongly supported Davitt (founder of the Land League in 1879) when his reputation had been attacked by Frank Hugh O'Donnell. Davitt's speech appeared in *Freeman's Journal* for 6 November.]

My dear Mr. Yeats

It is indeed most kind of you to think of writing so complimentary a letter.

I spoke, just as I felt, in my last utterance in the H of Commons, in the full conviction that I would serve the cause of Irish liberty best with right-thinking minds everywhere by spurning a craven expediency and basing Ireland's right & claim to freedom upon the Justice and Right which we should advocate for every People defending their independence.

I am glad I got out of Parliament on those lines. If you will read

my speech at Aughamore tomorrow (in Monday's Freeman) you will
see that there were good reasons why I was resolved to regain my
freedom from Party restraints.

What a magnificent struggle the Boers are making! And we
————————— are 25,000,000 of Celts in the world population! —
The Boers are 150,000 !!

With kind regards

Yours truly
MICHAEL DAVITT

From JOHN M. WATKINS

London

MS National Library of Ireland   2 March 1900

[Charter member of the Esoteric Section of the Theosophical
Society, Watkins founded the most renowned occult bookstore in
London. Lady Wilde was the author of many nationalistic poems and
two books on Irish folklore: *Ancient Legends, Mystic Charms, and
Superstitions of Ireland* (1887): *Ancient Cures, Charms, and Usages
of Ireland* (1890) (reviewed by Yeats in *The Scots Observer*, Mar
1890).]

Dear Yeats

Will you kindly read the enclosed & suggest to me if possible an
explanation. It is from a customer of mine in Co. Galway who is
evidently distressed & I should like to help the poor man if I can. I
know nothing of the man beyond the fact of his being a customer.

Your faithfully
J. M. WATKINS

Some months ago — all the country superstitious people I met began
showing me objects in the form of a ring and then another in the
form of a fork, to look through I suppose. Look through the ring
first and then through the fork. Did you ever hear of this? as I
cannot understand it. They also occasionally fixed themselves in
threes on the road before me and tried to make me pass through
them. Try to find out what this means for me if you can. I thought it
might be in Lady Wilde's book. — It was directed at me & meant
something mysterious.

From GEORGE MOORE
MS Berg Collection,   Llanfairfechan, Wales
New York Public Library   [early July 1900]

[This and the following letters from Moore in 1900—1 concern his collaboration with Yeats on *Diarmuid and Grania*, begun in the autumn of 1899. The play was produced in October 1901.]

Keep this letter

My dear Yeats
    You will be glad to hear that I like the II act wholly, I might say almost unreservedly. There may be a few changes to make but very little. The first act wanted more rewriting than I thought. The weakest scene was the scene with the Foster Mother. It is in this scene that these facts must come out (1) That Grania had once consented to marry Finn. (2) That she has mysteriously changed her mind. That, when in a sudden lightning she learnt that she was not to marry Finn, she went to the Foster Mother who by the act of magic discovered that Grania's prevision was quite true — that she was not to marry Finn. (3) That Grania for some mysterious reason has not told her father of the change that has come into her. I have written the scene; when I get to London I will get the act copied and will send you the type written copy for revision. I hope you will revise the scene with special reference to the three headings. For after all they are the basis of the entire action. Any thing you can write in to the scene to bring these points out will strengthen the play. I need not insist for these are points to which you attach even more importance than I do. We overlooked these points.

Always yours
GEORGE MOORE

If these points are not brought out Grania looks like a wilful girl who let things go to the last in order to make a row.

From GEORGE MOORE
TS Berg Collection,   London
New York Public Library   30 July 1900

My dear Yeats
    I have had a copy made of the second Act so that you may revise more easily. It does not differ from the last, or very slightly,

but it is all together and you will be able to make your revisions
easier than you would have on various M.S.S. The construction seems
to me perfect, and all the characters are clearly set forth in their
different attitudes and relations. What the Act seems to me [to]
want now is beauty in the dialogue, which is in places harsh and may
be occasionally disjointed. No one will be able to remedy these
defects as well as you. GRAINNE'S little monologue, in the middle
of the Act, might I think be improved; and the passages, in the
beginning of the Act, where GRAINNE and DIARMUID tell each
other stories might, I *think, be lengthened. The act is a little short.* It
only makes twenty-four closely typed pages, and it really ought to
make thirty or very nearly; so do not fear to lengthen the act, and do
not let any desire of further incidents hinder you. *The act wants no
new incidents; of that I am quite sure.* This is how it strikes me, but I
am longing to hear how it strikes you, so do write.

Always yours
GEORGE MOORE

From GEORGE W. RUSSELL

Dublin

MS Yeats   [autumn 1900]

[The controversies between Yeats, D. P. Moran (the editor of *The
Leader*), AE, Standish James O'Grady, and Moore formed the basis
for *Ideals in Irelands* which also included an essay by Douglas Hyde.
The novel is *The Speckled Bird.*]

My dear Yeats
The pastels are not sold separately from the box in Dublin and
you would have to order them from London from which they might
arrive in a fortnights time. I am sending you some ordinary white
chalks which I use myself rather than the pastel white. It is not soft
& crumbly and I like it better as it sticks better. If you want the
pastel white I will order it from London. I would have written before
but an Annual Conference & crowds of people from the country
have kept me busy. I am glad you see the conflict with the clerical
party is inevitable, and they are urging us into it. I want Moore to be
the martyr. He could very well expiate a life of sin by dying for a
good cause here. Moran was very confused in his explanation of his
attack but I gathered that he wanted to put life into the Catholics by

a vigorous onslaught on non Catholic things and thinkers. OGradys last letter on Moran was splendid. I hope you are working hard at the novel. I wish I could lie for a month on the greenlands. I am tired of work. But when I die I will go to Benbulben.

Yours ever,
GEORGE W. RUSSELL

P.S. Kind regards to Mr. Pollexfen.

From GEORGE MOORE

MS Berg Collection,   Dublin
New York Public Library   [September—October 1900]

My dear Yeats,

I have just scribbled a rough draft of the scene I wrote to you about yesterday. I dare say you will be able to improve it — I hope so for of course it wont do as it is. The speech in which Grania describes to Diarmuid their life in the woods is the improvisation of the moment and is only intended to put you on the track of a little poem in prose which you will write beautifully. I do not think much of writing across the table at each other, it results in superficial thinking and is only useful occasionally. I will come down tomorrow Saturday. I shall arrive about 12 — you will have had time to go through the enclosed — and perhaps to rewrite it.

Always yours
GEORGE MOORE

From GEORGE MOORE

MS Berg Collection,   [London?]
New York Public Library   [? late 1900]

My dear Yeats

I enclose the 2 act. I have put a great deal of work into it and I think it is stronger than it was. The scene with Grania and her foster mother was written when your letter arrived. But your letter was of use nevertheless and I think it is as good now as we shall ever get it. The evocation of the woods is I think better anyhow it will get across the footlights for it is all a temptation. If you alter it remember that everything she says must be a visible temptation offered to him, a sensible temptation I should say. The dramatic point is woman offering to a man a set of sensuous temptations. I count on you for the third act that is more your act than mine — I will send you it in dialogue on Saturday. I am afraid what I send will be thin.

Always yours
GEORGE MOORE

But do not alter it unless you are irresistably moved for it goes all right.

From GEORGE MOORE

MS Berg Collection,   London
New York Public Library   [? late 1900]

My dear Yeats
      I read the first and second acts to a friend and I could see that she was deeply interested, extraordinarily interested, I could feel that the play facinates the attention. The second act seemed to me to be quite perfect and *alas* your criticism of the scene between Grania and the foster mother is true, so true that the scene must be rewritten as you suggest or nearly. You are a wonderfull critic. There never was such a critic. The scene is made up of odds and ends of dialogue just like the scene in the scene in the second act before I rewrote it.
      But that the play is full of facination I have had the fullest proof tonight from within and from without.

Always yours
GEORGE MOORE

From GEORGE MOORE

MS Berg Collection,   London
New York Public Library   [? late 1900]

Wednesday

My dear Yeats ˙
      I have been through the act and approve of nearly all your corrections. I approve of the passage you propose to write into the

beginning of the act and shall like it better if you omit or lay little stress on the oath. You will not make the oath more impressive by speaking of it. The oath of fealty to the chief began 5000 years before Grania and to lay stress on it is like laying stress on the fact that a man must eat to live. You will only distract the attention of the audience from important matters — it will be an irritation. You had better leave it out. It comes in its place at the end of the act.

Always yours
GEORGE MOORE

From GEORGE MOORE

MS Berg Collection,   London
New York Public Library   [? late 1900]

[The "last emendation" to which Moore refers appears in Act I, lines 4—5, of the final version: "the chief man at a wedding feast is the man comes to be wed". Carden Tyrell is the protagonist of Edward Martyn's *The Heather Field* (1899); Moore had contributed an introduction to the published text.]

My dear Yeats,
   I will begin by telling you what you already know, viz: how much I appreciate the work you have done on Grania and how inspiring I have found your suggestions. Whatever merits the play may have are largely owing to you. Upon this question there can never be any question.
   Diarmuid is largely your conception and the character as it stands owes much to you — I do not try to say how much for fear of exaggeration on one side or the other. I think I can say however that your conception of Diarmuid was clearer in the beginning than mine was. You have rewritten his part in the third act — I have not seen it, but I am sure you have improved it; in the second act too he owes much to you. If we look to the other side we find that Grania was mine from the first, she was my clear idea; you always said that you approached her from the out side and I am bound to say you left me quite free to draw the character according to my conception of it. But now in the eleventh hour your wish to rewrite her character and in the very moment when I wish to reveal to the reader (or the hearer) the character in its essential essence. Why not choose two other scenes instead, the scene with the Foster Mother in the second act. Does this not seem to you fair for you to concede much to me

regarding Grania and I to concede much to you regarding Diarmuid. Is not this fair and reasonable – If you show this letter to your father I think he will tell you that it is. Do you take the hero and leave the heroine to me; of course if you take exception to any particular phrase I will alter it.

Your letter concludes with a reference to style on which you are to arbitrate. I can only repeat that I will alter any phrase I may write in the part of Grania if you object to it. You refer to a compact between us on this point. I am unwilling to believe that you under[stand] me to consent to your translating every line I write into what you consider to be your idiom, that when I write a good phrase as when I write a bad phrase it must be altered. I cannot think you approach the play in this spirit. I am unwilling to believe that you regard each scene as an exercise in translation. I am surely wrong to entertain such a thought. You are a man of letters if ever there were one and must know that any such writing would [be] like a still born child, as vague and as hopeless. I cannot answer all the points you raise it would make too long a letter. I have no slightest objection to your returning to your original bent in the opening scene if you are minded to do so. Your last emendation "The man who has come to be wed" is not grammatical. The character of Carden Tyrill I never touched, what do you say? a few words of terror may be in the scene where his wife tells him he is mad at the end of the first act – the writing of that scene amounted to nothing his part consisted in listening to what his wife said. I should not have attempted to add a word to the character of Carden Tyrill.

The best thing to do is to come down here and get the first act through. There is nothing to disagree about unless indeed you insist on writing special passages for Grania and will not accept my utterance what ever it may be.

Always yours,
GEORGE MOORE

PS I wish to act rightly in this matter and trust you will show this letter to Symons and to your father.

[no heading]
Since posting my letter to you I have looked through the act carefully and find hardly anything to object to except the passages where you have altered Grania's dialogue. You have said over and

over again that you could do nothing with her and you have asked me to supply insignificant scraps of dialogue in her scenes which you might have very well written yourself. Yet you chose to write the moment when her nature is most exultant and intimate. And mind you, you do not write an original passage but a paraphrase of what I had already written. The passage is not at all good; it seems to me to be as flat as anything could well be. It would be a miracle if it were otherwise for the character is foreign to you and you write from the out side.

I think you have deadened the dialogue in these two intimate scenes and I think we might hit on compromise passages — in fact there will be no difficulty unless you deliberately determine that we shant. In any case my dear friend

Yours most sincerely
GEORGE MOORE

Surely if anything in the world is clear it is that I must write the dialogue of a character so intimately mine as Grania's. Over and over again you are right on other points. Supposing I were to write psychological passages into the Countess Cathleen.

From GEORGE W. RUSSELL

Dublin
MS Yeats [? December 1900]

[*The Shadowy Waters* was published in book form in December 1900; the cover design by Althea Gyles consisted of a rose stamped in gold. The articles on Celtic cosmogony were published in the *United Irishman* (8 and 15 Mar 1902) and reprinted in *The Candle of Vision* (1918) under the title of "Celtic Cosmogony". "The Feast of Age" and "Dana" were included in *The Divine Vision* (1904).]

My dear Yeats,

Thanks for the Shadowy Waters, a most beautiful poem, which should have been printed faintly on dim twilight coloured paper and bound in skins with golden symbolism of stars and sybils and Druidic emblems. I feel that a nineteenth century person in this hideous world ought not to read it until he has cast aside his modern clothes and put on an ancient robe, and found out somewhere an old hall in a castle hung round with mementos of a thousand years ago to read it in.

I would have written before but I am terribly busy and am off tomorrow with about thirty lectures to deliver and my soul is for the present in the shape of the economic things I have to think about.

I am glad to hear from Lady Gregory that Grania is finished. I hope now that this is done that you will go back to your own work and you had better come to Ireland to do it. As for me, I have only little breaths playing on me from Tirnanoge and have not time to do anything, nor will I until February when I hope to go at the articles in the Celtic Cosmogony and also at my poem, The Feast of Age. At the rate I get along I don't think anybody else will ever feast in it except in very old age. It is made up at present of fragments like the "Dana" but is not a whole thing. Will you be in Ireland soon? I hear that the Saxon is deducting moneys from your royalties on account of your treasonable views. Do more for America and let the Saxon be damned.

> Yours ever,
> GEO. W. RUSSELL

From STANDISH O'GRADY

MS Yeats

[Dublin]
12 December [1900]

[O'Grady had published Yeats's "A Postscript to a Forthcoming Book of Essays by Various Writers" in his *All-Ireland Review* (1 Dec 1900). During 1900 O'Grady had written a series of editorials on "The Great Enchantment" (see *Ideals in Ireland*, 1901) or paralysis that had come over Irish "political understanding" since the failure of the insurrection of 1798. He was concerned that the Irish myths should not be "brought down to the crowd" by Yeats and his circle.]

Dear Yeats.

You wont see it yourself, perhaps; but there is a suggestion of log-rolling in your letter.

In all fair ways & natural I shall be glad to serve your interests & forward your fame.

Quite recently I devoted a good many pages of A.I.R. to that purpose.

Frankly, & quite between ourselves, I dont like at all the way you have been going on now for a good many years. You cant help it, I suppose, having got down into the crowds.

　　With *very* kind regards I remain

Yours sincerely
STANDISH O'GRADY

From STANDISH O'GRADY

MS Yeats

Dublin
12 December [1900]

[*A outrance* means "to the utmost".]

Dear Yeats.

　　I dont know what came over me to growl at you as I did. My only excuse is that in the midst of such tribulations as never before surrounded a man so little able to bear that sort of thing I am often as savage as a wounded bear or a baited badger & often write with a mind most disturbed.

　　I almost fear this is the second time I asked you to forgive me for something. The Bishop was only one & by no means the worst of these dogs that are round me & but for lawyers & friends & my own temporary prostration I would have fought him a outrance.

　　I hear your A.I.R. goes to Gort. I write today to tell them to send it to London.

　　Wishing you all happiness & good fortune, I remain

Ever yours
STANDISH O'GRADY

From STANDISH O'GRADY

MS Yeats

[Dublin]
14 December [1900]

Dear Yeats.

　　I wish to retract that letter as not as gracious & sympathetic as is my wont — I hope — written & posted in haste.

Ever yours
S. O'GRADY

From GEORGE MOORE

MS Berg Collection,   London
New York Public Library   [? early 1901]

[For what is probably Yeats's reply, see *L* 347—8.]

My dear Yeats
      I have rewritten the passage about the spring which Grania
speaks to her foster mother in the form which I should accept as
final if I were writing the play by myself. Ive done it for your
consideration. If you will bring your revisions of the first act we will
go through them after tea or after dinner and I do not think that we
shall fail to agree as to what the best shall be within an hour. I shall
remember and I'm sure you will that collaboration is mutual
concession. Perhaps the way would be simplified if we do not
attempt to do more than decide what is to be the acting test. The
publication of the play is unnecessary, at all events at present. The
book rights of a play are not worth £25 the acting rights of a fairly
successful play are worth from 4 to 5 thousand pounds.
                                        Always yours
                                        GEORGE MOORE

From GEORGE MOORE

MS Berg Collection,   London
New York Public Library   [? early 1901]

[Probably in reply to *L* 347—8.]

My dear Yeats
      If it was your intention all along to be supreme in command I
wish you had taken the scenario and written the play. I cannot
separate the invention of character and the invention and grouping of
incident from the dialogue once the play passes from the scenario
into dialogue. One of the characters I invented from the beginning
and through her I gave a psychological explanation to the legend. If
you had twice as much talent as you have you could not give living
speech to Grania. All you could write would be detached and
perfunctory.
      For me to hand over a play the greater part of which is written
by me, for *final* correction is an impossible proposal. We should be
one as ridiculous one as the other, you as the pedagogue I as the

pupil. The work now [can] only be done by mutual concession. A great many of your emedations I think very well of; the larger part pass without question.

If I may venture a word of advice I will ask you to show this letter to Symons: If I am not greatly mistaken he will tell you that it is impossible for me to hand over a completely written play for final correction — for you to write in bits of dialogue for characters which are foreign to you. I think he will tell you that you should repudiate such a proposal though it came from yourself. He will tell you that a play written by one man and corrected by another would not be better in the end than a carefully corrected Latin essay, repainted picture or stuffed animal.

To be precise: all those parts where Grania speaks of her intimate self must be written by me. If I dont satisfy you I must try again but they must be written by me. There are other places where you can help me out notably the scene with the foster mother in II act and the funeral oration in the III act.

Always yours
GEORGE MOORE

From A. S. SCANLON [?]

London

MS Yeats   22 January 1901

[Yeats had apparently asked Scanlon, a brother in the Golden Dawn, for this information to reassure some friend, possibly Maud Gonne. Initiated on 16 November 1891, she participated for a short time only, though she remained on the rolls as late as 1902.]

Dear Mr. Yeates,

With regard to the subject of confession in relation to the Society you wot of. I asked a very high Church (Anglican) person about it & he said if the Society has for its aim good it need not be mentioned in Confession & as it deals with others it cannot be — for one of the great things in Confession is that the penitent may not try to implicate others.

Later on [I] asked him what the Roman view was he said the same but he would ask a priest. The reply I got was as follows.

"The R C view is the same as ours. The Cardinal says that the Secret Societies wh: are denounced are those on the Continent. e.g. Freemasons who there do not now hold a belief even in a God.

A Person may not mention others in Confession — not knowing the nature of the Society of course approval of its work cannot be given."

Yours faithfully
A.S.S.

P.S. This information was of course *not* for publication but an answer to a special case: therefore I trust you to use it privately.

From W. J. STANTON PYPER

Clontarf, Ireland
MS Yeats   19 March 1901

[Pyper's walking companion was W. K. Magee ("John Eglinton"). Lugh's article, "Meeting of the Royal Trinity College Academy", was published in *The United Irishman*, 26 February 1901. Four more of his articles and reviews (including *Ideals in Ireland*) had appeared in January and February. Louis Claude Purser was a professor at Trinity College. A. P. Watt was Yeats's agent.]

My dear Yeats,

I am writing to tell you a little story which may interest you as it is about yourself. One Sunday in February Magee and myself journeyed to Lucan, whence we purposed walking to Maynooth, but finding the roads wet and the weather threatening, we changed our minds and decided to follow the Royal Canal and thus return to Dublin. We reached the Canal in due course and walked on for miles in the most utter solitude imaginable. We did not see above half dozen human beings, I suppose. We became very hungry, having eaten nothing since breakfast, and tried hard, but in vain to procure food at Clonsilla. Journeying on, discoursing of many things, we neared Blanchardstown, and fell in with a youth who obligingly offered to guide us to a place where we could get something to eat. We got talking, at first about the Language Movement, which seems rather backward in this district, though the youth's brother we were told, together with others was studying Gaelic. Then Magee asked him "Have you heared of a man called Yeats who writes poetry?" To our surprise the youth turns sharply on us and says "Is it W.B. you mean?" We said "Yes." "Oh yes, I know all about him and about his brother Jack too — the artist I mean: He's a good artist too, my brother knows him well." (the youth was a brother of Fagan who knows your brother & is in London now) The youth himself is a gardener. He gave us his brother's history in full, & told us he had been to "Jack Yeats's" exhibition. Continuing he said, "Yes, and I saw W. B. Yeats in the Park once, he was making a speech. He writes fine poetry, but he's *very aesthetic*. It's a great pity too, but there's no doubt at all about it, you can see it in his face, he's *very aesthetic*. Do you think he'll live long, for he looks terrible consumptive?"

We hastened to assure him that we could from personal knowledge certify that you were in excellent health and likely to remain so. He seemed much relieved and continued. "Ah, well, he looks very aesthetic all the same. But sure his poetry is great, and do you know how he writes it? The people say, he goes every summer to Achill Island, and there he does be lying out all night, and that's how the thoughts come into his head, and that's how he writes his poetry!"

After some further conversation, we parted. By the way, he had never heard of "A.E."

I have been writing off and on for Griffith over the signature of "Lugh." The Trinity College Academy article caused a mild sensation I have been told in T.C.D. I met Louis Purser the other day, and he told me they all enjoyed it very much.

If you see Watt, please ask him if he thinks my book has any chance at all. I don't think it's going to get published in London somehow. I hope you keep well, and are not becoming too "aesthetic."

Yours faithfully
W. J. STANTON PYPER

From MAUD GONNE

MS Berg Collection,   London
New York Public Library   [? June 1901]

[Maud had been in America with John MacBride raising money for the Irish cause. Her sister was Mrs Kathleen Pilcher. Maud had been assisting Yeats with the composition of rituals for the Celtic Mysteries.]

My dear Willie
Many thanks for your letter — I succeeded very well in America but will tell you all about this when we meet — I got back very well,

but caught a bad cold & sore throat on arrival in France, I am well of that now. I am engaged nursing my poor little sister who has been *very* ill indeed. She is better & has been allowed to sit up today. On Wednesday we are going to Norwood where the Doctor has ordered her to spend a week or 10 days to get up her strength enough to enable her to take a longer journey to some mountain place — I shall stay about a week longer with Kathleen. My address will be Queens Hotel Norwood — Then I am going to Ireland *73 Lower Mount Street* but will only be there till 1*st* week July as I have to return to Paris for a meeting.

I would like very much to see you & do a little occult work. I have not done much but on the boat I did a little, writing down some of my visions which may possibly be of use in the rite. I quite agree with your divisions of the ceremonies. I have a lot of writing to do for my sister so cant add more now —

With great pleasure at the thought of seeing you shortly.

> I remain
> Always your friend
> MAUD GONNE

From ROBERT BRIDGES

MS Bridges

Yattendon, Newbury
24 July 1901

[Bridges is replying to *L* 353—4, in which Yeats gave permission to Elizabeth Waterhouse, Bridges' mother-in-law, to include some of his poems in *A Little Book of Life and Death* (1902) and also described his psaltery experiments with Florence Farr. The novelist Thomas Anstey Guthrie used the pen-name "Anstie". Bridges' book was the new edition of *Milton's Prosody*, published in December 1901.]

My dear Yeats

Thank you for your permission to Mrs Waterhouse, which I will transmit to her. I do not warrant her book, in fact her taste is not as mine in anything. But these things have to be left to go as they will — and it is after all some sort of consolation that there shd be people who 'appreciate' that part of one's work which one does not care for oneself. I have always said that if I had published what I had burned & burned what I had published I shd have been a popular poet. Quite an echo of the age & a man of the day.

I am sorry we have missed you but you must come in the winter and make up – don't forget. And the dusk and the fireside will be a better atmosphere for you to tell the children some of your Irish legends.

I am much interested in all that you say about your work – and very much pleased that you are able to carry out your scheme. Your style in lyric & narrative is alike most charming* to me and I shd think that a combination of the two should show you at your best. The trouble of lyric verse is, I fancy, that it needs a mood which is fitful and really impossible to sustain – it is of its nature to exhaust itself and break off,– whereas the narrative, tho' it may really be as full of imagination, or seem to be, when once started has a tendency to run of itself. So that with this to fall back on you need never be idle.

I agree about the recitation, I think. It is a very difficult matter. Setting *song* aside – which has several degrees – the mere reading of poetry, if well read, is full of melodious devices, which it is the art of a good reader to conceal, so that he gets his effects without calling attention to them. The word recitation – and the presence of an instrument – makes open confession of his art, and without be-coming a singer he ceases to be a reader. The hearer has his attention called to the method itself – and as I have never had any experience of good chanting or recitation I do not know how I shd like it. There was a kind of recitation fashionable some years ago in London drawing rooms – satirised by Anstie – and it even crept into the churches. I have heard the Old Testament 'recited' in Westminster Abbey. This used to draw tears from me – tears of laughter. I shook as at a French farce. This is the only sort that I ever heard. I can't really imagine a recitation which I shd myself like as well as good reading (in which the same art wd be disguised) but I think that there must be such a thing – and I hope you and the lady will discover it.

I will send you a book with some interesting poetic notes in it before the autumn.

Yours ever
R BRIDGES

*In the right sense of the word

From "FIONA MACLEOD" (WILLIAM SHARP)
                                              Loch Fyne
MS Yeats   26 July 1901

[Sharp was assisting Yeats in the composition of rituals for the Celtic
Mysteries. Among the manuscripts of these still unpublished rituals is
a brief note from Fiona Macleod dated 12 November 1901.]

Dear Mr. Yeats
     In connection with my recent letter
(1) Would you object to a complete reconstruction of the Rite, as for
some reason we both still feel either an inveterate hostility or an
insuperable difficulty. By a reconstruction I mean a Rite identical in
end but wholly distinct in externals. In other words, has your Rite
finality to you?
(2) If you know or come across anything about 'the Queen's touch,'
or 'the Fool's laughter' in *November*, please tell me. By the way, be
very careful this November. It is always a month of suffering and
mischance for some of us and especially about the 21*st*. (the seven
days before or after) —
My friend recently has had five very singular visions, each unsought
and abrupt. Three of these I have been able to verify, and am deeply
impressed. Another I know to be a reflection of circumstances
unknown to us yet. The sixth is of a warning nature, at least I take it
so, though he is uncertain. "Put the four cups of light about you in
the seven and seven dark days of the month of the curlew" (. . . i.e.
November).
The steamer is coming down Loch Fyne, so I must hurriedly close.
                                         Yours Sincerely
                                         FIONA MACLEOD

Please answer through Mr. S. (who will at once forward to me) and
cancel now the Miss Rea address — as she has gone abroad for some
months — and also, please tell either Mr. S. or myself when the Irish
Theatre performance is to be in Dublin this year.
His address just now — later, in a fortnight or so he will be in
Argyll — is

                                         Spa House
                                         Cowley
                                         By Chesterfield.

From GEORGE MOORE
TS Berg Collection,   Dublin
New York Public Library   27 July 1901

[*Beltaine*, "the organ of the Irish Literary Theatre", was published for only three numbers (1899–1900). It was succeeded by *Samhain*, also edited by Yeats. Its first number (Oct 1901) contained Moore's brief article on "The Irish Literary Theatre" and Hyde's Gaelic play *Casadh an t-Sugáin*, followed by an English translation, *The Twisting of the Rope*. Augusta Mary Anne Holmes was an Irish-born, naturalized French musician.]

My dear Yeats,

You are quite right in thinking that FINN should speak the funeral oration and not CORMAC, but I do not think you are right in dividing it between *GRANIA* and *FINN*. I am afraid very few actresses could put off the personal emotion and become the formal queen, and I am sure that no one could do it unless she spoke the whole of the funeral oration; it would be more difficult for an actress to speak half of it than to speak the whole of it. It has occurred to me therefore that the funeral oration might be divided up between FINN, CAOELTE and USHEEN. I enclose my arrangement of it. I think you might even write USHEEN'S part in verse, six or seven or ten lines. You say that GRANIA lays Broad Edge on the litter forgetting that Broad Edge was left in the house. Pray put this right. If ever a situation leant itself more to music this is one. I do not like the introduction of music into a prose drama or into any drama, but if ever there was a situation in which music could be justified DIARMUID'S death is it. My notion for the musical scene would be that a musical phrase should be played at the words "It is by music that he leads the dead" and the same music could be sung by USHEEN and then with some variations the theme could be developed as the procession follows the body up the wood. I would not have a dead march, but the theme might by played by the clarinets in the orchestra and carried on by the harps which would be placed behind at the back of the stage. Music would exalt the end of the play, it would carry it one degree higher than words could carry it. There are always moments when one art has to seek assistance from another art. Beethoven in his ninth symphony had to seek assistance from the human voice. I do not know who would write the music. I might ask Augusta Holmes to do it when I am in Paris, there are many others who will be glad to do it. Now regarding Beltaine I will write whatever you want me to write for it. Shall I write an article explaining that the three years are not completed? That under some new conditions we should like to carry the Irish Literary Theatre on, and that if the corporation thinks fit we will give our services? I would propose to the Corporation that it should vote some four or five hundred pounds to be spent every year upon literary plays. I do not think I shall say anything with which you or Lady Gregory or Martyn would disagree, but if I did you would of course take it out and write in what you thought was suitable. Someone must write this article and the person to write it I think is he or she who has not any other subject in mind. I confess I have no other subject in mind. I have explained the degradation of London so often and I have explained that scenery is a hindrance so often that I feel unable to trot out all my little ideas once more. If you wish however to write the statement suggest some subject that I might write upon.

Always yours,
GEORGE MOORE

Or would you like me to write a little article on Hyde's play and our project to send it round the country?

From GEORGE MOORE

Dublin

TS and MS National Library of Ireland   31 July 1901

[F. R. Benson's company produced *Diarmuid and Grania* on 21 October 1901 at the Gaiety Theatre in Dublin, with Benson as Diarmuid and Mrs Benson as Grania. Moore's *Saint Teresa* was published on 3 July. Sir Edmund Gosse was a prolific and respected critic, poet, biographer, and translator. Moore's article in *Samhain* (Oct 1901) contains no mention of Father Peter O'Leary, a parish priest from Cork who wrote novels and plays and translated the Gospels into Gaelic.]

My dear Yeats,

I enclose you the article you wrote to me for — the article for Beltaine. I send it in a somewhat rough state because you will be able to put the finishing hand to it better than I shall, and because you may like to modify or add some lines, for in some places in the article I am not speaking of myself alone but in the name of the Irish Literary Theatre. I go to London on Thursday night or Friday morning, I spend a day with the Benson's. I got a letter from Mrs. Benson this morning and she says that she is perfectly satisfied and that they both look forward to great success. I hear that the articles about "Sister Teresa" have been all good, and that the book is selling well. Gosse writes to tell me that it is my best book, I can hardly think that, but to tell the truth I don't care. That one child should learn Irish interests me far more than the publication of a master piece, even if I could write a master piece.

With kind regards to
Lady Gregory.
I am, as ever,
yours
GEORGE MOORE

PS If I may offer a suggestion I will suggest that you do not omit what I say about Father O'Leary. I feel sure that these few lines will be immensely popular.

From DOUGLAS HYDE

MS Yeats

Frenchpark,
Co. Roscommon
1 August 1901

[Thomas William Rolleston helped found the Rhymers' Club and the Irish Literary Society, of which he was the first secretary. When in 1892 Rolleston and Charles Gavan Duffy failed to include Yeats in negotiations with Unwin for a "series of national books", Yeats felt that he had been betrayed, and he never forgave Rolleston. In 1898 Yeats conceived a "grandiose plan" for bringing together the "four parties in Ireland". The New Unionist Party was headed by Lord Bernard Edward Castletown, a leader of Pan-Celticism. The politics of the *Leader* under the editorship of D. P. Moran were frequently opposed to those of Yeats. Hyde, a peacemaker among warring factions, was the strongest force in the Gaelic League (founded 1893). Father Peter O'Leary was a strong advocate of Gaelic. "Lady Gregory's work" became *Cuchulain of Muirthemne* (1902), to which Yeats contributed an enthusiastic preface. The "scenario of a new play" may be a reference to a scenario received from George Moore (in a letter dated 3 July) upon which they planned to write *Where There Is Nothing*. When Yeats and Moore quarrelled, Yeats wrote the play "in a fortnight with the help of Lady Gregory and another friend [Hyde]".

Yeats wrote to Frank Fay on 1 August 1901 that he hoped "to collaborate with Hyde in a little play" in "the Irish language" (*L* 355).]

Dear Yeats

Your suggestion of the Conversazione has been a very pretty one, it bids fair to leave wigs on the queen! Rolleston is furious about the present state of affairs and threatens a secession under Lord Castletown. Indeed I'm not surprized. The tone of the Leader, though quite comprehensible, is certainly unpleasant, and he confounds it with the organ of the Gaelic League. I think myself that if a secession takes place it will be because the League will have become a declared Nationalist body rather than a declared Catholic one. Unfortunately we made a mistake in publishing a rather sectarian address to the Maynooth students by a priest called Forde [?], & this, added to the Leader's tone & Father O'Leary's arrogant and unbearable letter has naturally irritated people. As you say however, we have the extreme party behind us; but if they save the situation for us now, they will probably lose it for us later on by forcing us into declared Anti-Unionism or something of the sort! We must only try – avert the split as long as we can – & keep on at our own work, ignoring side-issues. I am quite weary corresponding with people & trying to smooth matters down.

I have now come to the conclusion that I will be doing best for the League & will create less unpleasant friction by keeping away altogether from the Nat^l Lit^y Soc^y's Conversazione. Rolleston proposed that the cards of invitation sh^d bear the inscription "to meet the delegates of the Pan Celtic Congress," or something like that. I should have no objection at all, but I would arouse furious animosity amongst the Munster & London Leaguers and a few of the Northern not to speak of the Kennelly-Borthwick-O'Reilly section in Dublin, who would say their President was betraying them & appearing in a semi-official postion. Hence, all things considered, I think I shall be acting most loyally by the League, who have always acted loyally by me, in simply staying away under some excuse, & I have written to tell Rolleston so, so that he may make it known to the Nat'^l Lit^y Soc^y. I let him know that I had changed my mind since writing to you.

Now, about Lady Gregory's work. I am delighted beyond measure that you think so highly of it. Please ask her to send me any portion she thinks fit, wch w^d make a little booklet & let me try my hand upon it, with a reasonable amount of latitude, and if she likes I can get it printed as a Gaelic League book. Let her send it to me anyhow & she'll soon see the result, whether it goes well or ill into Irish.

I shall be very curious about your scenario of a new play. I'll do my best on it. I am so glad that your Land of Hearts Desire has done so well.

I have not time to write more, I only got home from Sligo on Tuesday ev^g & have heaps of things to do.

Beannacht Leat [Blessing with you]
Yours ever
AN CRAOIBHÍN

From JOHN MASEFIELD

MS Berg Collection,   London
New York Public Library   15 August 1901

[The "poor silly yarn" was either the whole or part of his *Salt Water Ballads* (1902).]

My dear Yeats;

Here is my poor silly yarn about piracy on the long-shore, the Act of God, & other matters.

I have written it, I suppose, much as I should have told it to you had it been Monday night and you by your fireside. Much must be done to it I fear before it can be called a yarn in the proper sense of the word, but throughout I have tried to keep myself from attempts at brilliance, and have tried, though I am afraid hopelessly, to justify the kind of things you have said to me from time to time about my "capacity" for narrative.

D'Avalos makes a very twopenney villain, & Miguel, (hardly touched upon in this tale) scarcely reads as a "Sour" man, though I worked out the characters of both, more fully, in a yarn I wrote, and destroyed, a few months ago.

I haven't tried to put a polish on any part of the tale as you will see when you come to read. If the result disappoints your expectation of me I must ask you to let me try again.

> Believe me.
> Yours always
> JOHN MASEFIELD

P.S.

The practical seamanship I can absolutely guarantee.
I do hate to bother you with such rubbish —

From GEORGE W. RUSSELL

	Dublin
MS Yeats	[September 1901]

[Nuada of the Silver Hand was a Danaan warrior; Macha married her uncle and ruled all Ireland as queen. AE was one of many Yeats had been urging to help "get the talismatic shapes of the Gods done" (*L* 265). The articles on Celtic mythology AE describes did not appear in the *All-Ireland Review*, but a serialization of *Deirdre*, under three titles, did (6, 13, 20 July; 26 Oct, 2 Nov 1901; 8, 15 Feb 1902). Lu was the god of light; Bov the Red was king of the Danaans of Munster; Balor, the Fomorian with the baleful eye, was slain by Lu. Cullan the Smith (a Danaan divinity) dwelt near the mountain of Slieve Gullion (County Armagh), which is the setting for O'Grady's drama *The Masque of Finn*.]

My dear Yeats,

The colour of the ring in the Nuada symbol is gold or yellow, not blue. I have tried it with the gold circle and the true figure was seen. The other symbol (Macha) only requires a very slight modification. I had it at home here and in looking at it when I came back I saw there was some little differences which I will correct when you are in Dublin. They cannot matter much as you seemed to get it all right. I have also got the symbols of some other deities which I shall not tell you about until you can try them first. They bring very powerful beings.

I think you will like my articles on the Celtic mythology when they appear. I have a good deal written but they will stretch out, I am afraid, over a good many numbers of A.I.R. I am going to do the cosmogony first and then go to the local mysteries and the beings seen as the Tuatha. I will also deal with mountains, islands, fountains, words and symbols (not the ones I show to you of course). I hope O'Grady will be patient with them. I am not going to give any authorities. It is best to say this at the start so as to avoid discussion. I am sure I will irritate a good many people by them as I intend to show incidentally how much more poetic and complete the system is than our orthodox faith. Any scholar who reads it will go quite mad. When I think of the number of people it will annoy I grow cheerful and write better. I am afraid there is a warlike spirit let loose over Ireland. I suppose Moran's paper will be its organ. To attribute the A.I.R. to say Lu and the "Leader" to Bove or some other power, and all the other papers to their respective fountains should be one of our aims. I think the Express is Balor's paper. It certainly has got the evil eye and turns its readers into mummies or howling spooks.

George Moore will be in Dublin this week. He writes a note in which he compares me to St. Teresa! I hope she is all right. I hope to pay a visit to Slieve Gullion in a week or so. I have a longing to offer my services to the Great Smith. It was he who pitched O'Grady into the Financial Relations. After his visit there Mrs. O'Grady says the whirlpool sucked him in and he has never been the same. I am glad Hyde is trying his power in drama. I think he ought to have the dramatic power. Have you any more lyrics? The prologue to Shadowy Waters was very beautiful. Please thank Lady Gregory for her letter.

Yours ever,
GEO. W. RUSSELL

From "FIONA MACLEOD" (WILLIAM SHARP)

Midlothian, Scotland
MS Yeats   31 October 1901

[The American edition of *From the Hills of Dream* was published by Thomas B. Mosher in 1901.]

My dear Mr. Yeats
Now that at last I have an address to which I can write to you with surety I wish I could do so on magical matters; but that, I truly regret, is not possible yet. I have never known such continuity of

hostile will, of the which I am persuaded: and though, owing to the
visionary power of our common friend, much has been seen and
overcome, and much seen and avoided, there is still something to
avoid, something to overcome, and something to see. But very soon
now, possibly in this very month of November where the dark
powers prevail (and if so, a double victory indeed!) that which has
been impossible may become possible. Even yet, however, there is
much to work against: and not only here: for you, too, move often
into the Red and the Black, or so at least it seems.

So now I have only to send you a copy of the much changed,
cancelled, augmented, and revised American .edition of *From The
Hills of Dream*. It is, in effect, a new book, though there will be
much in it familiar to you. But even here there are changes which are
re-creative – as, for example, in the instance of "The Moon-Child",
where one or two touches and an added quatrain have made a poem
of what was merely poetic.

The first 10 poems are those which are in the current (October)
Fortnightly Review. But when these are reprinted in a forthcoming
volume of new verse, (perhaps in January), they will have a changed
sequence, with other (and I think better) additions: and the present
10th will be transposed to its right place in the "Dirges of the Four
Cities".

In the new book in question (which will also contain some of
the 40 'new' poems now included in this American edition) the chief
contents will be the remodelled and re-written poetic drama "The
Immortal Hour", and with it many of the notes to which I alluded
when I wrote last to you. In the present little volume it was not
found possible to include the lengthy, intimate, and somewhat
esoteric notes: among which I account of most interest for you those
pertinent to the occult myths embodied in "The Immortal Hour".

You will see, however, that one or two dedicatory pages –
intended for the later English new book – have here found a
sectional place: and will, I hope, please you.

Believe me

Your friend truly,

FIONA MACLEOD.

P.S. I should much like to have your opinion as to the title of the
new book of verse – whether
(1) For a Little Clan
(2) The Immortal Hour: and Poems
(3) The Silver Flutes

From "FIONA MACLEOD" (WILLIAM SHARP)

Midlothian, Scotland

MS Yeats   23 November 1901

[Sharp's "Celtic" essay was first printed in *The Contemporary Review*, then in *The Divine Adventure: Iona: By Sundown Shores* (1900). Revised and enlarged with a Foreword of explanation, "Celtic" was republished in *The Winged Destiny* (1904). AE, in particular, disapproved of the essay, as indeed he came to disapprove of Fiona Macleod.]

Dear Mr. Yeats

I send you a reprint of my "Celtic" essay, which has been so widely read and discussed — with a new introductory part which I would much like you to read. I believe you do not care for the "Celtic" essay: for that I am sorry, for I think it of my best, and that it will sink deeper and go further and last longer than anything I have written. Well, 'the star-crowned' will see to it, whether it go out on the flow or disappear on the ebb.

I hope to hear that you have found something to care for in the book I sent you and in what was addressed to you.

Your friend

FIONA MACLEOD

From FRANK J. FAY

Dublin

TS Reading University Library   17 February 1902

[Yeats's *Cathleen ni Houlihan* and AE's *Deirdre* were played on 2 April. Dr John Todhunter was a neighbour and friend of the Yeatses in London. Yeats liked — but overpraised — his work, especially *A Sicilian Idyll*. Todhunter's "Blank-Verse on the Stage" (*Fortnightly Review*, Feb 1902) compared Stephen Phillips and Yeats, to the latter's advantage. Phillips's *Ulysses* was produced by Beerbohm Tree at His Majesty's Theatre. In 1912 Phillips became editor of *Poetry and Drama, the Journal of the Poetry Society*. William Archer's article appeared on 15 February 1902.]

Dear Mr Yeats,

Your little play reached us safely through Mr Russell, and it is now in rehearsal. We are all delighted that Miss Gonne is to act Kathleen and I look for a great success for all of us. If we achieve it, I think it will result in our endeavouring to give more frequent performances of such plays by Irish authors as we can get. I may mention that our company for *Deirdre* includes two poets and that one of these has written several little plays and we hope to produce one for him when he is a little stronger in technique. But I think you spoke truth when you said that the Irish Literary Theatre had set people looking towards the stage, and if we see our way to follow up the Easter performance I do not think we shall lack a supply of plays; but perhaps I exaggerate. I should be glad to see sketches of the costume for Kathleen and to hear whether you wish anything special done with the play. There are some verses which the old woman sings. Could you send Miss Gonne the airs to which you wish them sung or do you wish them spoken.

I think it will be very difficult to get up regular performances without a hall. The only adequate hall in Dublin is that in which this performance is to take place; it is attached to St Teresa's Total Abstinence Association, Clarendon Street; but, even its stage, though well appointed, might be twice as large, and there are no dressing rooms. You want to concentrate people on one place and then I am convinced much good work could be [done]. It is impossible to count on haveing any Dublin hall regularly, and one could only be outspoken in one's own hall.

I should be glad to have your opinion on the enclosed which has just been written by a friend of mine who has been reading your Poems. Like many another here, he was, through lack of knowledge of your work, hostile to you; but you will see from his letter that he has changed. He is a Scotsman, very well read, and a searching critic; and moreover while like most Scots upholding the blessed empire, he is yet entirely sympathetic to Ireland. Because he is no gusher and because, as a lover of poetry, your work has forced this expression of opinion, I think it will interest you. You get more kicks than halfpence in Ireland because in some mysterious way we love belittling our gifted ones.

Have you read a most interesting article on Blank Verse on the Stage which Dr Todhunter contributes to this month's *Fortnightly*. I have found it very informing. He mentions you and your views. I hope you also will write an article and make it even longer than his. It has long been the custom of literary people to tell actors that they don't know how to recite verse; but here is a man who tries to help those who wish to learn. That is what is needed. Anyone can tell a person he is wrong, but the important man is he who can set right the erring one. Here we have a wretched paper *The Leader* which I have had to give up reading; it pulls many things to pieces but while it is disheartening some, it is hardening many. I had the pleasure of reading a so-called play which had received the blessing of Mr Hooligan and Mr Imaal and I can assure [you] it was one of the strangest pieces of incoherency and nonsense I have ever looked at. We were consulted about it but my brother was compelled to return the thing as impossible; and yet it is people of this sort who have the impudence to criticize those who know their business.

Have you been to see *Ulysses* and do you like it. Is the verse well spoken. The desire for a National Theatre seems to be strengthening in London. Already a request for a Municipal Theatre has been made to the County Council and now others are clamouring for a National Theatre. Certainly the statistics of performances of classical drama set forth in Archer's article in Saturday's *Morning Leader* proves if any proof were needed how inartistic English-speaking countries are dramatically. But I don't think those who long for a National Theatre in London will get it. The stage unless perhaps in Shakespeare's time has never been taken seriously there; and the average actor cares nothing for his calling.

I am reading and enjoying your Secret Rose.

Yours sincerely,

F. J. FAY

From JOHN BUTLER YEATS

Dublin

MS Yeats

[spring 1902]

[Lily was Yeats's sister Susan Mary, Ruth Pollexfen his cousin who lived with the Yeatses from 1900 to 1911. *Cathleen ni Houlihan* was produced on 2 April 1902. The last word of the play is "queen" not "dream".]

My dear Willie,

Lilly and Ruth come over tomorrow evening. That infernal woman, the present tenant of the house in Dundrum, can't be got to leave to let us in, although two months ago she promised to leave in two days. So Lilly is coming over to look for a house.

I hope the reading of the plays at Miss Gonne's went off all right.

In your *Kathleen* the last lines

"No, I saw a young girl,, and she walked liked a dream —" Patrick should step forward to the footlights and say the words frankly and straight out to the audience. It would, of course, be an innovation, but I think would have the right effect. The whole play is an appeal, a challenge, a rousing call to patriotism.

                                                    Yrs affectly
                                                    J. B. YEATS

From JOHN BUTLER YEATS

                                                    Dublin
MS Yeats   [summer 1902]

[JBY had come to Dublin in the fall of 1901 for an exhibition of his paintings arranged by the painter Sarah Purser. Not long after this letter was written, the family moved from London to Dundrum, where Lily and Lollie were to work in the Dun Emer Industries. John Quinn made his first trip to Ireland in the summer of 1902. While there, he commissioned JBY to paint several portraits of prominent Irish figures.]

My dear Willie,

I send you a post office order for £2. A cheque would be more convenient to you, but I have no funds at the bank as there is some delay in collecting Quinn's cheque. This is out of monies given me by Mrs. Byrne, the first I have received for some time, as things with me have been rather necessitous.

I am so glad about these plays given to Fay. Fay is a valuable citizen. I was greatly delighted with Quinn — and to think he is a rising barrister. At the railway station I introduced him to John O'Mahony. They both hope to be great friends in the future.

I also introduced him to Miss Purser, who looked at him hungrily, keen to paint him. I have a lot of commissions coming to me, but at present we are all at our wit's ends how to manage the move which will cost £48. How to get that £48 is the problem — a seemingly insoluble problem.

                                                    Yrs affectly
                                                    J. B. YEATS

From GEORGE W. RUSSELL

Dublin

MS Yeats   [?late June 1902]

[Valentine Grace played the part of Shemus Rua in *The Countess Cathleen*. AE misquotes a proverb from Blake's *Marriage of Heaven and Hell*. Yeats's "Baile and Aillinn" was published in the *Monthly Review* (July 1902). Yeats helped found the Dublin Hermetic Society in 1885 but did not affiliate.]

My dear Yeats,

I saw Fay yesterday. The objections to Grace are political. I have come to the conclusion that everyone in Ireland is incapacitated from joining with other Irishmen on account of his principles or lack of principle. I must confess I like this "stiff upper lip." "If the fool persists in his folly he will become wise." Every prejudice has its root in the Oversoul and if men sacrifice enough for their prejudices their prejudices will widen and deepen into universal laws.

I am delighted to hear you are writing verse again. The story of the Baile is a little fantastic but I am sure you will make a beautiful thing out of it. How are the pastels? Have you begun to draw the opal beings? My hermetists are all beginning to see and hear and I have great hopes of them. We will put down the mighty prelates from their thrones in Ireland in due time.

Yours sincerely

GEO. W. RUSSELL

From GEORGE W. RUSSELL

Dublin

MS Yeats   [?July 1902]

[The novel is *The Speckled Bird*.]

My dear W.B.Y.

I have not heard from Fay to whom you were to speak. Did you? I cannot arrange for him to meet Grace as I do not know his address. However if you have spoken to him he may turn up and I will bear what you say about the Countess Cathleen in mind. Will you tell Lady Gregory that any one of the three rooms I have been enquiring about would do well for Jack, and all have been used for pictorial exhibitions. But it is the devil to get a reply from these unbusinesslike people about the cost of the rooms. Anyhow I hope to have the matter settled at the end of this week. I hope the novel is incarnating. By the way I hear of a wild outburst of phenomenal spiritualism in Trinity of all places in the world! Tables moving about in a divinity students room of all places in Trinity! I am trying to meet the three men who are concerned. So far as I could find from an account given they see opalescent beings, and I really think the gods are taking violent measures to nationalise Trinity and are beginning at the bottom. The gods coming into a divinity students room in Trinity. It is the land of wonders.

> Yours in a hurry
> G.W.R.

From JOHN BUTLER YEATS

MS Yeats

Dublin
[?20 July 1902]

[John Quinn, a New York lawyer and patron of the arts, had begun his long relationship with the Yeatses through correspondence with Jack B. Yeats in the fall of 1901. In November 1901 Yeats told Lady Gregory that his father "is quite welcome to sell the portrait I have" (*L* 359). George Moore and Edward Martyn had been discussing *The Hour-Glass*, subtitled "A Morality Play" in its first printings. JBY recalls two lines from Blake's "Auguries of Innocence": "The Poison of the Honey Bee/Is the Artist's Jealousy." The poem may have been "Baile and Aillinn".]

My dear Willie,
   Thanks for £2 — will let you have it back as soon as possible.
   I've had a letter from John Quinn of New York He buys y^r portrait, the one hanging in y^r room in London. — He left New York 15th of this month for London and writes, "I shall esteem it a favour if you will let me know by a line to my firm's office at No. 3, Fenchurch Lane, E.C. London when I may get the picture."
   He hopes to be in Ireland end of July or beginning of August.
   He also wants a portrait of AE, and a copy of John O'Leary's, about which he will speak when he sees me. These paintings are no longer decorations, but symbolic pictures.

Last night I was at Moore's. Martyn for half an hour talked of nothing elses but y^r Morality play — "Superb, magnificent, most dramatic, far the best thing he has ever done — and the things he has got into it."

It was beautiful to see Moore's restlessness — the jealousy of the artist, which Blake says is like the sting of the honey bee, as you remember. He questioned and questioned, and was something relieved when he heard it could be acted in thirty minutes.

Moore is like a Doctor who remembers all his cases but is without theory. I am just the opposite of this. He w^d be a great curer, but I w^d advance medical science.

I suppose you will give me a letter entitling John Quinn to break into yr premises and carry off the portrait.

Yrs affectly
J B YEATS

I like y^r poem better and better.

From FRANK J. FAY

Dublin

TS Reading University Library   25 July 1902

[The brother is William G. Fay. The Fays remained with the Irish National Theatre Society until 1908, when they resigned, primarily because William was not made Director of the Abbey. *Everyman* was produced at the Rotunda on 24 October 1902. *The Hour-Glass* and Lady Gregory's *Twenty-Five* were produced on 14 March 1903 in Molesworth Hall. James H. S. Cousins, a Belfast Theosophist, was the author of *The Racing Lug* (produced on 31 October) and *The Sleep of the King* (produced on 29 October), referred to as *Connla* after one of the characters. The Reverend Patrick S. Dineen, who compiled the first modern Irish—English dictionary and edited *The Poems of Egan O'Rahilly*, was the author of one novel as well as plays in Gaelic. Teresa's is a reference to the hall in which *Deirdre* and *Cathleen ni Houlihan* were played. Frederick Ryan was co-founder with John Eglinton of *Dana* and the first secretary of the Irish Literary Theatre; *The Laying of the Foundations* was produced on 29 October. Arthur Griffith was the editor of *The United Irishman* (changed to *Sinn Fein* in 1906). Padraic Colum was the author of *Broken Soil* (produced on 3 December 1903), *The Land* (produced on 9 June 1905), and *Thomas Muskerry* (produced on 12 May 1910).]

Dear Mr Yeats,
      I heard from my brother on Tuesday and have sent him your letter. The two plays reached me this morning and I have read them with much interest. *The Hour-Glass* will be compared with the *Everyman* but your play has the advantage that the story is an Irish folk tale whereas the *Everyman* is, I think, a Buddhist legend. I think *The Hour-Glass* very fine though I do not like the holding of an unbeliever up to the scorn so to speak of this pretentiously pious country. Of course I know that it would be impossible to plead for unbelief in a play here; but I know that unbelief is a sincere thing. You, I am glad to see, draw your unbeliever with sympathy for him. I think you have cast the piece well; but I doubt I could act the Fool. It is hardly my line. Of course if you insist I will try but I 'hae ma doots' of my success. When I told my brother the story, he said he'd like to act the Fool because he thought he could do something with the part. Have you any objection to it being played by him. I wish you would give me your ideas on each part, but chiefly on the Wise Man and the Fool; the others are I think obvious. What age is the Wise Man? How do you see him? Has he a beard? Do you want the Fool played on the 'village idiot' lines, or as a Shakespearean Fool? What is the period of the play? If of today, how do you wish it dressed; city fashion or country? I think we will have to substitute something for the dandelion. These 'what o'clock is it's' as I have heard them called are only to be had a special time of the year. The butterfly is impossible and will have to be left to the imagination. The farce will I think give my brother a great opportunity and it will I think be a great success. It's easy enough. Yes we must have humour. We haven't half enough; but I doubt it's in the land except the sort that appears in the *UI*.
      You have misunderstood me. *The Racing Lug is* to be done; in fact it's nearly ready. *Connla* is quite ready. I do not agree with your estimate of the former; a professional who heard Cousins read it was delighted with it. I don't know nor do I care about what is called construction; but the play will act. The fault I find with all the plays written in Irish is that they won't act. I have just finished rehearsing Father Dineen's *Enchanted Well*; it has been praised hugely because it's Irish and everything in Irish must be good at present. But to me it seems a long-winded dialogue. *The Racing Lug* is founded on an

incident that actually happened; if it doesn't tell anything new about human nature (and the plays that do are I should think rare), it is a very human story. I quite agree with your estimate of Martyn's play so far as I have heard it, but I only heard some of it read. However the people who run *The Oracle* don't know any better. I have a thing which recieved their blessing called *The King of West Briton*, which would open your eyes as to what judges they are

I wonder whether Mr Martyn would give a loan of sufficient money to build a hall and on what terms. I must say, I think he has been prodigal in the matter of *Palestrina*; of course it's a fine thing to encourage great music; but there are other things that at present would be more useful and have a wider effect.

I shall tell my brother what you said about Dr Hyde. This fear to touch politics makes one despair. In spite of the League, the Language Movement is becoming and must become a political force.

I doubt whether we ought to talk much about a national theatre yet. It's rather a large order. After ten years work we may have something to say. I look on our work as pioneer work. We, even in a stronger measure than 'L'Oeuvre' represent the protest against commercialism: of course I don't mean to compare our acting with theirs, but both have something of the same aim.

I had an idea of printing and selling *Connla* and *The Racing Lug* at the hall in which they will be acted. Would it be possible to incorporate them with *Samhain*. I know nothing of these matters; but *we cannot indulge in expense*. Every penny we have to spare must go towards getting wigs, costumes and scenery. Of course we have the *Deirdre* scenery; but the *wigs* which were used with the first act set belong to Teresa's. We shall have to get some for ourselves and also a cottage interior. Are you able to sketch? Would you send me a few samples of interiors of cottages, if you can do so without wounding the occupiers. I have written again to my brother. Personally I think *Samhain* would be useful, and interesting, and I can't see what objection there could be to its being sold in the Hall; but I can only speak for myself.

Besides *Connla* and *The Racing Lug* we have *Deirdre*, we have Mr Ryan's *The Laying of the Foundations* and Mrs Gore-Booth's *Cuchulain* to rehearse, also *Kathleen*. With your two plays our hands will be full. I don't see why all shouldn't see the footlights this autumn. People are still asking for *Deirdre* and *Kathleen*.

I have just been talking with Mr Griffith about the *necessity* for having a play on 'Robert Emmet'. I had some time ago and again yesterday suggested the subject to Mr Columb. We don't want the 'Irish Drama' sort of thing. Whitbread, the manager of the Queen's Theatre, has offered a prize for a drama and the reptile press have been backing him for all they are worth. He has tabooed 'Robert Emmet', but whether from fear or because he intends to write a play on the subject himself, I don't know; but we should be ready and if possible *anticipate* him in the matter. His theatre is the home of the shoddiest kind of melodrama and is only a little less harmful than the music hall. His patrons are or ought to be Nationalists but are of the music hall type, and they applaud the English play as soon as the Irish. I think we frightened Whitbread a little last April and the prize play is a bid for popularity; but it must be a melodrama; his audience wouldn't, *at present*, understand anything else.

By the way, why did you put the fool in place of the *child* which I think is contrasted in the folk play with the wiseman.

Will you let me have a reply to such parts of this as require an answer by next post.

I trust your sight is improving.

When will you be in Dublin? If you are going to England previous to the production of these two plays, I think you should see some rehearsals so that we may know whether our work is in the right direction.

Yours sincerely,
F. J. FAY

From FREDERICK RYAN

MS Yeats

Dublin
10 August 1902

[W. G. Fay rented the hall on Lower Camden Street for £40 yearly. AE declined to be president and urged the Society to approach Yeats. Besides AE, Maud Gonne and Douglas Hyde were vice presidents. Yeats did in fact deliver a lecture on "The Reform of the Theatre" at the production (on 14 March 1903) of *The Hour-Glass* and *Twenty-Five*.]

Dear Sir

As I believe Mr. Russell has told you the National Dramatic Society which Mr. Fay organised has been placed on a more definite basis, and has rented a Hall for twelve months, capable of accomodating 200 people. This gives a permanent prospect of carrying on the work and is in every way preferable to spasmodic performances.

At a meeting of the Society held yesterday it was, on the motion of Mr. Russell (A.E.), unanimously decided to ask you to be President, Mr. George Russell being Vice President; and as Secretary I was instructed to convey this to you and to inquire if you would kindly honour us by accepting.

When the Hall has been put in order — which I fancy will be in about a week — and when the Company is ready to give perform- ances we are very anxious that you should "send us off" with a lecture, if at all convenient, in which we could explain our objects, hopes, ambitions etc and let out what are our plans & prospects. Personally if I may say so I think it absolutely necessary to do this, by way of preface, and of course there is no one who could do it as you. If it is not trespassing I shd be glad if you would let me know as to this so that we could make arrangements. Doubtless Mr. Russell & Mr. Fay have written or will write you on the matter.

Yours Sincerely
FREDERICK RYAN
Secretary Irish Natl
Dramatic Socy

From FRANK J. FAY

Dublin

MS Yeats

12 August 1902

[André Antoine founded the famous Théâtre Libre in Paris in 1877. Yeats and his friends managed to change the law prohibiting the performance of plays in halls. The Samhain productions were on 27 October–1 November.]

Dear Mr. Yeats,

You have heard of the hall. It is not large and would perhaps seat 200; the Theatre Libre started in a hall that seated 300. Of course the comparison does not go much further. The hall is in Camden Street close to Harrington Street, and is No. 34. The trams pass the door, but it is so far from the street that there is no annoyance from tram bells. The stage is as deep as Clarendon Street but not so wide and we will have to resort to the simplest of scenery so as to have room to dress and store props during the shows.

If you have a copy of Kathleen ni Houlihan would you lend it to me. I have mislaid my copy and we cannot commence rehearsals without a book. You said something about it being about to be printed. Perhaps you could get me a rough proof. I want it at the earliest possible moment.

Mr. Ryan will reply to your kind letter re President. I dont think there could be any row. We have played frequently during the past ten years in I suppose every hall in town; but have never been interfered with. Once some six years ago the Gaiety tried to stop amateur shows; but the other theatres would not join and the matter dropped. My brother has however some notion of a sort of private theatre where no money would be taken at the door. It is very kind of you to promise to lecture.

The Hour Glass has been cast as you suggested. Would you tell me where I could get some of the folk-tales you mentioned in your last letter in which a fool similar to yours occurs. Can you give us or get us sketches of the dresses. They would want to be put in hands soon, as seven or eight will have to be made.

We are, I believe, to play at Samhain for five nights; but Mr. Ryan will write about these matters.

It was a matter of waiting until doomsday for a proper hall or taking the present one and I think we can do our work here small though the place be.

> Yours
> F. J. FAY

From JOHN QUINN

TS Manuscript Division,   New York
New York Public Library   27 September 1902

[The play was *Where There Is Nothing,* as yet unnamed. John Lane was co-founder with Charles Elkin Mathews of the Bodley Head publishing house, New York and London. Yeats did not go to America until November 1903. The revised and enlarged edition of *The Celtic Twilight* was published in July 1902. The American novelist Henry Harland was literary editor of *The Yellow Book.* Yeats's novel was *The Speckled Bird* (never finished); the plays, *The Hour-Glass and Other Plays* (1904). the essays, *Ideas of Good and Evil* (1903). Yeats and Moore planned to collaborate on *Where There Is Nothing*; when Yeats wrote it alone, Moore threatened suit. Dilke was owner of the *Athenaeum*. The "fine pieces" were in *The Countess Cathleen*, included in *Poems* (1901). Quinn refers to "A Remonstrance with Scotsmen for Having Soured the Disposition of Their Ghosts and Faeries" from *The Celtic Twilight* (1902). The third play referred to was *The Pot of Broth*. Quinn had made his first trip to Ireland in the summer of 1902. He refers to an unsigned review of *Poems* (1901) in the *Athenaeum* (8 March 1902). Mansfield produced and played in *The Devil's Disciple* in 1896.]

My dear Yeats: Enclosed herewith I send you a short memorandum prepared in our office on the law of copyright in the United States and also a copy of the same, so that, if you care to do so, you will have a copy to send to your agent, Mr. A. P. Watt. The practical suggestions I would make are the following: (1) That the title of *the play* should be deposited in Washington, in accordance with the memorandum; (2) That it should be printed simultaneously in each country (printing here being a condition precedent to the allowance of copyright here); (3) Next that the copyright performance should be had in England; (4) Then should follow the deposit of the two printed copies in Washington; and (5) Finally the publication simultaneously in the two countries.

I shall be very glad to attend to the obtaining of the copyright here if you will send me the title of the play and let me know in whose name you wish to have the copyright taken — it is usually taken in the author's name or in the name of the publisher. Of course whatever publisher Mr. Watt puts the play with in America will attend to the printing and depositing of the two copies, but I shall be glad to see that the law is complied with in all respects — of course without any charge to yourself or to your publishers.

As to the American publishers here, Mr. Watt will be best able to inform you. Dodd, Mead & Company who published your *Shadowy Waters* are an excellent firm and are very honorable in their business dealings. Scribners would be good people, if they could be induced to take the play. Stone & Company of Chicago, who published Moore's *The Bending of the Bough*, would, I imagine, be very glad to publish the play. Mr. John Lane also would, I should think, make it a "go," as they say in America.

I should not submit the manuscript to any manager or actor until your rights have been secured both in America and in England — not that you would thereby forfeit any rights but because there is always the danger and the temptation that scenes or ideas

may be stolen from what might strike the actor or manager as a fine
play.

In view of the fact that you are coming here, I would suggest
that you have all your books copyrighted here as well as in England,
at least all of them that there is a fair business reason for
copyrighting. When you come here your name will be much better
known in America than it is today and a great many people will want
to buy your books. It seems a pity that the new edition of *The Celtic
Twilight* was not *printed* in America and the copyright thus
secured — I mean in the same way that *The Shadowy Waters* was
printed here by Dodd, Mead and *The Wind Among the Reeds* by
Lane.

Henry Harland, the novelist, whom I visited while I was in
England and who is coming to the United States this Autumn, told
me that the chief reason for his coming here was that Lane, his
publisher, was urging it upon him as the best thing to help along the
sale of his books. In the same way your coming here, while not at all
with that object in view, would inevitably increase the demand for
your various books. Before coming I would therefore advise that you
secure the copyright both of *the play* and of your novel, when it is
ready for publication, and also of the book of plays and the book of
essays. There would hardly be such a demand here for the book on
Irish Folklore as would, in my opinion, justify its separate
publication here.

I mailed to you a week ago my copy of Nietzsche's *Thus Spake
Zarathustra*. I don't know whether you are acquainted with
Nietzsche's writings or not. While his so-called philosophy is utterly
abhorrent to me — the philosophy of the "blond beast," of the
exaltation of brutality, the philosophy that would make Bismarck
and Chamberlain the greatest men of their time — nevertheless he has
a wonderful epigrammatic style, and in recalling some of the dialogue
of your play I was reminded of certain passages in *Zarathustra*. But
since I sent the book to you I have received Lady Gregory's letter
telling me that the play is finished so that you probably will not
want to bother with the book at all.

Another reason for my sending it was that I saw a copy of it in
the French edition on Moore's library table when I called at his
house in company with your father the Saturday night before I went
down to Galway. *If* he is writing a novel on the subject, he may be
reading *Zarathustra* with the plan of the novel in his mind. This is
only a supposition on my part. The two things may have no

connection. Now that your play is finished you will not of course care to waste time on Nietzsche's *rhetoric*.

I shall be glad if you will let me know how Moore acts in regard to his absurd claim. I agree with Lady Gregory in believing that he will not go so far as an open rupture with you and attempt by proceedings in court to enjoin the publication of the play. He would have the laboring oar in such a contest and would, in my judgment, never be able to make out his case. As I understand his claim, it is that you and he were collaborating on the play and that at a certain time you decided "to throw him over and go on without him." He would never be able to make out this contention, *unless* you have committed yourself by admissions in writing to him. He is an astute controversalist and if I may venture the suggestion I should not, in your place, commit myself in writing except in so far as to deny his charges. I would go ahead in your own way and arrange for the publication of the play as you have written it. If Moore thinks that you are afraid of him, he may persist. If you go ahead without any apparent apprehension concerning his threats he may not go any further. If it comes to the worst you will have to fight him and your friends will, I am sure, see you through. At any rate one of them in this country will be glad to do all he can in helping you. It would be a ugly fight and while your publisher for business reasons might not fear but might welcome it, you would not want to be dragged into an open rupture with Moore on a charge of appropriating his ideas.

I sent Sir Charles Dilke, whom I met at a dinner in London, a copy of your *Poems, The Shadowy Waters, The Wind Among the Reeds, The Secret Rose,* and *The Celtic Twilight.* He and I had a long talk about poetry and I was astonished to hear him state that he had never read anything of yours. In sending him the books I told him that I was surprised that he was not familiar with your work in view of the fact that a very appreciative review of it had been published in *The Athenaeum* only a few weeks ago. In thanking me for sending him the books he states in a letter forwarded to me from London: "I knew that he had been written about in *The Athenaeum* but had, after many disappointments, closed, but for you, the book of new poetry."

In a later letter also forwarded to me from London he states that in *The Wind Among the Reeds* he admires "The Secret Rose" and "The Travail of Passion" and that the "prose notes are attractive and the little Irish stories fine." In the volume of poems he says that he admires the "Pity of Love," and adds: "There are some fine pieces in *Cathleen* and on the whole I like it best. The prose stories are pretty. He is so delightfully Irish that I wonder if it is on purpose that he writes 'shall' for 'will.' The folklore is pleasantly varied by the charming 'admonition' addressed to the Scots on their treatment of fairies," and he thanks me for having made him acquainted with your work.

Mr. Mathews has just sent to me one of the eight copies, in vellum, of *Cathleen ni Hoolihan* just printed for Bullen & Co. It makes a very fine little book and I am glad to have it. The play itself is beautiful. It seems to me that when you print the three short plays — *Cathleen, The Hour-Glass*, and the third play — you can find a much more fitting name for the book than "Plays for a Barn." That title does not *sound* like Yeats. It conveys no definite meaning and would, I fear, be misunderstood — at any rate in this country — if you were to publish them under that title here.

I am sorry that my time was so short in Ireland. I had many things I wanted to talk to you about. I hope that another time we will be able to have what the Indians would describe as some "long talks" together. My few days in Ireland were the pleasantest part of my trip abroad and my visit with Lady Gregory and yourself was the pleasantest part of the time I spent in Ireland.

Sincerely yours,
JOHN QUINN

Richard Mansfield is the actor who played Shaw's "Devil's Disciple" here — a very good actor — one peculiarly fitted — it seems to me — for your play. But I should publish the play as a book and arrange later for its staging by some good actors — Mansfield here best of all.

JOHN QUINN

From GEORGE W. RUSSELL

Dublin
28 September 1902

MS Yeats

[AE refers to Moore's threat to sue Yeats over *Where There Is Nothing* (published 1 November 1902). AE contributed "The Dramatic Treatment of Heroic Literature" to *Samhain* (Oct 1902), printed by Sealy Bryers & Walker.]

Dear W.B.Y.,

I returned here late last night. My wife tells me that George Moore called in the afternoon and told her to tell me that he had decided to take my advice in the Yeats affair, "old friends" &c. I have not seen him yet but write to tell you of this change which I expected to come when he had brooded over what I said to him. I will write when I know more. Please tell Lady Gregory I returned proof to Sealys. With kind regards,

yours sincerely
GEO. W. RUSSELL

P.S.

I told Moore that if the matter was fixed up that I would see that a version of it would circulate which would hurt the feelings of neither of you and that neither he nor you must claim any triumph over the other. I will as I say write when I see what the good man has decided. I am glad that the matter seems to be clearing up. G.R.

From HENRY G. O'BRIEN

H.M.S. Argonaut

MS Yeats
6 October 1902

Dear Mr Yeats

I must start by apologising for taking up your time considering that I have no earthly claim to it, as I am only acquainted with you through certain books of yours which I have enjoyed more than I can say. Except for this and the fact that I am Irish and deeply interested in all concerning my country I should not presume to trouble you with my personal hope and aims. To put it clearly the facts are these. I was educated at Clongowes College in Kildare in 94 when it was first decided that I should enter the Navy. I was then 11 years of age being born in Cork in 83, and had no decided tastes in any direction. I left after a year there and went to a private school in England a year later, that is in the end of 96 to prepare for the Naval examinations. I passed my examination in December 97 and joined the Britannia training ship in Jan 98 and after the customary 18 months joined a sea going ship the Jupiter until April 1900 and enjoyed it very fairly, especially as we spent the greater part of our time cruising around the home ports, and while in Ireland at Berehaven and Queenstown very often obtained a few days leave to

my friends and relations in Cork and Mitchelstown. In April 00 as I
have said I was appointed to this ship but we did not leave England
until June owing to defective trials and other matters. We reached
Hong Kong in August, just too late to go North and take any part in
the Boxer troubles which were then nearly over, and we remained at
Hong Kong for 3 months instead.

To turn now to my chief reasons for writing to you, I may first
say that having been in the service that is to say in sea going ships for
3½ years (April 99–Oct 02), I am now forced to the conclusion
that I am absolutely out of my sphere as far as purely service matters
go. I certainly have no zeal, as I would willingly retire if occasion
only offered, my feeling being, the hopelessness of retiring and
finding no opening for me and a consciousness of my own ignorance
of the sort of work I might be compelled to take up for lack of other
employment. My ability in service matters is perhaps questionable as
only last September I failed to pass for Sub lieutenant and I go up
again in December, but I consider of course that the one brings out
the other, or that a person having any zeal will probably either pass
or otherwise gain by hard work and increasing interest in everything
around him, the requisite ability to please his Captain, senior officers
and examiners. I have failed to do this, not only to the two former
but also the latter as I have previously mentioned.

The only reason I can assign to this is that my interest, quixotic
as it may seem, is wholly and entirely devoted to my country. My
spare time is devoted to reading such works about Ireland, country,
language and people, as I can get hold of in so far removed a part of
the world as this. The fact is I cannot get away from them. They turn
up at awkward moments when I am on duty, and for these moments
I lose all idea of what I am supposed to be doing and consequently I
have got a reputation for being one of the slackest officers in the
ship, which of course I do not disown for an instant, as my idea of
misery is panic, and that is the requisite of a smart officer. I must
conclude by asking your advice in my own case, as I should dearly
like to know your ideas on the subject and if it will not trouble you
to reply to this appealing letter. What I should like to have done
myself of course would have been, to be a farmer in some part of
Ireland and my idea of happiness would be to write verses or prose,
compliments apart, such as you do in the Celtic Twilight and John
Sherman and Dhoya which I believe are also yours, and which have
given me more pleasure than anything else I have read so far. To
conclude once more, I have to thank you sincerely if you have

troubled to read so far, and hoping that you will consider this letter as a purely private question to you from

> Your Sincere Admirer
> HENRY G. O'BRIEN
> Midn.

From FRANK PEARCE STURM

MS Yeats

Aberdeen
23 November 1902

[On 21 April 1900 Yeats had been the leader of a committee which suspended Mathers from membership in the Isis-Urania Temple (London) of the Golden Dawn. Yeats knew Adolphe Smith in the Society for Psychical Research. Pope Honorius III was the author of *Clavicle de Salomon*, sometimes called *The Black Book*. Apparently Sturm did not write about *Samhain* in *Bon-Accord*.]

Dear Mr Yeats

I am writing to you on an unconventional kind of notepaper. I hope you will not mind. Today is Sunday, and I have run short of letter paper. If I wait for tomorrow, a thousand and one things may prevent my writing.

Let me thank you for your letter, which reached me on Thursday morning. That you like my work means a great deal to me, for I would rather have your opinion than that of anyone else I can think of. You placed a certain finger on my weakness when you said my thought is shadowy. I know it is, for I am ever the victim of a struggle between the dream in my heart and the inadequate form of expression that crystallizes into words in spite of myself. I get an idea that seems of a very subtle beauty so long as it is not written down, but when I have made the inevitable compromise between the dream and my immature power of expression, the result is neither beautiful nor subtle, but often banal.

When I have written more and thought more, I hope to gain a mastery over myself. In the meantime I can only try to purge myself from those faults of style that are as obvious to me as they can be to any critic. Your letter has done much to encourage me. I feel I can now write with a greater delight than ever, and a more certain hope.

It would be an ill thing to repay your kindness by boring you. I hope never to do that. But I have it in your own words that you are interested in my articles and poems, and so I take courage to enclose more verses with this letter. Perhaps thay are better than the ones you have already seen. They please me better. Do not trouble to send them back. I hope you will be careful of your eyes; you have my deepest sympathy. I know what it is to read and write until lamplight is an agony not to be endured.

You warn me against Mr Macgregor Mathers. You are not the only person who has found occasion to break off all connection with him and with his brotherhood. If I can possibly manage to get to London I shall say more to you. The man I spoke of in my letter was not Mr Mathers, whom I have never seen, but a Mr Adolphe Smith, who entered into correspondence with me over certain of my articles, and who claimed to have worked with you. He came to see me in Aberdeen. We performed some experiments together and made exchange of a number of manuscripts.

Surely you cannot dream I would repay your confidence by showing your letter to anyone for whom it was not intended. Your cause is my cause, and your enemies mine. I am a stranger to you, but you have been my friend for years, and a far greater friend than many whom I spoke with day by day.

Last night, looking over my papers, I found a memorandum, copied from some forgotten book, which I am sure will interest you. In the British Museum Library there is a Latin MS of the fourteenth century. It is catalogued as "Sloane 313." There is no title page, but from the text it appears to be the famous "Sworn Book of Honorius." If that is so it would certainly repay the trouble of investigation. The introduction to the book accounts for the condemnation of Magic by the prelates of the Church on the ground that they had been deceived by demons. The result was a convocation of all the masters of Magic, who came out of Naples, Athens, and a place called Tholetus. They deputed a certain Honorius to write a summary of the magic art. This he did, "giving the Kernal to us and the Shell to others." From this he afterwards extracted a still more condensed work, "which we term the sacred or sworn book." In the meantime, the princes and prelates, having burned "certain fables or trifles," deemed they had destroyed the magic art, and were purified. The magicians, however, took oath among themselves to preserve the "Sworn Book" in the most secret manner; only three copies were made and the owner of each copy was bound to bury it before his death. The only existing copy is Sloane 313. If that is true, it should be priceless. I have another note to the effect that the Sworn Book of Honorius is quite different from the

Grimoire of Pope Honorius, which is of later date, and of doubtful authenticity.

Does not your Hanrahan, in "The Secret Rose," first enter upon his sorrows when he buys this very book? I often think his fate is the fate of all who open the Book of the Great Dhoul. Do any of us escape? I think not.

Yours sincerely,
F. P. STURM

P.S. The editor of the "Bon-Accord," the only weekly in these Highland parts, has bidden me to write an article about the new issue of "Samhain." I will post you a copy when it appears.

From FRANK PEARCE STURM

Aberdeen
MS Yeats   26 December 1902

["The Sorrow of Deirdre" was published in *Bon-Accord* (1 May 1902) and republished in *An Hour of Reverie* (1905), this time inscribed "To W. B. Yeats". Sturm may have been recalling Yeats's description of "the beauty of white Deirdre" in "The Twisting of the Rope and Hanrahan the Red" from *The Secret Rose*.]

Dear Mr Yeats,

Bald thanks are poor things to express the gratitude I feel for your last letter of advice and criticism. Never fear but that I shall take your words to heart. Your censure is just what I needed to open my eyes to the defect I have felt but have been unable to locate. I have written much and destroyed the most of what I wrote, and when I published anything have felt miserable because I knew there was some great blemish somewhere. I will try and do as you say, I will 'dramatize myself', catching the moods as they come and go, instead of building up futile words that never express what I desire them to express.

As for poets needing a movement that shall urge them to go to nature alone for information, surely you should be the last man to complain of the lack of such a movement, when you are the leader and head of a school whose every thought and word is a breath of the innermost subtlety of nature herself.

I send you in this letter a copy of "The Sorrow of Deirdre." It is strange that it should be the poem you like above all the rest, because when I wrote it last summer and showed it to a man who wished to print it in his journal, I said "If I knew Mr Yeats I would put his name under the title of this poem," and was only kept from doing so by the thought that it would be a liberty to inscribe my poem to a man without his knowledge or permission. It was through you that I wrote it. I had been reading something you had written of Deirdre, I forget where now but I think it was a sentence in "The Secret Rose" that moved my imagination. Because you like the poem I have dared to put your name to it now, and with your permission it will remain there when I publish it in my book.

If ever I do anything that succeeds I shall go to Ireland. You can write there with a contented heart; you have people who are worth writing for, good Catholics with imaginations, and with traditions not entirely forgotten. Here there are black, dour Calvinists for the most part, except in the Islands, and they look upon all literature and all poetry as vanity and foolishness, with the exception, of course, of the unmentionable Burns.

I think, if my opinion is worth anything at all, that in after days this Celtic Movement will be looked upon much as we look upon the great Classical Renaissance which had its birth in the medaeval times and has altered, almost, the face of the world.

It is my ambition, and always has been my ambition, to add one brick to the temple of phantasy and romance you are building, where men can worship and forget for a little the selling of tea and sugar. Since you have written to me I begin to think I may perhaps find the material for that brick.

With many good wishes for the New Year.

Yours sincerely
F. P. STURM

From WILFRED SCAWEN BLUNT

Garden of Sheylch Obeyd
Ezbet el Nalchl, Egypt

MS Yeats   4 January 1903

[A friend of Lady Gregory and strongly opposed to the policies of the British government, Blunt wrote *Fand* for the Irish Literary Theatre. Based on the account in *Cuchulain of Muirthemne* (1902) (for which Yeats had contributed a preface), *Fand* was not produced until 20 April 1907. Lady Day is Annunciation Day, 25 March.]

My dear Yeats,

I am delighted to have a line from 'you. Lady Gregory has kept me supplied with Irish Literature, so I know pretty well what you have been doing & congratulate you very cordially. Of all the plays she has sent me I like your Cathleen ni Hoolihan the best. It seems to me to contain in it all the tragedy of Ireland. It must have had a great success.

For myself, I fear I have been rather dilatory in what I undertook. I wrote a first act of Fand which satisfied me fairly well, but I have dawdled over the rest, & now I have unfortunately left my Cuchulin book in England & am rather at a loss how to finish. I have written a play also on another subject which has distracted my attention & I am writing other things as well. Still I hope to have Fand finished soon, & as soon as it is so I will have it set up in type & you can see whether it w^d be of any use to you.

This place is an excellent one for writing as one is absolutely undisturbed by visitors & with a quite perfect climate. Indeed it is the terrestial Paradise, wild beauty, serpent & all.

Yours very truly
WILFRED SCAWEN BLUNT

I hope to be back in London by Lady Day.

From GILBERT MURRAY

Farnham, Surrey
10 January 1903

MS Yeats

[Best known for *The Rise of the Greek Epic* (1907) and *Euripides and His Age* (1913), Murray became Regius Professor of Greek at Oxford in 1908. He was for many years a member of the Council of the SPR. Murray changed *six* to *seven*: if his memory is correct, he is probably speaking of the trip Yeats and Arthur Symons made to Ireland in early 1896.]

Dear Sir,

May I, without impertinence, write a thank you for the extraordinary pleasure which I have received from your Countess Cathleen & Land of Heart's Desire. It is late in the day, and I ought to have read them years ago; but it so happened that I only came across them last week, & have been so living in the thrill of them ever since that I cannot resist the desire to write to you.

I did not know there was anybody living who could write such poetry.

I have, of course, bought all your books (as far as my bookseller knows them) and shall read them with great care, though I will not trouble you by writing again.

I once met you at Mr. Gosse's about seven years ago, at a time when I was writing a History of Greek Literature for a series that he was editing, & you were just going to Dublin to celebrate some Nationalist anniversary.

Yours Sincerely,
GILBERT MURRAY.

From GILBERT MURRAY

Farnham
TS Yeats   24 January 1903

[Murray refers to two passages in his *Euripides, translated into English Rhyming Verse* (1902): the first, from *Hippolytus* (p. 39), begins "Could I take me to some cavern for mine hiding"; the second, from *Bacchae* (p. 125) begins "Will they ever come to me again, ever again".]

Dear Mr Yeats,

I should like exceedingly to read your prose plays, and will tell Heinemann to send you copies of my two. In the mean time I rather wish you would read a couple of lyrics — by Euripides, not by me; or rather by Euripides with me interpreting — on pp 125 and 39 of the book that I am sending to you. That from the Bacchae, on p 125 seems to me extraordinarily like some of the Old Irish longing to "dance upon the mountains like a flame," and the same feeling is often recurring in Euripides.

I feel quite at a loss about the proper form for a modern play . . . and the proper sort of representation, too. The Hippolytus seems to me right, for one style; and your three, especially perhaps The Land of Heart's Desire, strike me as right for another. I used to believe in a sort of Ibsen-Dumas form of prose play, but it now mostly seems to me ugly and all wrong — a form created to suit a bad style of representation.

I do not quite know what your Dublin plan is, in essentials. My personal experience of the English theatre has been rather excruciating — and that, I believe not through anybody's fault in particular. The system and atmosphere of the modern English theatre seems somehow to kill out any poetry that there may be in a play, to wring it out, sentence by sentence, and produce the play crisp and dry. (Of course, if one could master the medium properly, it might be all right. I would not judge from my own case without making ample allowance for my personal inexperience and lack of skill. But I think it is the same with practically all ordinary plays.) I should imagine, therefore, that our general feeling on the subject was much the same.

I am ill, also — a slight breakdown from overwork &c. May I add, as to my Euripides, that I quite realise that you may not want to read it now — or ever! — So please do not let it be a weight on your mind, as books thus sent so often are.

Yours sincerely
GILBERT MURRAY.

I get writer's cramp when ill; hence the machine.

From WILLIAM G. FAY

Dublin
30 January 1903

MS National Library of Ireland

[*Cumann na nGaedhal* was a party formed by Arthur Griffith. Lady Gregory's *Twenty-Five* was produced with *The Hour-Glass* on 14 March 1903. Padraic Colum's *The Saxon Shilling* was not produced at the Abbey.]

Dear Mr. Yeates

Yours of 29th to hand. I am glad to hear Miss Gonne wrote you her complaint as now every member of our little Society knows of it except Dr. Hyde who I shall not write to as I do not think he would be interested. Now you may remember you and I had a long discussion here in Autumn about a literary veto by individuals and I pointed out the fact that we could not run a voluntary society with an individual veto. It seemed to me that Miss Gonne wished a political veto and I objected on the same grounds that I did about a literary veto. I will state my side of the case —

We wanted a play to go with *The Hour Glass*, hadn't time to get up Lady Gregory's so I said we play the *Saxon Shilling* it was caste at the first Rehearsal. I found that the ending though it read well did not act at all so strong. I suggested to Columb to take the piece and see if he could not make a better shot at it. He wrote a new ending not in my opinion very great but it gave my actor more to do and a better show. Now Miss Gonne turned up to the 3rd Rehearsal at which neither ending was acted as the lines were only being read, she told me before the company that I had ruined the piece and that Cuman no Gaedhal would be vexed and I replied that I thought my ending best and I was not playing the piece for Cuman no Gaedhal and I did not see what they had to do with it.

A further discussion arose in Mr Russel House at which a lot of strangers were present and at which Miss Gonne accused me first of Terrorising Columb into changing the ending and secondly that I was afraid to play the piece as written. The whole thing appears to me absurd, why I should be afraid, I don't know. I take a devel of a lot of scaring for I dont care a damn for any man woman or child alive. Ive been in the mud and walked on velvet but I wont scared of any political play that anyone in Ireland has backbone enough to write, political life in Ireland dosent called for Heroism of anysort. If anyone want to see trouble here let them tackle Mother Church as you did in "Where There is Nothing." Let them act freethinkers and Orangemen and then see how the people will carry on. As for the piece in question its puny enough from a political point of view, and could be done much better at the Queens Theatre than we could manage it for they have more soldiers coats and rifles, there are plenty of ordinary Irish melodrama twice as strong from Miss Gonne's point of view. But I grow wearisome I think the final part of the matter is I altered the piece from a technical point of view Miss Gonne holds I did it from fright. I dont care, and I cant help other people thinking me a funk if they want to, so I have let the matter drop, as I think it is the best, for I think that when all comes to all the piece is the property of Cuman no Gaedhal *though they have never claimed it* and if so we have no right to it at all. If not its Columbs property and he can do as he chooses with it.

To prevent the recurrence of these nasty discussions we have drawn up a set of rules with Mr Russel aid and Miss Gonne approval, (provided the company agree to them). A copy will be forwarded to you next week, and will you let us have your opinion on them as President as soon as possible. About offending U.I. or people like that I have only one opinion that a Theatre is no more a Political Party than its a Temperance platform or can exist at all as Preaching shop for one set of opinions. For pity sake let Art at least be free. I think this puts my view of the matters in question in the best way I can, if I have failed, attribute it to my want of skill in putting my ideas into writing or ask me again.

> I remain
> Yours faithfully
> William G Fay

From GEORGE W. RUSSELL

MS Yeats

Dublin
[?February 1903]

[Althea Gyles was a member of the Golden Dawn and a minor poet and artist whose reputation rests chiefly on the Rosicrucian covers she designed for several of Yeats's books. Cecil French, a London artist, was a patron of Gyles. One of his pencil drawings hung in Yeats's sitting-room. AE refers to the productions of 27 October–1 November 1902. *The Hour-Glass* and *Twenty-Five* were produced at Molesworth Hall on 14 March. Cousins's farce, *Sold*, was not produced by the Society.]

My dear Yeats,

Thanks for information about Althea. I would be glad to hear from you again if I get any definite information from French. I have told Dr Maguire what you wrote.

About the Theatre Society, I have been so busy this last autumn & winter that I have only been twice at the room since the Ancient Concert Rooms performances. I went down a few weeks ago because I heard the Society was likely to split up unless some definite rules on a democratic principle were drawn up. There was a rebellion going on which was natural among voluntary workers at the way in which plays were accepted or rejected without their consent so I drew up and got them to pass the only rules which were possible under the circumstances. I think you got a copy of them. I knew you would not like them but if they were not passed I do not think there would be a theatre society. All the company contribute equally to the finances and neither Fay nor Miss Gonne nor you nor myself would be allowed to veto or accept any play or to do more than give an opinion which naturally has weight.

Your play I believe will be produced about the 14th March in Molesworth Hall. So I was told today. I saw part of it rehearsed and I think it will go well. I think the delay was caused by the rows. If the rules had been drawn up long ago the play would have been performed before this. The company had learned two plays against their will & both had been withdrawn and neither would ever have been given to the company if the rules had been in existence and carried out. Cousins farce was handed to the company by Fay and they were told to learn their parts, and then it was withdrawn I think because you did not like it. Now if the company had been asked to vote on it, it would never have been accepted at all, and all the waste of time learning parts would have been avoided and also the rage at learning parts for nothing when it was withdrawn. Colums play similarly was handed to the company by Fay and withdrawn I think because Miss Gonne objected to its ending, and the company had got its nerves in disorder, so I drew up rules making all this hasty acceptance and repentance impossible. Now you will get copies of plays & can write your opinion before the company learn parts, and you will find it will work much better. You might be able to arrange better if you were constantly here but the rules are the only possible alternative. The Hermetic would be delighted to have your lecture on the Fairy Kingdom. I will speak to them at your next meeting. The room would be too small for an audience of fifty and I could easily borrow the room from the Theatre Society for the occasion. Please let me have a fortnight or three weeks notice and I will find the audience of fifty or one hundred.

Yours ever
GEO. W. RUSSELL

From FRANK J. FAY

Dublin
TS University of Reading   23 March 1903

[Colum's *Broken Soil* was produced on 3 December 1903, *The Shadowy Waters* not until 14 January 1904. Probably because of the productions in London (afternoon and evening of 2 May 1903), there was no "May show" in Dublin. Marie Walker ("Maire Nic Shiubhlaigh"), who played Dectora in *The Shadowy Waters*, quarrelled with Yeats and left the Abbey in 1905 but returned in 1910.]

Dear Mr Yeats,
    We had a full meeting last night and the Secretary will give you details. We have hit on a rather good idea, or rather the brother did

so. He has got the Society to appoint three people to look after printing and business details, one to look after costumes and another to look after properties. The work of the Society is thus being thrown on several instead of one or two and all those who have been appointed will be held responsible for what they have undertaken. For the next show, which has been arranged for the third week of May, the Society has decided to do *The Shadowy Waters* and Colum's play. And this letter is to ask you what about the music which Forgail is to play on the harp. We will need this at the earliest possible moment. We cannot have it too soon because it will be necessary to rehearse it a great deal unless what I think would be impressive is to be bungled. You might write to my brother anything you have to say about *The Shadowy Waters* at the earliest possible moment so that he may have it from the start. But this music is all important and urgent.

I got your letter and am glad the show has pleased people. There are signs that the smaller parts are going to be made go better.

I had a long letter yesterday from a man who has seen every kind of play that has been in Dublin for 25 years and who has written and thought much about the stage. He is very outspoken and has come to our shows for years. He liked *The Hourglass* very much. I asked him to contrast it with *Everyman* and he said that the latter went home to each individual in the audience but the *Hour Glass* he says enabled those who saw it to congratulate themselves that they were not like the Wise Man. He says that a gentleman beside him insisted that he had seen a white flame so the piece must have worked on the imagination of at least one member of the audience pretty strongly. This gentleman who has written the letter of which I am telling you said that the decoration had exactly the effect we wanted — keeping the attention concentrated on the words. That is the second who has said the same. He says that he thinks it would be better to make no reference to the commercial theatre and personally I agree with him. He thinks this last show our greatest success. I am very glad of all this because I did not think we had a strong bill of plays but that is always the way, one can never tell what an audience will think a good bill. If we don't get mauled in London and if we do as well with the May show, we won't have done a bad year's work. We shall have by the way produced eleven plays — already we have done nine. *The Foundations* and *A Pot of Broth* have been acted each half a dozen times or more. Our finances are healthy.

I am glad to hear your opinion of my brother's acting. He is the one 'live' actor in the company. I think with you he would do well in serious parts: but then he is using his hands and brains all day from early morning and not having much time for private study he possibly fights shy of a new class of work. But perhaps he will change. He is to play Nolan, the Socialist in *The Foundations*, on Monday.

The gentleman I have spoken about considers that Miss Walker has improved more than any one else since he saw her in St Teresa's. I too am of this opinion.

Please remember me to Lady Gregory.

Yours sincerely,

F. J. FAY

P.S. Are the battle axes to be ordinary shape. What shape are the swords to be or do you wish any but Forgail to have a sword. I have a *crown* — that which we used [in] *Connla*. There will be the *hats* or *helmets* to consider and if Forgail wears a helmet or hat, do you wish him to remove it at the lines commencing 'The harvest's in, the granary doors are shut', which I take to be the entrance of Love. Am *I right* as to the interpretation of that speech. Forgail says 'give her to Aibric if he will, I wait for an immortal woman, as I think'; and then he goes to Dectora and gazes on her, eventually giving utterance to the speech 'The Harvest's in', which I interpret — I don't know if rightly — as above. If helmets are necessary and swords we will need designs at once so as to get them put in hand.

From JOHN MASEFIELD

MS Berg Collection,   London
New York Public Library   27 April 1903

[Masefield married Constance de la Cherois-Crommelin, of County Antrim.]

My dear Yeats.

I am writing (though only hurriedly) to tell you that I am engaged to be married to Miss Crommelin, and that I am very very happy and full of sky. It is goodbye to all my plans of travelling with the tinkers (you must tell Lady Gregory this) as if things go well we may be married in July. Will you, do you think, be able to wave a flag on that occasion?

I hope to see you soon and speak at greater length. Please remember me to Lady Gregory and believe me

> Yours ever
> JOHN MASEFIELD

From SIR SYDNEY C. COCKERELL

London
4 May 1903

MS Yeats

[A partner of Sir Emery Walker in a process and general engraving business from 1900 to 1904, Cockerell had been secretary for the Kelmscott Press (1892–8) and became Director of the Fitzwilliam Museum in Cambridge (1908–37). Five plays were performed at the Queen's Gate Hall, South Kensington, on 2 May 1903: *The Hour-Glass, Cathleen ni Houlihan, A Pot of Broth, Twenty-five*, and *The Laying of the Foundations*. Florence Farr Emery received considerable attention for experiments in speaking verse (chiefly Yeats's) to the accompaniment of a psaltery designed by Arnold Dolmetsch.]

My dear Yeats,

I congratulate you & your friends most heartily on the unqualified success of Saturdays performances. It was very wonderful that they should go without a visible hitch, considering all the difficulties. I thought the staging of the Hourglass was admirable, as well as the costumes & colouring – but I do not hold with the sentiment of faith without works damning or saving – & in this connexion there seemed to me to be a touch of insincerity which made the whole thing unconvincing. 'Twenty five' & a Pot of Broth were both quite perfect in their way. Every word told – & the acting was firstrate. In Kathleen ni Houlihan, which is a beautiful piece of writing, the intonation seemed to me a little overdone – but this may be because I am not in sympathy with the attitude that you & Mrs Emery wish us to adopt when anything poetical has to be read or declaimed. I am no poet & in these matters I remain a Philistine.

How fortunate you are to have such a good actor as Fay at your command! He was so good in each piece that I scarcely know which he did best.

> Yours always
> S C COCKERELL

I enclose a catalogue of astrological etc. books that has come to me from Germany.

From "FIONA MACLEOD" (WILLIAM SHARP)
                                          Midlothian, Scotland
MS Yeats   6 June 1903

[Sharp's "forthcoming book of essays", *The Winged Destiny*, did not appear until the summer of 1904. One section of this book is entitled "The Sunset of Old Tales". From another section, "The Gael and His Heritage" is concerned with the collection and preservation of legends and myths. Thomas B. Mosher published *The House of Usna* in 1903. Yeats's new book was *Ideas of Good and Evil* (May 1903).]

Dear Mr. Yeats,

I hear that you want to know from me any hint or clue to a Gaelic 'Centaur' from the notes on the subject you were told I had.

In a sense I cannot say that I do know anything of a Gaelic Centaur — for though I have twice at first hand come upon as it were the fragmentary crest or tail of an all but vanished legend, I have no reason to believe the latter to be authentically Gaelic. For example, one day last summer an old man of the island of Skye told me a story he said was "an old ancient *sgèul* of the Gael, older than the grey brow of Ben More yonder that the minister's brother The Professor was for telling us was once no more that a *machar* (i.e. a sandy plain) by the sea or maybe was a ledge below the sea itself, though I misdoubt me where he got that wisdom — too manny books, too manny books . . . they get some confused they who read owre manny books." Well, to give it as briefly as I can, his story was of a woman named Alb — "because she was white, or because all her long hair was white, tho' for sure I don't see the why o' that for I've never heard Alb put upon any whiteness at all at all — " who came to the West out of the East, and had two sons born there and that near a great river. And she died there. And the heap of the cairn that was afterwards made upon her was like a cairn of mountains so big and high and great was it: and it could be seen from the three oceans and the two seas. But the two sons would have died, had not a grey wolf come to them, and suckled them, (and then certain strange phrases and allusions with which I needn't trouble you): and when they were grown they were called Alpein and Crumein, "and they made the biggest Dûn in the world and a great city and that no other than Dunedin (Edinburgh)." And nations came of them like to the tribe of the *sgádan* in the sea or the salmon in the river. And they called the land after their mother."

Now this sounds Gaelic, but it is only familiar history gone through the sieve of men's minds in days when there were no books, and since then handed on with Gaelic names and Gaelic colour and the ingenuity or mythopoeic fancy of the Gaelic teller. For it is just the tale of Rome and of Romulus and Remus. Alba or Albyn is the old gaelic (and Gaulish or European-Celtic) name for Scotland, the land of high hills or white (i.e. snow-capped) mountains — preserved in the familiar *Alp* — and the cairn of great rocky heights in Scotland itself, seen from the three oceans (on the east, on the north, and on the West) and from the two seas (the Moyle or Mull of Cantyre, or Irish Sea, and the Solway Firth dividing Scotland from England). As for the names, they are the two most ancient in gaelic Scotland — for no clan-names go back so far as MacAlpine and MacCrimmon (and the latter, curiously enough, is also in Old Gaelic readable as Son of the Wolf . . . the house-name *Crimthann*, the Wolf, too, you will remember, was given to St. Columba in boyhood.)

And so, too, one may find the Tale of Troy with Gaelic names and colour, though it is not gaelic but only like many other tales sucked along on the ebb from old history. So inevitable is this tendency that I would undertake (if among peasant Gaels unable to speak English) that a story told let me say of Charlemagne or the Cid would be retold among them a year or two thence with a gaelic colour, and say in seven years thence would be "an old ancient sgéul of the Gael" that had been told "to my mother's mother by her that was old then and had all the old tales and poems."

Well, this long preamble is to explain why I do not believe there is any authentic "Centaur" legend.

I have, however, gone into the matter in one of the sections ("The Sunset of Old Tales" . . . . of which a part appears in the *Fortnightly* of this month) in my forthcoming book of essays and studies in Gaelic literature and legend, which has been delayed for a year past by illness and other causes.

My essay in question is on the sculptured symbols of the Centaur and the Salmon, as found on a few of the most ancient Pagan stories in Scotland. The 'Centaur' is so rare as to be practically unknown except to a few specialists. I have drawings and all particulars of the only three that exist: and of these one is remarkable — tho' the concurrent secondary symbolism is difficult to determine.

(W. S. has made a tracing — and could show you in London if you are to be there till after mid-June: he getting there about the 14th.)

The puzzling thing is that most of the sculptured symbols of which these are two are practically found only in Gaelic Scotland – which would seem to tell against their being solely derivative from Roman sources. But the whole thing was to be gone into very carefully. (I have also, I may add, a very curious tracing of an ancient symbol on a stone in the north of Scotland – of a *horse-headed salmon*, unique I suppose.) However, W. S. will I am sure show you all the tracings and memda he has made, when you see him in London. (It is likely I may reproduce the remarkable forest-branch bearing Centaur to which I allude above.)

It may interest you to hear that Mr. Mosher of Portland, Maine, is to reissue this autumn a revised edition of my version of "The Tale of Deirdrê and the Sons of Usna" (from the "Old Tales Retold" volume) and also of the drama of the close of the Deirdrê-cycle, "The House of Usna." I much wish the latter could be performed by the Irish Literary Theatre.

I have read your new book with deep interest, apart from its charm and beauty.

Sincerely yours
FIONA MACLEOD

From SIR ERIC MACLAGAN

MS Berg Collection,   York
New York Public Library   29 July 1903

[Director of the Victoria and Albert Museum, Sir Eric Maclagan was a close friend of Yeats for several years, having "at one moment actually shared lodgings" with him. According to Professor Michael Maclagan, his father loaned "Yeats a copy of *Luitprand of Cremona*, who is the prime source for the trees and birds of the Byzantine court." St John Hope was Assistant Secretary of the Society of Antiquaries. The volume he recommended was *A Description of All the Ancient Monuments, Rites and Customs within the Monastical Church of Durham before the Suppression* (1842). Maclagan and A. G. B. Russell edited Blake's *Jerusalem* (published by A. H. Bullen in 1904). In the Preface (dated July 1903) the editors acknowledge their indebtedness "to the patient and sympathetic labours of Messrs. Ellis and Yeats, and our personal obligation to the latter for his ready help and kindness". The *Jerusalem* was part of a projected series of Blake's Prophetic Books. *Milton*, the only other volume in the series, appeared in 1907. "Another play" is a reference to *The Hour-Glass*, one of the plays produced in London on 2 May. The Gregory referred to is Robert. *In the Seven Woods*, the first publication of the Dun Emer Press, was published in August.]

My dear Yeats

(Forgive me for writing to you on this paper, but there is no writing paper left in my room.) I have looked up all the books within my reach about banners; they certainly were in very early use in Byzantium (under Constantine) and in France (Gregory of Tours and others); but from the two or three representations of the Byzantine banners that I have seen (none of them very satisfactory) they tended to be rather like the Roman standards, i.e. elaborate poles with quite a small square cloth at the top; which probably only bore the ☧ or some such symbol. Yesterday I consulted Mr. St. John Hope, a very learned antiquary, about mediaeval banners, which were considerably used in England, and he tells me that there is an elaborate description of the Banner of St. Cuthbert at Durham, in a mediaeval account of the rites of that church printed by the Surtees Society. This I will look up as soon as I can get at the York Cathedral Library. Meanwhile he tells me that the only correct traditional shape is square or oblong; the banners with peaked and scalloped ends are a device of ecclesiastical milliners only. Such banners generally bore the figure of a saint with an emblem, as you describe the ones that A. E. and your brother have designed: from motives of economy they were often only of painted cloth. Certainly for use in processions they are generally made too small nowadays. Please write and tell me if I can be of any use finding out symbols for you; I shall be in London at the end of August and could look out anything that you wanted in the Museum.

I am very glad you liked the page of our Jerusalem; I got eight or nine sheets of proof the other day and I think Bullen is having it done very nicely. We are keeping to the original spelling absolutely, which seems to me the only thing to do; and we are publishing the text quite by itself, except for a page of notes and an index that has cost us much weary toil! I do hope it will induce people to read Blake, now.

The hymns I showed you at Oxford were all in the "Irish Liber Hymnorum" published in two volumes by the Bradshaw society in 1897. All the Irish hymns in that book have got English prose translations; but many of the hymns are Latin. I'm sending you two translations of the latter, very fine in the original; but I think the Irish hymns interested you most, and theśe are very hard (to me) to put into rhyme; I can only get one little one into shape at all, and that I'm sending with the others. I have not got a copy of my own of the book, or I would send it to you; it is full of most interesting things, references to legends etc.

I'm so glad you've done another play; but I hope after this year's English success that it won't be only in Dublin that it will be performed. I was so sorry to miss the Irish plays in London, but I was in Munich at the time.

I saw Masefield in London the other day, and his intended wife, who seemed a very charming lady. When are you coming back to London again? I hope that Ireland is making you feel well and doing your eyes good.

> Yours always
> ERIC R. D. MACLAGAN

Please give my love to Gregory if you are seeing him. Did Bullen tell you that Swinburne has accepted the dedication of our Blake.
By the way, when are the new poems going to come out at the "Dun Emer" press? I can't remember whether I ever wrote and subscribed.

From FRANK PEARCE STURM

	Aberdeen
MS Yeats	22 September 1903

[Sturm received a medical degree from the University of Aberdeen in 1907, having tried unsuccessfully to earn a living by writing. Apparently Sturm published no articles in the *Theosophical Review* or *L'Initiation*. *Piacula sunt* means "let them be offerings" and *salve*, "be well".]

Dear Mr. Yeats

I will take your advice in all things. I will give your formula of the "egg of light," but I do not think it will do much good, and I will tell you why. The woman who sees this elemental bear is very easily thrown into an hypnotic trance, I am told, and has her head full of things she has heard and read about hypnotism.

When I tell her about the "egg of light" she will think I am trying to put her under the influence of "suggestion," and that will cause her to "auto-suggest" a contrary influence. I know these nervous women. However I will try, and I thank you greatly for your advice.

You are entirely right about "hysteria and mania." There is a little circle of occultists in London to which I once belonged and with whom I still correspond. One of their number, while at a seance where the darker powers were being invoked, was siezed with hystero-epilepsy, though he had been healthy before, and he is now a constant sufferer from that frightful malady. I am a medical student by profession, and I have seen too much of hysterical disorders to be sure that they can always be referred to a material cause. One of the first neurologists in the world has lately made the statement that hystero-epilepsy can never be so explained. He has even hinted at "spiritual influxes," which is a long way for a scientist to go.

My silver pentagram may be the death of me yet, but the results I get with it are so interesting that I can not find it in my heart to cast it into the Sea just yet awhile. I am not exactly "playing with thaumaturgy," as you suppose. All my experiments are planned with care and precision, and they are working towards a definite end. I hope soon to publish some article on my experiments either in the "Theosophical Review" or "*L'Initiation.*" I expect you see both periodicals, but I will send you the numbers containing my articles. You may be angry with me for playing with fire, but I can promise that you will be interested in my results. *Piacula sunt!*

As to my poems. I do certainly read much contemporary poetry, especially Shelley and Rossetti, but I do not read much poetry that is contemporary in the strict sence. Arthur Symons, for instance, has had no influence on me, for his poetry is frequently a bit disgusting, though I like his prose immensely. Stephen Phillips I read once, but not twice – his work is too cloying – like a diet of chocolates. The poems of Robert Bridges are the ones I like best and read the most, with the single exception of your own.

You yourself have influenced me more than any writer living or dead, except, perhaps, Poe. When I am writing verse I find it difficult to escape from echoing you. Since I read "The Shadowy Waters" I have been so haunted by its strange rhythms that I cannot write unrhymed verse at all, for that very reason.

I read also much French poetry, and have the most of Baudelaire and a good deal of Verlaine off by heart. Years ago I translated the the more lucid of Mallarmé's poems into what I then supposed to be English verse. It was not verse, as a matter of fact, but I cannot think the effort was wasted. As to Latin poetry, I have

read Lucretius many times, and know Virgil as well as I know
Shakespeare.

Someday perhaps I may be able to make a style for myself. I am
only twenty-four years old, so there is time enough yet. Certainly, I
will publish no book until you give me permission. I chose you for
my master long ago when I read your tales and poems in "The
Savoy" ("Rosa Alchemica" and "The Tablets of the Law" kept me
dreaming for weeks) and now that you have practically given me
permission to show you my work, I will not apologize for submitting
poems from time to time.

If you ever have a photograph of yourself that you feel you can
spare, I know well who would like to have it. I have a copy of
Whistler's portrait of Stephane Mallarmé, and a steel-engraving of
Baudelaire, hung up in my room, but I have no portrait of you,
except one I cut out of some weekly paper. It isn't very good, nor is
it autographed.

If I am too much presuming upon so slight an acquaintance,
please forgive me and take not notice.

Yours sincerely
FRANK STURM

P.S. I was at a dinner the other night where a priest became much
excited about your *"Where There Is Nothing."* He hadn't read it, but
he had been on the continent for a holiday and had read something
about it in a French paper. I broke into the conversation and fought
your battle. If we hadn't both been guests at the same table, I believe
he would have excommunicated me on the spot. He held forth small
hopes for your future salvation. You are a heretic. Salve!

F.P.S.

From GILBERT MURRAY

Farnham

TS Yeats   12 November 1903

[The Masquers Society was founded on 28 March 1903 to give
performances of "plays, masques, ballets and ceremonies". Yeats,
Murray, Symons, T. Sturge Moore, Edith Craig, and Pamela Colman
Smith (see her letter dated 16 December 1903) were members of the
managing committee. Miss Craig, sister of Gordon and daughter of
Ellen Terry, was also a member of the managing committee of the

State Society from 1899 to 1903. Acton Acton-Bond was a Canadian-born actor.]

My dear Yeats,

You will hear with mixed feelings that the Masquers Society is no more! As you know, I have long been in favour of its decease, and some ten days ago Acton Bond (whom Miss Craig had put on the committee as an active theatrical person who could "run" it) moved that the society should cease until such time as there might be a prospect of working with more success . . . i.e. principally, when you and Symons and Moore and Miss Craig and himself should all be available for work. I promptly supported him, and told the committee that I had mentioned the point both to you and to Symons and that, though I was not authorized to speak for you, I had had letters from you inclining in the direction of winding the society up. Symons, I said, had expressed the same opinion definitely and had even authorized me to vote for him, though I would not have used the vote had there been any real difference of opinion on the committee. Everyone was for winding up and returning the subscriptions except Miss Craig, who contended that she could put a piece on the stage in a fortnight, and do it well. (It is the latter part that I doubt. I have no doubt that we could produce scratch performances like the old Independent Theatre &c, as much as we like. But that is not what we were started for.) Eventually Miss Craig moved an amendment to Bond's motion for hibernating, that we should cease altogether. She pointed out that, if we were liable to resurrection, the ghost would hamper her in dealing with plays that might turn up. If we were really dead, she would devote herself to improving the Stage Society. I advised Bond to accept the amendment, and it was carried unanimously. We are returning subscriptions, and explaining that, though we had enough money and members to justify us in starting, we found other circumstances unfavourable and thought that the attempt at a "Theatre of Beauty" should be postponed, though we still keep our faith in it.

It is a great weight off my mind! We shall actually end our life without having swindled anybody, and I shall no longer shrink from the eye of a policeman. But what bad luck we have had, in the way of marriages and foreign travels.

I hope America is behaving herself nicely to you.

Yours very sincerely,
GILBERT MURRAY.

From PAMELA COLMAN SMITH

London

MS Yeats   16 December 1903

[A psychic American artist of some talent, "Pixie" Smith came to London in 1899 and called on Yeats, who was probably instrumental in having her admitted to the Golden Dawn. When the Order split in 1903, she joined the group led by A. E. Waite. She is known among occultists for seventy-eight plates illustrating Waite's *The Pictorial Key to the Tarot* (1910). John Singer Sargent, well-known London artist, was a long-time friend of Yeats. The little red fox is in "The Rider from the North" (originally "The Happy Townland") from *In the Seven Woods* (August 1903). "The dream of the Wandering Angus" is a reference to "The Old Age of Queen Maeve" from the same volume.]

Dear Mr. W. B —

This is to say howdee and wish you good luck for the new year —

I am lilting and storytelling at a great rate. I had an amusing argument the other day with John Sargent about the meaning of the little Red Fox! —

The Masquers is dead — at least for the present — The Dancers — came out with a flourish of news paper notices — and thinks its self *very* grand — Most people I know, won't join — Edy Craig & I think of getting up a *grand* mock dance & offer to do it for them! —

I think the sale of your books should go up — ! for the numbers of people who have asked where the Red Fox comes from — & The dream of the Wandering Angus — & then they dash out to get the book! —

With best wishes for good luck
from yours
PIXIE
PAMELA

From PAMELA COLMAN SMITH

London

MS Yeats   3 February 1904

[Yeats was in America from November 1903 till 9 March 1904. Robert Laurence Binyon was a good friend of Yeats, who selected

Binyon's *Odes* (December 1900) as one of the best books of 1901. Edward Calvert, a disciple of Blake, was one of Yeats's favourite artists. Miss Smith's project came to nothing.]

Dear Mr. W. B —
Miss Horniman tells me that you will be sailing soon — and so I am writing to tell you of a plan that Mrs. Fortescue & I have in our heads — which you might be able to think over on your trip home —

We want very much to get up a hand press — to print small editions of books — (by subscription) hand coloured — and have thought of Blake's "Songs of Innocence" & "Songs of experience" — & hand colour them in facsimile of the original copies — Since our first proposition we have heard that *Methuen* is going to do the two-in-3 colour process — & with an introduction by Laurence Binyon.

Do you think that this would interfere with our small edition (limited) 500 ——— copies. *hand coloured?*

Or do you think it better to do a book on *Calvert* — with reproductions of the woodcuts ——————? ———————

In either case will you do the text for us — ? With Blake it would be an introduction ——————— if you would take what we can afford namely — *£10.10.0.* In the case of the Calvert it depends on you — what text there is — & we should have to think over — our business arrangements. The Unicorn Press have been so long about the book on Calvert they announced — that if it can be made practical commercially I see no reason why we should not do it.

You have been having a great time we hear — and are looking forward to hearing your adventures —

Yours
PIXIE
PAMELA

P.S. *Please* keep this to *yourself!*

From JOHN QUINN

TS Manuscript Division,   New York
New York Public Library   [6 February 1904]

[Hull House was founded in Chicago in 1889 by Jane Addams, social reformer and co-winner of the Nobel Peace Prize (1931). It was Miss Ada Smith, daughter of the proprietress of a boarding house where

Quinn lived, who made the black tie. George Brett was head of Macmillan in America. O'Grady's paper was *The All-Ireland Review*. Quinn probably refers to the first production of *The Shadowy Waters*, performed without Yeats's approval on 14 January 1904. An unsigned review in *The United Irishman* for 23 January, probably by Arthur Griffith, called the play "indefinite as a whole" but admired the speaking of Frank Fay and Maire Nic Shiubhlaigh.]

My dear Yeats:

Greetings and congratulations on your success at the Coast. I am very glad that you were so well received and have a little glow of pride in the vindication of my judgment in having you go to the Coast.

This letter should have gone yesterday. It did not go because yesterday (Friday) I received a telegram from Mrs. Coonley Ward, who had engaged a lecture for Tuesday at 10:30, saying that she wanted the lecture in the evening. I wired her that this was impossible. Since that time I have received a letter from Miss Mary R. Smith asking for a lecture at Hull House in Chicago next week.

You will see from the statement I enclose regarding the lecture for Mrs. Ward that *Tuesday morning the 9th at 10:30 was the hour agreed upon.* I send you the chronology of my communication with Mrs. Ward. Please read it. You will see that I suggested *Thursday* morning, if Tuesday morning as arranged is impossible. However, if Miss Addams, the head of Hull House, wants you to lecture on *Thursday* I should advise giving her the preference over Mrs. Ward. I enclose herewith a copy of my letter to Miss Addams today. Please read it. You will see that I suggest Monday afternoon or Tuesday morning for your lecture at Hull House. If Monday afternoon *or evening* or Tuesday morning does not suit Miss Addams, then if she or Miss Smith calls upon you please say to them that you can lecture for them Thursday at 10:30.

You must start east Thursday afternoon at 3 o'clock, so Thursday morning is the very latest that you can lecture. If Mrs. Ward calls upon you just let her read the schedule of my communications with her.

I send you herewith your schedule of engagements which follow out very carefully. Be particular about leaving Chicago on time Thursday. This will be a hard week's travelling for you, but next week you can rest.

The first thing you want to do Monday morning after reading

this letter – the very first thing – is to call the porter and have your laundry attended to. I am sure that at the Auditorium Annex, if you give them your shirts and collars on Monday, *with special instructions*, they can have them washed for you and delivered to you by Tuesday morning. Don't give them to them without special instructions. If you give your linen without special instructions you may not get it back until about the middle or end of the week, and you will need all your linen to last you until Saturday.

You will see from your schedule of dates that you have short stops and long trips. It will, therefore, be inconvenient to have your trunk with you. I had a small extra dress suitcase sent to you today. Use this to carry your shirts in and put in the two dress suitcases such things as will last you until Sunday the 14th. It will be much less inconvenient for you to have your things in the two dress suitcases than to be bothered with the trunk. Put the things that you don't need into the trunk; have the trunk locked; have the porter address it to John Quinn, 1 West 87th St., New York City; have it sent by express; get a receipt from the expressman; and send the receipt in a letter to me *with the key* of the trunk enclosed. I can open the trunk if you send the key and have your underwear and linen washed and taken care of and ready for your return.

Miss Smith told me yesterday that your black tie might be soiled and she very kindly offered to make you one. She made it today and telephoned to me this afternoon that she had sent it to you at the Auditorium Annex.

If your trousers need pressing, or your dress suit needs pressing, you can have this attended to on *Monday* at the hotel.

I have taken up the question of publishing your works with Scribners. I went over all of your different books with them this morning and I think that by the time that you return they will be ready to make you a good offer. Much better than Brett, who acts like a Jew.

I send you also herewith three letters from Lady Gregory, one from Miss Horniman, two from your sisters and one from your brother. I also send you a letter which I opened from a Miss Ethel Middleton of 151 Dunn Avenue, Toronto, Canada. You lecture at Toronto Saturday evening the 13th. You arrive there on the morning of the 13th. At some point in your travels you ought to send a letter or a telegram to Miss Middleton.

Andrew Carnegie sent an invitation to you to dinner for the 11th. I sent a note saying that you would not return from the West until the 14th and that you would be glad to meet him upon your return. I will no doubt receive a reply from him in the next few days. I think you ought to meet him if possible. He might want to establish a Carnegie theatre in Dublin. Or he might want you to invest the proceeds of your lectures in steel stocks.

I also send you last week's *United Irishman* and O'Grady's paper. The U.I. seems to speak fairly well of the play.

I am sorry that you have to hurry back so soon after the 28th. I had arranged for a lecture at Newark on Sunday evening the 6th of March and for another lecture at Dobbs Ferry on the 8th (Tuesday). If you think you cannot wait until after the 6th, telegraph me on Monday and I will cancel the Paterson lecture. You could sail on Wednesday the 9th and reach Ireland by about the 17th. Wouldn't that be time enough? I hope that you can stay at least that long? Please let me know whether you can or not. On Monday I will look up the sailing dates of the White Star boats and will write you so that you can recieve the letter by Thursday at the Auditorium Annex. My letter will give the names of the boats and the dates of sailing and the dates of arrival at Queenstown.

I am sorry that you have such a hard week before you, but it was impossible to arrange the lectures otherwise. You will have plenty of time to prepare for the Emmet lecture. I am sure you will do it well. I will read up a little about Emmet and between now and Sunday make a few brief notes which may be useful as suggestions for your lecture.

Don't worry about the lecture at all.

Don't forget any of your things at Chicago.

Don't forget about your linen on Monday.

I think that I have given you enough to do at Chicago to provide you with a good excuse for declining invitations to the stock yards or to the university. Chicago boasts of but two things, first the stock yards and second the university; but the stock yards always come first. Now that you have been to the university (which I forgive only because it was a *pretty* girl that invited you) they will surely want you to go to the stock yards. I hope that the play at the university was badly performed. I have a great many more things to say but it is getting late, and so Good Night!

If my suggestion about the use of the second dress suitcase and the return of the trunk does not seem convenient, then just have the porter send back the dress suitcase by express, to me at 1 West 87th St.

If you should happen to run short of money telegraph me from any point where you may be a day and I will send you more money *by telegraph*. I'll be glad to see you back. It has all been a big success. Sincerely,

JOHN QUINN

[Enclosure]

FACTS OF MRS. COONLEY WARD'S LECTURE

Jan. 19.   Mrs. Ward wrote asking for lecture.

Jan. 23.   Wrote suggesting afternoon Feb. 11.

Jan. 25.   Mrs. Ward wrote asking if you could stay until six o'clock in afternoon.

Jan. 27.   Wrote suggesting beginning lecture earlier.

Jan. 29.   Mrs. Ward telegraphed: "Please give me other dates, eleventh afternoon impossible, evenings suit."

Jan. 29.   Telegraphed suggesting several dates *including morning of ninth*.

Jan. 29.   Mrs. Ward telegraphed: *"Ten thirty Tuesday morning ninth is perfectly satisfactory."*

Jan. 29.   Wrote confirming telegram of this date.

Feb. 1.   Mrs. Ward telegraphed: "Your letter received, *have finally decided on Tuesday ninth*."

Feb. 5.   Received, to my great surprise, letter from Mrs. Ward dated February 2nd: "I have finally decided on Tuesday evening, Feb. 9 &c." This letter was not received until Feb. 5.

Feb. 5.   Immediately telegraphed "Evening of ninth engaged; you can have evening of eighth or morning ninth."

Feb. 6.   Mrs. Ward telegraphed: "Telegraphed Friday waited till Monday then issued three hundred invitations impossible to change."

Feb. 6.   Telegraphed: "Your telegram said Tuesday morning. No other arrangement possible now unless Thursday morning. Do you want either."

From GEORGE W. RUSSELL

Dublin

MS Yeats   [March 1904]

[Rearden was one of thirty commissioners who represented the Louisiana Purchase Exposition in St Louis, Missouri, which opened

on 30 April 1904. J. Dudley Digges, P. J. Kelly, C. Caulfield, and
Maire T. Quinn were early members of the Fays' company. Elizabeth
Young ("Violet Mervyn") had played the lead in a performance of
the first and second acts of AE's *Deirdre* on 3 January 1902 in the
garden of George Coffey's house. Miss Quinn played the lead in the
first full production of the play (2 April 1902). Yeats refused
permission for the use of his plays. After Yeats threatened suit,
through John Quinn, if the company did not cease using the name
"The Irish National Theatre Co. of Dublin", the Fays' American
manager, Charles Frohman, changed their advertisements.]

My dear Yeats,
        I have been troubled about your letter. I have no knowledge of
Rearden beyond the fact that he is some sort of a commissioner & I
spoke to him a couple of times. I would be sorry to think he was
intending to carry on a game of false puffs in the states. What I know
about Digges and his people is as follows: First, no company is going
out. Digges, Miss Young, Kelly (of Fays co.), Caulfield, who was in
Fays co. a year ago & Miss Quinn are going out. Miss Young, who is
very competent, will do all the leading parts with Digges. The
remainder of the company will be made up in U.S.A. or from Irish
musicians & singers who will be there & who will fill up the minor
parts. When Fay refused to go Digges asked me if I had any objection
to his trying Deirdre as he had been engaged by Rearden along with
those I have mentioned. I told him I had no objection. Fays people
not wishing to go, I did not see any reason why I should refuse
especially as I thought that with Digges Kelly & Miss Young, they
would not give a bad show. If Miss Quinn was leading actress, I
would have been much more disinclined to allow them. It never
occurred to me that your lectures in the states might make any
difficulty. I see now of course that if Digges had *your* plays there
would be confusion. I am altogether unknown as a writer of plays
over there & I do not suppose the use of my play would lead to
complications. Martyn I understand has given permission for the
Heather Field & Moore for the Bending of the Bough & I believe for
his share of Diarmuid & Grania. I don't know exactly what to do
about the matter now. I am going to ask Rearden to put on any
programme of Deirdre "Performance by permission of the Irish
National Theatre Society who are owners of the copyright". This will
I think distinguish Digges from the National Theatre. So far as you
are concerned you have a good case in refusing Diarmuid & Grania.

About your other plays I cannot advise you unless you wrote to Rearden more or less as you wrote to me, and stated that you hoped to have national theatre society out later on & did not wish to have minds of people confused. If you wished to be goodnatured and let them have one or two plays like the Hourglass if you exacted a written agreement that on all programmes of performances it should be distinctly set out that the plays were acted by permission of Irish National Theatre Society of Dublin it would prevent confusion to some extent. But you have more knowledge of U S A than I and can judge best. For small plays it is likely the performances will be quite as good as the National Theatre Society could give, Digges Miss Young & Kelly being quite as good as any remaining here. I doubt altogether their power to do the big plays competently but I daresay the Pot of Broth Cathleen ni Houlihan & the Hourglass would be done well enough especially as both Digges & Kelly have been in them already & so has Caulfield in Cathleen. Cousins plays are not going only those I mentioned of Moore & Martyn. I wish I had known all you write before. The matter has been hanging fire here for months. I am sorry I cannot see my way to withdraw permission to act Deirdre though if I had thought there would be any reason against letting them have it I would of course have refused.

Later — I have seen Rearden & have got his promise to put on programme of all performances of Deirdre "by permission of Irish National Theatre Society." This I think will distinguish the company from ours. My own advice to you is to act as you think best about your own plays except Cathleen which I understand you did not retain for the Theatre Society. Your plays are of more importance than mine & may be a source of income to you later on so you have other reasons for not letting them go out of the company at present. I have scribbled this in a hurry as you want reply at once but I am too hurried & busy here to have time to think it out.

Yours sincerely,
GEO. W. RUSSELL

From GEORGE W. RUSSELL

Dublin

MS Yeats   15 March 1904

[*The Hour-Glass* had been published by Macmillan on 13 January 1904. *New Songs* was published in March 1904, *The Divine Vision* in January. Count Casimir Joseph Dunin-Markievicz, who married

Constance Gore-Booth in 1900, was a minor painter and play-wright.]

My dear Yeats,

I am delighted that you are over on this side of the water again. I congratulate you on your success in the States. There is no living Irishman who could more fittingly and favourably represent new Irish ideas to our kin in America. I have just returned from the country this morning & found you had sent me, I am sure it is an error, *two* copies of the Hour Glass, both with my name written in it. What does this mean. I have examined the problem with such light as a slight acquaintance with Poes detective stories can give me, and assume either of the following:

1st that you have another book similar in binding to the Hour Glass which you intended to send.

2nd that your wits were woolgathering

3rd that you intended to enclose with a copy for myself a copy for some other person whose address you did not know, but — here supposition 2 comes in somewhat you forgot to whom you were sending.
Which of all these is true? and is there any body here you want me to pass on the second copy to?

Did you get a copy of "New Songs" which I posted to you at Woburn Bldgs a couple of weeks ago & did you get a copy of "The Divine Vision" I sent c/o Quinn in U.S.A?

I am in my spare time painting as many pictures as I can for I am going to exhibit during Horse Show Week together with Markovitch the Polish painter all the best in a collection of pictures "Ireland Visible and Invisible." I hope it will irritate a good many people. I would never have thought seriously of it but Markovitch who is a medallist in Salon & a really fine painter thinks my things are good and like nobody else's & He has persuaded me; so I am going to adventure with my suggestions for a Celtic art. Markovitch is devouring Lady Gregorys books & is going to do cartoons of old Irish subjects for the show. I hope it will pay its expenses for if it doesnt Ill be "broke."

With kind regards,
Yours ever
GEO. W. RUSSELL

P.S. When are you coming over here

From CHARLES RICKETTS

London

MS Yeats   [*ca.* 1 April 1904]

[Ricketts and Shannon attended the evening production at the Royalty Theatre in London on 26 March 1904. Frank Fay played the lead in *The King's Threshold* and Colum's *The Broken Soil*, but his brother W. G. Fay probably played in *The Pot of Broth*.]

My Dear Yeats

I am shocked at my not having written to you before now to say how greatly Shannon & I enjoyed your new play on Saturday. And how pleased we were with the friendly reception it met from an audience which seemed more intelligent than most audiences.

I like the motive of The King's Threshold, the telling simplicity and effectiveness with which you develop your situation, and the sense of variety & progress, or should I say climax you put into each situation notably when the bride is brought on to the stage. I was charmed by many beautiful & fresh things by the way which I should like to quote, but I became so angry at the end with the exchange of compliments and protracted life of the poet that they have slipped my memory. – I like the touches of humour which are fresh & direct, I like the reference to leprosy over the white hands of the princess. I do not like the curses; curses are always conventional or spoken conventionally. I like the poet's reference to a place in his world, instead of that more comfortable place his bride had in mind. – All through I found myself deeply interested; once or twice annoyed by the intoning of pieces which were quite delightful enough in themselves, without that vocal form of limelight. I liked the farce it was also telling, fresh & simple with a touch of old Greek or early form of freshness which characterized the situations in the King's Threshold. The King's Threshold suffered of course at the hands of your players who were mostly inadequate but never offensive, and that is a compliment when romantic play acting is concerned. Fay is really a remarkable actor, he was good in the Kings Threshold, superlatively good in the Second Play and capital in the Pot of Broth, some of his dumb play was quite extraordinary. I have met several friends who were at the plays all were interested, some of them delighted.

With every cordial wish for the future of the Irish National Theatre.

Believe me

Sincerely yours
C. RICKETTS.

From GEORGE W. RUSSELL

Dublin

MS Yeats   [? June 1904]

[Probably because The *Sleep of the King* and *The Racing Lug* had been produced only once (in October 1902) by the Irish Literary Theatre, Cousins joined the group of dissidents which founded the Theatre of Ireland. AE refers to John Lane, the publisher, and to poems which were to be included in *Irish Literature* (10 vols, 1904), ed. Justin McCarthy. *The Bell Branch* was not founded.]

Dear Yeats,

I will read your letter to the committee. Just as it happens Cousins writes resigning his connection with the Theatre Society & withdrawing his Sleep of the King & Racing Lug. There has been too much wirepulling & bickering for him he says & he has altogether assumed the tone of an aggrieved person. Of course he was badly treated by Fay who accepted "Sold" at first with joy & got three rehearsals & then withdrew it without giving any particular reason, but if Cousins carries out a threat he made to Ryan of writing all the facts to the United Irishman I do not think he will gain anything, as it is a personal matter between himself & Fay there being no Theatre Society until I drew up the rules.

I am writing to Lane again pressing for an answer about the poems. He is a nuisance.

I am thinking of getting out a monthly magazine and am getting quotations from printers. It is to be called "The Bell Branch" price sixpence – in appearance something like Samhain with brown paper cover & a design in black and gold. It might serve as the organ of drama, literature & art in Ireland dealing with all these things from a spiritual standpoint. If I could get 250 subscribers at seven shillings a year each, six for paper & one shilling for postage, I could do it. I will take no advertisements & am inclined to issue it only to subscribers & not have it on sale in the shops, but that is a detail. Magee has promised to write, so has George Moore whose contributions by the way will have to be carefully considered and I will certainly refuse them if objectionable. The magazine will acquire force if its standpoint is definitely transcendental and while I asked him to contribute something I did so because in getting out a preliminary circular asking for subscribers I wanted names. Will you write something. I know you cannot very well afford to give away articles but if you would promise a page or two sometime I will put your name down as a contributor. You might find the magazine useful as a means of educating people here and I think our subscribers would soon include most of the thoughtful people we want to get at. I believe Lady Gregory is staying near Rosses Point. Would you ask her whether she would give me an article if I can get the thing underweigh. If I can get 250 people to become subscribers I will do it; every copy sold over that number will be profit which I would use to illustrate & enlarge the paper. I would like drawings coloured by hand of the Sidhe auras &c. Reproductions of pencil sketches of your fathers & other things which might be interesting. How long will you be in Sligo? I get my holidays on the 16th July and am thinking of going Rosses Point for a couple of weeks & for a week to Donegal. Kind regards to your uncle.

GEO. W. RUSSELL

From JOHN MASEFIELD

MS Berg Collection,   London
New York Public Library   24 August 1904

[Lady Gregory's *Spreading the News* and Yeats's *On Baile's Strand* were the first productions (27 December 1904) of the Abbey Theatre. Masefield was present, representing the *Manchester Guardian*. The "buccanneer book" is probably *A Mainsail Haul*, published 1 June 1905. Masefield did not include either of the poems in this letter in *The Collected Poems*. Four years later *Ballads and Poems* (1908) included a poem in praise of London which echoes the one on Liverpool: "Oh London Town's a fine town, and London sights are rare".]

My dear Yeats,
     It was very good & kind of you to write me so charming a letter. I will come over for Lady Gregory's play unless my buccanneer book is too backward to let me go. It is being written under an agreement & I must make every effort to get it done in time. I wish to God I were as Synge is; going along a lane with a fiddle, the lucky dog, and playing tunes to the milkmaids. One gets so mouldy in this grisly place, where one never sees a living human being after you have gone back to Ireland.

I joined with ancient shipmen beside the galley range
And some were fond of women but all were fond of
    change,
They sang their quavering chanties all in a fo'c's'le drone
And I was finely suited if I had only known.

I was rested in the alehouse that had the sanded floor
Where sailors sat a-drinking and chalking up the score
And talked of ships and mermaids, of topsail sheets &
    slings
But I was fond and foolish: I looked for better things.

I heard a drunken fiddler in Billy Lee's saloon
I seared an empty belly with thinking on the tune
The beer-mugs clinked the tables, the drinkers roared the
    song
But I was tired, and left them, and that's where I was
    wrong.

We are going to live at Greenwich, in a little lonely house not
very far from the river, and I hope that sometimes, when there are
some fine ships to see, you will come with me to see them & to talk
of Bowlines, and the Dry Tortugas, with the men on board. It is a
wretched river after the Mersey & the ships are not like the Liverpool
ships, & the docks are barren of beauty. But the sailor-town is yet
the one human part of London, & I hope I shall find happiness, if no
ballad poetry, in walking about among the crimps, by the marine-
stores, with a sailor as a comrade, and a quid of jacky in my cheek.
But it is a beastly hole after Liverpool; for Liverpool is the town of
my heart & I would rather sail a mud-flat there than command a
clipper ship out of London.

Oh Liverpool's a fine place for any lad to be
For there the stately clippers come & tarry sailors go
And sails are hung a-drying from the wettings of the sea
And one may buy a parrot for a silver piece or so.

And there the bonny steamers swing with funnels red &
    black
And bold Blue Peters flapping, and an anchor down,
And ships are sailing daily and never coming back,
And crews are cheering daily while towing into town.

Oh a stirring port is Liverpool when all the clippers start
With brass-work brightened finely and the topsails set
I have a surging fleet of them a-sailing in my heart
With all their royals drawing, & their fore sheets wet.

It was a pity I ever left the sea; there is nothing like it.

I am afraid I shall never be able to do much verse from now on, for I have to work to keep the fire alight, & I cannot write prose all day, and verse when the prose is done. I have written 160,000 words (the length of 2 novels) this year, and also arranged a picture-show, and I have had my hatreds to spoil me for poetry, in addition to all the work. Campden had to be abandoned, for had we gone thither the enemy would have followed, & the place is too little for a feud of the kind.

Please remember me very kindly to Lady Gregory & thank her for her kindness in typing me so long a letter. Good luck to your theatre & its poets.

Yours ever
JOHN MASEFIELD

From GILBERT MURRAY

Farnham
TS Yeats   27 January 1905

[Henry Irving, manager (with Ellen Terry) of the Lyceum Theatre, and Herbert Beerbohm Tree were well-known London actors. In *Samhain* (December 1904) Yeats had written that "*Oedipus the King* is forbidden in London". Murray translated Euripides' *Troades* and *Bacchae*. "Fand of the Fair Cheek" is a reference to Blunt's *Fand*. In 1902, Edwyn Robert Bevan "rendered into English verse" *Prometheus Bound*.]

O Man,

I will not translate the Oedipus Rex for the Irish Theatre, because it is a play with nothing Irish about it: no religion, not one beautiful action, hardly a stroke of poetry. Even the good things that have to be done in order to make the plot work are done through mere loss of temper. The spiritual tragedy is never faced or understood: all the stress is laid on the mere external uncleanness. Sophocles no doubt did many bad things in his life: I would not try to shield him from just blame. But in this case I am sure, he was in a trance and his body was possessed by a series of devils — Sardou, the Lord Mayor of London, Aristotle, the Judicious Hooker, and all the Editors of the Spectator from its inception to the present day. It has splendid qualities as an acting play, but all of the most English-French-German sort: it is all construction and no spirit.

I am really distressed that the Censor objected to it. It ought to be played not perhaps at His Majesty's by Tree, but by Irving at the Lyceum, with a lecture before . . . and after. And a public dinner. With speeches. By Cabinet Ministers.

When free from his affliction, Sophocles wrote some very beautiful plays, the Antigone for instance. And Aeschylus has all the great qualities always, though not the second-rate. I shall translate some Aeschylus some day when I feel I can do it, but really I can, as a rule, only work at the people who have got my own religion. And Sophocles hasnt. (The said Religion is not perhaps very visible in the Hippolytus, but it is there. And it is plentiful in the Troades and the Bacchae.)

Many thanks for Samhain, the whole of which I read with great pleasure. The second Hippolytus chorus was indeed "too large." The words are admirably chosen. I have tried to express the fact in many ways, but I never thought of that simple adjective.

Fand of the Fair Cheek seems to me a beautiful thing. I have just received it. I have been rehearsing the Land of Heart's Desire with my daughters, who are going to act it at school . . . a long cherished plan.

Seriously, I rather hope that you wont do the Oedipus. It is not the play for you to cast your lot with. Do the Prometheus (Bevan's transln not at all bad: or I might at a pinch attempt it, though I cannot promise without rereading) or even the Persae with a seditious innuendo. Or the Antigone.

Yours ever,
GILBERT MURRAY

From A. E. F. HORNIMAN

Dublin

MS National Library of Ireland 9 February 1905

[The "friend" was George Moore.]

Dear Demon,

I want you to clearly understand that though I acknowledge that I have no right to interfere with your social life yet that I am publicly connected with the Irish National Theatre Society.

If by any writings of your "friend" they appear to be his "protegées" in any way I shall look upon it as a public insult offered to me by the whole Society severally and collectively unless those writings are publicly repudiated. I shall carry out all the promises I have made most scrupulously and I shall alter the stage costumes to the best of my ability but in that case I shall do no more. It is your duty to carry out what you think best for your country and if pleasing Mr. Quinn and your "friend" will serve your aims better than what I can do, I have no right to blame you. But I will not raise a finger, beyond carrying out the pledges I have already given, to anything with which your friend is allowed to connect himself in any way, without public protest from the Society.

Yours sincerely

A. E. F. HORNIMAN

From ARNOLD DOLMETSCH

MS Berg Collection, Chicago

New York Public Library 2 April 1905

[*On Baile's Strand* (first produced by the Abbey on 27 December 1904) was performed in Chicago, where Yeats had lectured in February 1904. Sir Phillip Benjamin Greet was an actor, manager, and producer.]

My dear Yeats

I saw the first performance of this last Friday and enjoyed it very much. All women, *not* made up. The fool was exceedingly good. The audience was small, but included the foremost litterary men in Chicago. They made me talk about you for ever so long afterwards. You have made a very deep impression in this country. You should come again soon.

I have been loosing a lot of money in the beginning of my tour, through very bad management. But, I am my own manager now: I have not only made good all the loss, but some profit is in hand, and I see more coming. I shall not come back before May 10 or so, and will only stay in England a few weeks. I shall return to America for an indefinite period. Alas! They are willing to support me here, whilst in England they let me starve ... I am now doing a "Shakespeare Festival" here, with Ben Greet. I am looking forward to see you. I *should like* to make some music for such a morality play, Angelic music, introduced as you would. It would be beautiful. I am staying here long enough to get an answer, if you feel inclined to write.

> Yours very sincerely
> ARNOLD DOLMETSCH

From WILFRED SCAWEN BLUNT

MS Yeats

Sussex
9 May 1905

[Blunt refers to *Fand*. Francois Coppée was a French poet and playwright. Yeats's long essay on "The Dramatic Movement" appeared in *Samhain* (December 1904).]

Dear Yeats.

Many thanks for your letter abt. the play, as to which I quite understand the difficulties there may be with your company in acting it, it being so much a woman's piece. But I have so little sympathy with the heroics of male courage, even in the heroic ages, that I cd. not have written it otherwise, and I chose that particular episode in the Cuchulain Legend because it was comparatively free from the bombast of fighting. As to the metre I equally cd. not have written it in blank verse. I have been preaching against blank verse any time for the last five & twenty years as the one thing which has always stood in the way of any progress in the direction of good verse drama on the English stage. It is a most unfortunate metre because unless it is of the very highest quality (and Shakespeare alone wrote that in dramatic form) it is almost undistinguishable from prose so that the actor is obliged to mouth it to show that it is verse at all. I was brought up, as far as play going went, mostly in Paris & used to attribute the success of the French poetic drama largely to their having so infinitely better a medium than ours in the Alexandrine — for the metre of Fand — I wd. have you remember — is precisely that of all Victor Hugo's great tragedies to say nothing of Coppée's & the rest of the successful verse plays written in France down to our own day. I had therefore hoped that a new start might be made which shd. get us out of the terrible old Elizabethan groove in which we have stuck so long, & I thought perhaps in Ireland the tyranny of English custom would be less hindering than in London. Your actors however know their own business best & I never placed any great reliance on the play being acted any where. Certainly I have no wish that it shd. be so in London, where the school of acting is so unintelligent & so ignoble. I shall have Fand properly printed now & published so that it may have its place among my literary works which I am setting in order, & there I shall be quite content it should remain. Latterly my health has become so bad that I cannot hope to do more than clean up my poetic rubbish heap, & finish prose works long on hand. I have taken great interest in all your stage propaganda during the past year & especially in the success of Lady Gregory's Kincora & what you wrote in the autumn in the Samhain. I agree with most of your ideas though as you know not with all.

Yours very truly,
WILFRED SCAWEN BLUNT

From A. H. BULLEN

Stratford-upon-Avon
21 May 1905

MS Yeats

[Joseph Hone was the financial backer of Maunsel & Co., George Roberts its managing director. AE had included poems by Roberts in *New Songs,* published by Bullen in 1904.]

Private

My dear Yeats,

Young Hone came on Friday. He appears to have a thorough dislike of his manager Roberts; in fact cannot speak about him with patience. Evidently he would be glad to back out of the arrangement if he could find a decent excuse; but he stands in some fear of 'A.E.' I found Hone pleasant enough & felt some sympathy for him; for Russell wants eventually to thrust Roberts on him as a partner, &

Hone's alarm at the prospect is tempered with disgust — as Roberts is of course his social inferior. He asked whether I would co-operate with him if he were to throw over Roberts (this ex-Knight of the Garter); but I did not commit myself to anything definitely. We can talk over the matter when you come down: let me hear when you are coming. Hone has a great admiration for you, & would like to work with you & me if Roberts could be got out of the way; but he says that A.E. won't allow Roberts to be ousted.

Yours Sincerely

A. H. BULLEN

From PADRAIC COLUM

	Dublin
MS National Library of Ireland	3 June 1905

[See Colum's letter of "November 1905".]

My dear Mr. Yeats,

As you are aware I voted for the establishment of a limited liability Co in order to save the Society from a disastrous split. I come back to Dublin and I find the Society hopelessly shattered. The one thing to be done is to re-unite the Society. Until this is done the dramatic movement is hung up. I appeal to you — I earnestly appeal to you to take steps to re-unite the group.

Please write to me at once and let me know what steps you are about to take.

Yours sincerely

PADRAIC COLUM

From PADRAIC COLUM

MS Berg Collection,	[London]
New York Public Library	[? November 1905]

[After the first production of *The Land* (9 June 1905), the Irish National Theatre Society became the National Theatre Society, Ltd. It was apparently one of the plays produced on 27 and 28 November 1905 in St George's Hall, Langham Place, London. Arthur Griffith, editor of the *United Irishman*, had praised the Irishness of *Broken Soil* in contrast to Synge's *In the Shadow of the Glen* (produced on 8 October 1903). *Broken Soil* (produced on 3 December 1903) was

revised and renamed *The Fiddler's House* (produced in a hall in the
Rotunda, Dublin, in 1907).]

My dear Mr. Yeats
Of course it's not true that I blamed the society's arrangements
about "the Land". It's quite true that I expressed my disappointment that the matinee would prevent many of my friends being
present. I expressed it to Miss Horniman herself. But I knew it was
due to inevitable circumstances. As a matter of fact I am almost
indifferent to the show I get in London, and anyone who knows me,
knows this. I wouldn't have come to London at all only Lady
Gregory asked me to play. I am very distressed about the matter
being spoken of. I see a reference to it in the "UI". I would have
written to Griffiths, only I know from a somewhat bitter experience
that this would be no use. It may be that I am not so intensely
interested in the artistic side of the movement as you are, but I can
assure you that you can always reckon on my loyalty to you
personally & to my school. I will have some of the play finished soon
after I get back. The alterations in "the Land" were not a success and
I am determined to finish "Broken Soil". I find the material difficult.

Yours sincerely

P. COLUM

From GEORGE W. RUSSELL

Dublin

MS Yeats   [December 1905]

[When Annie Horniman subsidized the National Theatre Society, Ltd
in 1905, Yeats agreed that the players should also be subsidized —
that is, become full-time professionals. Marie Walker ("Maire Nic
Shiubhlaigh") was one of several who opposed the new organization.
She left the Abbey on 15 December 1905 and joined a rival group,
the Theatre of Ireland, organized in 1906. Yeats, Synge, and Lady
Gregory were directors of the new organization; they held the bulk of
the shares and maintained the power. AE suggests that only Frank
and Willie Fay, Sara Allgood, and Udolphus Wright would remain
loyal if a break should come, and in fact many of the company did
follow Miss Walker. Thomas Michael Kettle, author and politician,
was Professor of Economics at University College Dublin. Maurice
Joy was at one time secretary to Horace Plunkett. Yeats wrote a

series of letters about the Queen's visit in 1900 (see, for example, *L* 335). Also, see *L* 466 for what is probably Yeats's reply to this letter from AE.]

My dear Yeats
    I heard you wrote to Miss Walker but have not seen her or spoken to her about the matter. The only time I spoke to her on these points since the new company was formed was a little afterwards when she came up to me to ask my advice. I advised her to join you then & never advised her in any contrary way since. I told Roberts, who mentioned about Miss Walkers refusal to go on with the arrangement made, that she would have no ground unless you on your side had broken through some understanding and if not she must go on whether she liked it or not. I did not imagine that you were in earnest anyhow, and of course you may be acting in the best way, but I am inclined to think it is unwise considering the very insecure hold you have on the old society. If you irritate the members they will certainly elect a new President & Vice Presidents at their next meeting and you Lady Gregory & myself who are not members except ex officio from our position will drop out & have no grounds for interference. Synge was elected a member & will remain, but if they adopt this course, with whatever new President or Vice Presidents they may elect, the voting power will give the old society completely into their hands. In all "resolutions" a three quarters majority is necessary, but an election will go by majority of votes. I myself thought I was elected a member of the old society but I found I only can act ex officio and if I was not renominated as a Vice President I would be out, so would you & Lady Gregory. The books contain the list of members formally admitted. I believe the rules have been submitted for a legal opinion on this point. Of course if you are prepared to let the old society go you can act regardless of any irritation you may arouse. I think if you do you will lose Dublin completely. You have managed to upset the nerves of all the younger people who write in the U.I. the Nationist and other papers. You will get no defenders in the press here, however matters may stand in London where of course your reputation will carry a weight which it would not in Ireland. What I think is wrong about your way of getting a movement to work is that all movements need volunteers and you cannot afford to pay everyone, and when you talk in Dublin about "singing canaries" and "poultry gardans" it all comes back to the people for whom it was intended, and with very vivid

exaggerations. There is probably not one of the younger people of whom you have not said some stinging and contemptuous remark. They may have been justified. But if you wish to lead a movement you can only do so by silence on points which irritate you or by kindly suggestions to the people. A man without followers can do nothing and you have few or no friends in Dublin. Their irritation leads them to tear to pieces everything you write until they persuade themselves that it has no merit at all. Of course if an angry man read Homer he would see nothing in it and would describe it as a series of brutal rows. You are committing the great mistake of so many people about Ireland "the twenty years of resolute government" theory. Irish people will only be led by their affections. Wake their affection and they will move heaven and earth to help you. Look at Hydes power compared with your own and you have twenty times his ability. Fall out of the circle of their affections and they will turn on you like Healy or Parnell. You may lose all your present actors who are not paid, as they will probably meet continually the young men in the clubs who will say you are confessedly not a Nationalist, and if a new company was formed it would get all the old group of actors except the two Fays, Miss Allgood and Wright. I am giving you the situation as it appears to me. Remember there is Martyn, Moore, Colm who is young and who may be swept from you by the tide of popular resentment & the Gaelic League which has no affection for you, and an amalgamation of all the dissenters with a Gaelic dramatic society associated with it would leave you Synge, Lady Gregory, & Boyle with yourself and none of these have drawing power in Dublin. The others will get tremendous houses as the National Players did crammed to overflowing. Griffiths, Ryan of the Nationist, Moran of the Leader would all welcome another society. You who initiated the theatre movement in Ireland will be out of it. You irritated the Cork people, the Belfast people would work with a new nationalist society & get them good houses there. You will be as out of everything in Ireland as Dowden & with as little influence. Your last Samhain did you endless harm it was so badly written and more patronising in its references to other writers than the quality of thought or writing displayed by yourself allowed. I imagine you get few people to tell you the truth because you are all too ready to fly in a rage, they have not your vehement power of language and while they remain quiet, they go away to work against you. There have been greater artists in literature than yourself but it is not always recorded that their position impelled them to speak contemptuously of everyone not their equal. The fact is the position you wish to hold of general autocrat in literary, dramatic and artistic matters in Dublin or Ireland is a position accorded through love and cannot be assumed and without a press to back you up or a band of energetic propagandists to carry your opinions about, you may be as right as God Almighty in his secrecy but with as little influence in the lives of men. You may say you dont want a popular influence. You only want the educated intellectual opinion on your side. But you know Dublin and are Magee, Moore, Colm, and the small crowd of young people like Starkey, Kettle, Joy with you. I dont think they are. There is society but there are strong social influences against you and I doubt whether anything but a recantation of your Queen's letter would help you much with them. You must not take this letter as written in spirit of antagonism. I have had no particular reason to support you and many good reasons to fight you if I wished to do so. But I have always recognized your genius as a poet, and have always fought for you there where I could. I have felt for some years past that the old friendship between [us] was worn very thin. But at least you are one of the few people in Ireland who have done something and are still trying to do something, and I do not wish to fight you unless your track of action interferes with my own, and a question of principle arises. I have always tried to avoid any friction, and have decided that as I did not wish to write plays myself I should not interfere with you who did. I have no doubt I have been represented as always thwarting your views but as a matter of fact I have lost a great deal of my influence among the young men by defending you. When the society was started you may not be aware of the fact that I was unanimously elected President, and it was with some difficulty I induced them to put you into that position. I mention this merely to show you that I did not wish to take any position which I felt rightly belonged to you. There was I think hardly a time since then when if I wished actively to oppose your views I could not have carried the society with me. I have a kind of honour of my own and did not think because you went round sneering at "Deirdre" as a bad & popular play and at my opinions as valueless, that that was any reason why I should try to upset your work. Of course I do not deny that I have laughed at most of your dogmas, and have never disguised my opinion that in trying to write plays you are deflecting a genius which is essentially lyrical & narrative from its best manifestation and that your want of logical constructive power unfitted you for dramatic writing, at least for the stage. You spoke once to me of two courts of appeal the "popular" and the "intellectual". Neither one or the other have awarded you any other position than as a writer of beautiful verse, and I think it a mistake which later on you may regret that you should lose time managing a business bringing endless annoyance with no added influence. As a poet you could and would exercise an immense influence on your contemporaries, as a dramatist you lose influence. The few dozen people who come to the Abbey Theatre are a poor compensation for the thousands who would read another Wind Among the Reeds or another Usheen or work like that. However as you have begun it and tied the Theatre round your neck you must go on with it, and my advice to you is let Miss Walker alone and do as little as you can to irritate those who are against you, or you will find that a man with no friends and many active enemies may for all his genius have less influence on his time than some person of one half his abilities. This is my advice. Ask yourself whether you did not bully and worry Miss Walker into joining you against her own wish and whether as a gentleman you are right in trying to bully and threaten her into remaining whatever your legal rights may be.

Yours sincerely
GEO. W. RUSSELL

From WILLIAM SHARP

Sicily
MS Yeats   [December 1905]

[This letter was written only a few days before Sharp died on 12 December. He and his wife were visiting his "dear friend" Alexander Nelson Hood near Taormina in the Sicilian Highland. Following "veiled mission", Sharp wrote the following lines which are carefully crossed out: "At the same time that a certain person sought you and that you did not recognize the person, the occasion, or the significance." Sharp fell dangerously ill in the spring in West Scotland, where he finished work on the "new Tauchnitz vol.", *The Sunset of Old Tales* (1905).]

My dear Yeats,
    Your letter of the 4th has reached me in Sicily some 9 days later.
    Frankly, I have been much hurt by your continuous and apparently systematic ignoring of any communication from me, and

had made up my mind to keep silence henceforth. I knew of your dislike of writing letters (common to all of us who have so much pen-work to do, & fully shared in if not exceeded by myself) and ever bore in mind your overstrained eyesight – but naturally I thought that in the course of more than a year, and after letter-after-letter, you wd. have sent even a P.C. – or, what seemed simple, dictated a message through Lady Gregory or some other friend.

I have a very strong feeling as to the *Nobless-oblige* of friendship – and as I do not regard you as a mere acquaintance, I feel it the more.

Now, however, that you have at last written, and that I have explained my feeling in the matter, I'll endeavour to put it aside among the discharged things.

I am in a remote and wild part of the Sicilian Highlands, staying with a dear friend: and expect to remain here till Christmas. Thereafter we shall be in the French Riviera (probably at Cimiez near Nice) for three months. So I fear there is little likelihood of our meeting till after Easter.

I am unfortunately not in a position to say anything definite on the matter which you broach. If we meet, we may speak of what cannot well be written about. I may add, however, that neither I nor any person *personally* known to me "sent" any one to you on a veiled mission. As you know, we are in a crucial period of change in many ways, and there are circles within circles, veiled influences and good and evil (and non-good and non-evil) formative and dis-formative forces everywhere at work. Obscure summons, obscure warnings, meetings & partings, veiled messages, come to us all.

All which sounds very absurd, or mysterious, or conveniently vague. However, you'll understand. Also my present silence.

As you are likely to be in France (Paris?) in April or May, we may possibly meet *there*. Perhaps you know nothing of any such likelihood, and it may be mere wildfire of supposition. Bien, nous verrons.

I hope the dramatic undertakings will be a success, above all in reaching the psychic nerves, the living thought, of those to whom their appeal is made.

For many months this year I was ill – dying – but there were other than physical reasons for this, & I survived thing after thing and shock after shock like a swimmer rising to successive waves – & then suddenly to every one's amazement swam into havens of relative well-being once more. But the game is not over, of course: and equally of course is a losing game. Nevertheless I'm well content with things as they are, all things considered.

Have you heard of or from Miss Macleod? If I can get a copy from the Catania bookseller who occasionally sends foreign books by courier to this remote place, I'll send you a copy of her new Tauchnitz volume of revised, augmented, and selected matter called "The Sunset of Old Tales" — or I may get some one to do it for me at home, or in Germany — yes, that will be simpler. If in the course of a week or two one does not reach you, write to Miss Macleod who wd. like you to have one.

I wish you'd dictate a line to me of your own literary work. Is any new vol. of prose or verse to come out soon? I hope so.

As for myself, I have much on hand, but for long I have had to do little. Now, if the Gods permit, I hope to recover some lost ground.

I dreamt of you some time ago as going thro' a dark wood and plucking here & there in the darkness seven apples (as you thought) — but they were stars. And you came to an edge or cliff, and threw three away, & listened, and then hearing nothing threw three more idly away. But you kept, or forgot, one — & it trickled thro' your body and came out at your feet, and you kicked it before you as you walked, & it gave light, but I do not think you saw the light, or the star. What is your star, here, — do you know? or can you interpret the dream?

Yours as ever,
W.S.

From ELIZABETH A. AND WILLIAM SHARP

London and Chorleywood

MS Yeats
28 December [? 1905]

[Sharp died on 12 December. His wife wrote from London; Sharp's undated statement is headed "Chorleywood".]

Dear Mr. Yeats

My husband wished that you should receive the enclosed immediately on his death. Unfortunately I found it today only.

As you will see, he and he only, was, and wrote as, Fiona Macleod.

Sincerely yours
ELIZABETH A. SHARP

This will reach you after my death. You will think I have deceived you about Fiona Macleod. But, in absolute privacy, I tell you that I have not, howsoever in certain details I have (inevitably) misled you. Only, it is a mystery. Perhaps you will intuitively understand, or may come to understand. "The rest is silence." Farewell.

WILLIAM SHARP

It is only right, however, to add that I, and I only, am the author — in the *literal* and literary sense — of all written under the name of Fiona Macleod.

From A. E. F. HORNIMAN

London

MS National Library of Ireland   9 January 1906

Official
To the President of the
Irish National Theatre Society
Dear Mr. Yeats,

I am informed that various of the members of the I.N.Th. Soc., yourself amongst them have formed a Ltd. Co. called the National Theatre Society Ltd so that the promises made to me in the letter of 1904 can be better carried out. I highly approve of this for as I have spent so much time & money on my side I consider it to be fair that every precaution should be taken by the members towards carrying out the objects as announced by you. I hereby transfer my gift of the free use of the Abbey Theatre (on the same conditions as before) to the National Theatre Society Ltd as I consider that the Ltd Co. will honestly carry out my intentions. Those members who have not followed you, have completely ignored me and so I have no reason to believe that they wish for my further help in any way. They have never formally protested to me against your new plan & so under whatever name they may choose to call themselves, I can have nothing to do with them. The theatre is a means for carrying out a certain theatrical scheme & as long as you continue in the same path, the theatre is at the disposal of you & your friends under whatever title you may choose to use.

With kind regards

Yours sincerely
A. E. F. HORNIMAN

P.S. A copy of this has been sent to Mr. Synge.

From FRANK J. FAY

Dublin

TS/MS National Library of Ireland   16 January 1906

[William Boyle's *The Eloquent Dempsey* was produced by the Abbey on 20 January 1906; Lady Gregory's *Hyacinth Halvey* on 19 February 1906. The "pars" are "paragraphs" of news sent to the newspapers for insertion as news items; "adverts" were paid inserts. The newspapers mentioned by Fay were nationalist in sentiment, and most were generally opposed to the National Theatre Society as not nationalist enough. Vera Esposito ("Emma Vernon") had played in Boyle's *The Building Fund* on 25 April 1905. *The Well of the Saints* had been produced by Max Reinhardt at the Deutsches Theatre in Berlin. Above the phrase "because my pars are crude" is written: "I asked Synge to help him".]

Dear Mr. Yeats,

My brother asks me to write and tell you that all is in readiness for Saturday night. Last Saturday we had an inch in the *Times*, *Freeman*, and *Independent*, and pars in the *Herald* and *Telegraph* and the *Telegraph* par appeared in Monday's *Freeman*. I also sent a par to the *Times*, but *they didn't insert it*. Possibly they will do so on Saturday; but just as likely they will not. *They need looking after badly*. The theatre bills are up on the boards here since Saturday last; crimson and black, and Allens are posting their boardings on Thursday. Mr. Darley has arranged about the Music, and his name is large on all the advertisements and bills, and is mentioned in the pars. Last night we sent advt. to *Leader, U.I., Nationist*, and *Claidheamh* for one inch.

We are rehearsing *Kathleen*, in which Miss Allgood promises to be very fine, and *The Building Fund*, in which she promises to beat Mrs. Esposito. We have taken up *Halvey* again, *but have nothing to go with it for next month*. This is very important. With the people we have, I don't see how *The Shadowy Waters* could be got up in that time. Synge got news that the *Well of the Saints* was played last Friday night at the Deutches, but has not had press notices yet. The *Nationist* by the way wrote asking for an advert. Oh these incorruptibles! I hope you will be here soon, because my pars are crude, stiff things, and a great deal more could be made out of the election-side of *The Eloquent Dempsey* than I have been able to make out of it. We are right in the middle of the elections — municipal and others — and if this could be brought out properly in the pars, it might help to draw good houses. Power has not left us. *Riders to the Sea* will I think go very well.

Our friends the enemy are saying the wildest nonsense. I met Colm today. My God, the samee gamee. Said he was coming to interview me or be interviewed, said you were on the wrong track. I said "How?" "Not with the popular voice of the country." I said, "What is the popular voice?" "Griffith, Moran, or the *Nationist* or *Claidheamh Soluis.*" He said the *Nationist* is out of it and if he thinks Moran is popular voice I said on What or How popular. No reply. I asked if you were on the wrong track was he on the right one he said he didn't know. I asked him if he was ever introduced to the Popular Voice or would know him if he met him. No reply. Says he is awaiting more evidence and will come round and see me again. Great Lord they are beyond anything. I would as soon teach Metaphysics to babies in arms as try to talk common sense with these people.

[unsigned]

From PADRAIC COLUM

MS Berg Collection,   Dublin
New York Public Library   18 February 1906

[Colum joined the dissident group who left the Abbey. He wrote again on 21 April 1906: "Please accept my resignation from Society". In May he was one of the signatories of a letter inviting various people to come to an organizational meeting to found the Theatre of Ireland.]

My dear Mr. Yeats,
    First of all I must inform you that I was altogether unaware of the letter sent to Lady Gregory. I have read her reply to that letter. One clause in it has affected me very much. Lady Gregory says "The Theatre was given to Mr. Yeats to carry out his dramatic projects." This is disclaiming the notion that the Abbey Theatre is the Theatre of a Society aiming at the creation of a national drama. It is altogether a personal adventure. I do not think it would be fair to take advantage of that adventure, especially as I feel that I am developing ideas that may be altogether opposed to yours. I am still young enough to believe in a movement that will express itself in drama, and from this out it will be my study to get in touch with the life & ideas that underlie that movement, & to turn them into personal experience. I shall work with any Society that has the aims of the Society to which we first belonged. If I am a member of the

National Theatre Society, Ltd, please lay my resignation before the Directors.

I feel this situation very keenly. I may develop ideas opposed to yours, but I shall always by proud of being a contemporary. To you and W. G. Fay I owe much as a dramatist.

Yours sincerely
PÁDRAIC COLUM

From A. E. F. HORNIMAN

Edinburgh

MS National Library of Ireland   24 June 1906

[Yeats's birthday was 13 June, not 23 June. Miss Horniman refers to W. G. Fay. Members of the Gaelic League and other "patriots" were frequently opposed to the aesthetic premises of Yeats. Miss Horniman's letter concerning the "use of the Abbey Theatre" appeared in *Samhain* (December 1904).]

My dear Demon,

I have only just remembered that yesterday was your birthday — may you have a very successful year & a happy one too. I feel much relieved in mind now that I have planned definitely to put things completely into the hands of the Directors. It would have been impossible for me to keep Fay on as my representative after he was so rude. Apart from that interview he had gone on obstructing me in so many ways that were most foolish, matters in which I should have consented at once if I had been asked clearly. You will have to get someone to see after the business matters because otherwise *your* time & strength will be wasted. I will write my proposed plans, only for discussion with you, *not* as settled on the other side of this paper so as to make you know exactly what I mean. You will be free to do just as you like about making it up with the Gaelic League or anyone else. I know that I need make no proviso as to anything you have published. My letter in Samhain is not affected at all.

Yours
ANNIE

Abbey Theatre to be completely in the hands of the Directors.

A sum of £500 a year to be paid quarterly in advance to pay salaries.

A sum of £100 a year to be paid quarterly in advance to cover cost of attendants etc for my tenants.

The proposed right to sell refreshments to belong to the Directors for their profit.

Any price of seats to be charged to the public by the Directors. But tenants must charge as at present.

The money paid by tenants to Cramers to be put in my bank as at present & with it the gas & electric money from the Company. These monies, with the rent from the house in Abbey Street, to be used by me towards paying rent, rates, and taxes. I bear the expenses of rents, rates & taxes.

For scenery such as would be required by my tenants or useful to them, I will pay half the cost.

In case of repairs, I will bear the expense of such as are necessary when applied to by the Directors. But these matters have just been done & so should not occur again for some time.

I retain the right to forbid Maunsell & Co. to put plays into the Abbey Theatre Series which have not been acted by your company, if I think fit.

That the prices charged to my tenants remain as before until I see fit to alter them, also the rules in the business circular.

That no alterations nor additions be made to the Abbey Theatre in public parts without my full consent.

Proposed by A.E.F.H.

From A. E. F. HORNIMAN

MS National Library of Ireland

London
22 July 1906

[Lady Gregory's next play was *The Canavans* (produced 8 December 1906). Stephen Gwynn was a director of Maunsel until his election to Parliament.]

My dear Demon,

I got all your letters thank you, that from Longford was a little delayed. What does Mr. Synge mean by telling you that Fay "has fallen off in his acting" & yet he objected to my presumption in seeing it for myself! I'm one of the *educated* public who mar or make & whose verdict is the final one. It was an impertinence of Mr. Synge to write about me to you as he did, now it is *impudence* to avow an opinion as his own, which he had not the courage to express until he found that *I* had support. Perhaps cowardice is the root of what I call impudence. I don't mind people disagreeing with me & opposing me, but I do mind being virtually told that I'm too great a fool to judge for myself, especially by one who should know that my opinion was founded on a patent fact. That carelessness was not accidental, it was an intention to obstruct the success of the tour. And Mr. Synge being encouraged to aid in the want of discipline was very clever. Fay may have foolish motives, but he is no fool. Either some person or his own vanity alarmed him between Nottingham & Cardiff & he determined to behave so that we should not make a good position for ourselves on the road where he would be only one of a company, not the Jove threatening you & Lady Gregory with thunder-bolts & keeping me at bay. He will dismiss and engage people, away from Dublin you two can't prevent this and he will make it impossible for anyone to stay if he wants to get rid of the poor man. He does not know anything about the make-up of any characters except those in his own line & he will not be taught. Fines on that matter would be absurd unless the people learned what to do & who should judge the matter? The two of them, Fay & Synge, will comfort each other & to my mind the only way to save Synge for Art is to keep him away from Dublin. The Mollie Allgood affair is not as serious in one way as the influence of Fay; if he marries her & she gives up acting, he will be freer from Fay; yet on the other hand he may keep close to Fay so that she shall have good parts & have in time a larger salary. I had a very nice letter indeed from Miss Darragh; I think that she is inclined though to over-rate the influence I had in your scheme. I hope that she will be able to help you effectually. If opportunity offers I wish that you would tell her how I advised giving away paper through Miss Taylor so that the class of people who won't believe that the shows are over-political should see for themselves. Fay never objected to papering amongst the friends of the actors; at the time I felt that he would have annoyed Lady Gregory I am sure & she would have been forearmed against the later scandal. *You* would have considered me well able to bear the annoyance.

I feel as if growing popularity in Dublin will be a snare unless we can depend on some amount of solidity in the stage-management. The care taken in getting things right is now waste of time. It would not be a business manager's work *at all* to see after anything but "the front of the house" & if you tried to make the poor man see after anything else, the unfortunate fellow would have "a Hell of a time."

I'm glad that Lady Gregory's next play will be in three acts — what beautiful but impossible material she has at hand. Fay taking to his bed to terrorise over her is delicious. Mr Synge will gloomily wander by the lake side & threaten suicide in silence. If I were there I should establish myself on a sofa in curling pins & an old dressing-gown & refuse to move & only moan & drop ashes on the carpet. Now that Mullingar has had two of your autographs you won't get your hair cut nor be in time for meals nor put cherry-stones anywhere but in the fire-place.

I had Boyle here yesterday. I told him of the want of discipline in travelling (omitting the spooning, my courage failed there) and he was annoyed. In regard to the slovenliness & the carelessness about the acting & "mise en scène" he agrees with me that there was some obscure purpose behind it, I did *not* suggest this to him. I thought it only fair for him to know that though I have completely withdrawn from interference that the Home Rule would be accompanied by a subsidy. The little dog detail, he said, gave him a clue to the whole situation.

The new play interested me intensely, I see great difficulties in casting it, not only because of the clever characters, but the fact that one of the men requires geniality as well as blatancy. The later part of the third act must be a little pulled together & there may be some few cuts here & there. The rhyme about the lake, the recurring prophecy, will be most effective in performance. It should be printed under the title of the programme. Roberts won't condescend to tell Mr. Boyle anything about his sales & accounts. Gwynn had a row with him about the Irish Literary Society, so I advised him to write & worry Hone.

Sarah Allgood's over-playing has another cause besides big theatres — it comes from the terrible drag on her when the rest did not condescend to act at all & she had to make a great effort to keep things going. Your great romantic poetic imagination (of which we all read in reviews), cannot build up the horrors of Spreading the News at Edinburgh, when no one else did anything but say the words & dolefully half do the "business."

I don't advise a Greek or any poetical play until you get a hold on things again. Rather begin with Boyle or Lady Gregory. If Miss Darragh will play she must be billed as a Star ("Gast") and there must be extra advertising & that would be expensive. Out of pure kindness of heart I spare Lady Gregory a letter — she ought to be grateful. Perhaps she will gently "rub in" some of this although our poor dear Poet will suffer.

Yours
ANNIE

I shall go away about July 31st, not earlier.

From A. E. F. HORNIMAN

Bayreuth, Bavaria

MS National Library of Ireland   14 August 1906

[W. A. Henderson became Business Secretary on 1 October. Seaghan Barlow played minor roles and did odd jobs. Jack Smith is a character in Lady Gregory's *Spreading the News*. Quinn arranged Hyde's American tour. Miss Horniman refers to AE's *Deirdre* (produced 2 April 1902). Pan Karel Musek, stage manager of the National Theatre in Prague, translated two of Synge's plays into Bohemian. Jessie L. Weston's new book was *The Legend of Sir Perceval* (1906–9).]

My dear Demon,

What is the use of my sending you my address I wonder! I shall be here until the 21st.

I am glad that you feel in good spirit about the theatre & have got a Business Manager in view. He is a necessary person but something else is necessary too. I quite understand the idea of the authors stage-managing their works; this is quite right when practicable, but something must be done to make it certain that their orders will be carried *out in their absence*. Until this is done all your toil is just making ropes of sand! Fay will never do this, his carelessness & slovenliness are *not* unreasoned I am certain. The payment of the actors and the acceptance of Miss Darragh's help he may be persuaded to permit, but he will try to obstruct them & the pull will come in some other direction eventually. We are all determined to make the company "an expert thing" but that cannot be done until everyone *acts* instead of simply using themselves. This was perfectly shown in the case of Barlow (Shawn). He was so good as the red-haired Jack Smith at first when he was fresh & natural but when he got used to the part he became the dull wooden useless amateur for he had no *Art* to fall back on. It's of no use to think of

America nor any place that matters until the whole company have got an *Art* back-bone to fall back upon. The idea of Art may be only the very common-place professional idea of earning a livelihood & getting a bigger salary, but that is at anyrate honest & gives one something to rely on. I've had enough of the old idea, the Edinburgh experience made me understand that *"it does not wash."*

I heard from Boyle that Fay told him that his plays are not worth copyrighting in America, that naturally was not a pleasant remark for him to hear. I presume that Quinn has given us up since "the very gifted man" Hyde has been in America; so if he thinks it worth while, should not Boyle get it done by an agent? I do so wish that you would write to him about it. You authors (some of you) *really* care, but Russell does not care & if your sister makes a mess of the status of Dun Emer, *she* does not care. You know perfectly well that your "real passion for good work" gets no sympathy from the emotional people. It is this worship of sentiment and emotion which is used as means of keeping down the artistic standard; it is *sloth* on the part of those who want to keep on top with the least possible trouble.

It is as if you were to become satisfied with a Deirdre only rather better than Russell's scare-crow!

I've got you a pair of unique candlesticks, they come from a village near here, & are 18th cen. I think; each holds three candles with room for guttering. Rough brass-work & not easily knocked over. Own up that I treat you much better than you deserve! You take no notice of my wish to see Dr. Musek at Prague. Have you taken any notice of Miss Weston's new book yet which she sent to you? She is here *now* at 51 Richard Wagner Strasse. The weather is delightfully warm. All the tickets are sold. Does not this sound ideal – in March they had about £20,000 advance booking & so did not advertise at all, even in Munich! Let us keep up our spirits & remember that in 1876 they had to sell off the scenery to pay their expenses!

I enclose a cutting for although it will give you no fresh information you may as well see what the Chronicle prints.

As to the mystery as to no "lets" – I should like to know whether there are similar legends in Dublin to that absurd one I heard in March, that we objected to Trinity College so would not let their new club have the Abbey for less than £50 a week. Fay told me at Cardiff very gaily that there were "no lets for June." I shall be very suspicious if no cheque comes in October, it will be serious if there is a complete stop to the letting. But that won't stop us, I'll hold on as long as you & Lady Gregory think it worth while.

I'm getting fat, the heat and the beer agree with me & there are no mosquitoes. I arrived here a terrible spectable with *both* eyes damaged and a swollen cheek as well.

Yours
ANNIE

From A. E. F. HORNIMAN

London
MS National Library of Ireland 22 September 1906

[Alfred Wareing, Sir Herbert Beerbohm Tree's publicity manager, arranged the Abbey Company's tour in spring 1906. The entrance to the Abbey was on Marlborough, an unfashionable street. Sir Charles Hawtrey was a well-known English actor-manager. "The Dana affair" refers to Moore's article "Stage Management in the Irish National Theatre", *Dana* (Sep 1904), published under the pseudonym of "Paul Ruttledge".]

My dear Demon,

There is absolutely nothing for us to talk out, I wrote nothing fresh to you, I only repeated what it was necessary to impress upon you so as to force you to believe that my "letter to the Directors" is genuine in its fullest application. I did not want to pain you more than was absolutely needful, indeed I was foolish enough to imagine that you would be glad to know how much relieved I feel at the ceasing of the continual sources of disagreement between us. I don't remember ever having wished to sacrifice your work or ambitions to any personal idea of my own; only when worn out & obstructed I got cross from mental & physical fatigue. This I am most sorry for, I strove against it in vain. I failed to carry out the costumes properly, partly from my own incapacity and partly from being treated so badly in regard to measurements etc. All that grievance I have laid aside completely & now I want you to know that I lay aside my efforts in regard to the theatre as completely.

I know that my intense distaste for any manifestation of "national feeling" is unpleasant to you, that you are repelled by it & so I have tried to keep it in check. I accept "national feeling" as part of your nature but you cannot accept as part of my nature what is personal to me. I would not knowingly and deliberately pain you as

an ardent nationalist & then delight in it as you pained me as a
self-respecting person about Moore. You never will remember that
when I first made a fuss on the subject in Dublin that you said that
you were *glad* of my attitude. Then without any warning you made
it up with him. I cannot write what you told me last Winter what he
said to you about me — you said it with a smile which I must strive
to forget. I told Miss Darragh that you publicly called him your
friend, but I never hinted that I had any personal grievance against
him. I also told her that Mrs McBride had once been a Vice-President
but after leaving had done us all the harm she could. I said that Dr
Hyde used you as an advertisment in America but that the Gaelic
League did not support the performances. She said exactly the same
things to me as Mr Wareing said in regard to the means of success,
that Fay had some hidden reason against it. It is obvious to me that
the only way that prejudice can be overcome is to get the people to
see for themselves.

Yes, I'm gratified that Miss Darragh thought that light green
would have been better for the Angel, but your text demanded red.
That poor halo, how carefully it was made, with a device to hairpin it
on exactly! I always did my best & it was only after a fight against
too heavy odds that I found my incapacity. I'm very glad that the
people had the sense to like "The Hour Glass."

If Mrs Pat Campbell will take Deirdre I *beg* you to raise no
obstacles in any way. A play by you, toured over England & taken
to the Theatre Royal Dublin would indirectly help the Abbey
Theatre most powerfully. It would shew your work to the class of
people who would not be seen coming down Marlborough Street. It
would prove to them in the clearest way that the work was not
political; & because a well-known actress had paid you for it, there
was most likely some merit in your other works. I believe firmly that
if Lady Gregory wrote a comedy ten times better than "Spreading
the News" that its production in London would do us more good
than if we had it at the Abbey. Fay has put a barrier between the
company & the real stage — if any of the authors can cross that
barrier it would partly undo the mischief. I feel most strongly on this
subject — you can only gain the ear of the decent ordinary educated
people in Dublin by proving to them that the Abbey is not a political
side show; as long as they feel this they are quite right to stay away.
To *beg* Mrs Pat Campbell to play your Deirdre in Dublin would be
wise policy. For Hawtrey to act Boyle's footman play there too &
for a first-class comedian to do one by Lady Gregory would prove

the truth to some at least. Neither of you will agree with me I know, but that does not take away my strong feeling that this is the great fact of the situation. We are stranded — our actors have proved themselves un-fit for a wider public — our authors have proved themselves fit & they should go on & not let Fay & his intrigues do any more harm. If any of you choose to give the royalties gained by your plays in Ireland as a donation to the Ltd Company, no one can prevent you. As they would be paid (or reckoned) by the week it would be quite simple to arrange.

Now this is a personal bit, you often have said that I act "by the book" or "by a rule"; I don't even know what you mean by that. I only try honestly to act uprightly, partly because of my own feeling of self-respect. I don't care about money for itself but I have a great sense of responsibility & just because of that strong feeling I will not be really foolish even in regard to small sums. One must make mistakes but even mistakes do less harm when there is a reasoned plan behind them & one owns up to them & tries to undo them. It was as soon as I realised the unwisdom of the divided authority that I saw that my right to interference of any sort must cease at once. The only matter (except the "mise en scène") in which I ever interfered was at the very beginning when I was so firm that I would never let Moore be introduced to me, (I mean *before* the Dana affair). Yet the wish that you all knew perfectly well carried no weight with any of you, it would have been only a very ordinary courtesy to me to have told Russell my feeling about this when he proposed him as a Vice-President. This not being done, Russell and Fay, & the rest saw that my intensely strong feelings were not to be considered in the very least. (I'm not referring to the course of action which you took to please Mr Quinn against Lady Gregory's wish as she told me herself. He got his own way & then stopped his subscription! He is a friend of Dr Hyde (an enormously "gifted man") & so as soon as the hint was given him Quinn would try to harm us in a most subtle way or perhaps he was used as an unconscious weapon against us). Since that time, it was *before* the application for the Patent even, I always knew that my *personal* feelings would never be considered, but I never let that come in the way of energies & my efforts. Otherwise the breaking off would have been far more painful to me. I could not have done more for I always did my best, but that awful snub given to the average man

would have made him wash his hands of the whole thing & stop the
negociations for the leases. I remember that it was on the very day
that I signed the draft agreements. Yes — in one way I did act
"finely," that I did not let a personal matter stop what I knew to be
the right course. But when I saw after Glasgow that subservience to
Fay would not be "fine" but would eventually ruin the scheme I saw
that I must go. Now don't think me ungenerous for referring to all
this — I have really written it so that you should clearly understand
that, do what I might, I always felt myself to be an outsider amongst
you & it was a very painful position to be in. My wish for myself
was one that would *not* have hurt the theatre. I wished to protect it
& myself from any connection with a person whose name alone
carries an idea of a want of dignity to say the very least. What is done
cannot be undone; a few firm words might have made Russell &
Fay take me seriously but they were unspoken & the results have
been distinctly damaging.

I tried to get a chrysophrase & gun-metal cigarette case in vain, I'll
search for one in Germany & perhaps in Bohemia next month. This
one will do quite well for when you go out fishing for the servants'
Friday dinner. You can shew this to Lady Gregory, she may as well
know that there is some relief in my present feelings.

Yours
ANNIE

P.S. The tooth-brush box & soap envelope will be useful I know. I
have similar ones myself. The candlestick is too big to send, I'll keep
it safely for you. I expect to go abroad again about Oct. 8th.

From FLORENCE DARRAGH

| | London |
| MS National Library of Ireland | 22 September 1906 |

[Miss Darragh began acting for the Abbey Company in the autumn of
1906 and left in January of the following year. "P.C." refers to Mrs
Patrick Campbell.]

Dear Mr. Yeats
    Many thanks for yours which of course I kept private. I'm so
glad "Deirdre" has risen & is in full flight & that everything your

side is so smooth. — Now as to Miss Horniman — she lunched with me on Tuesday & in her own words burst into song from 1.30 to 5. So I listened & said about 6 sentences which resulted in her asking me to go and see her on Monday to meet a Miss Spencer who would tell me more grievances etc. She is dining here on Thursday so you see I am paying her all those ridiculous little attentions which she values so much and which she has firmly fixed in her mind none of the Irish Theatre have paid her. Of course she is in a state of seething fury about the whole thing and says she hates everything and nearly everyone apparently concerned with the Irish Theatre. However thro' it all she has a tenacious hankering after it partly hatred and partly to prove herself right in her judgement of art and acting — her views are perfectly sound & in the main she is right. My common sense tells me that. Fay is of course her obsession & one that will remain too — till he is put in the position of a paid leading actor & producer *only* of peasant plays I doubt her doing anything more for the Co. I think her difficulty could be solved later on by having a Stage-manager and let Mr Fay be Producer. But the long & the short of it is she is dissatisfied because the theatre has neither made money nor acquired réclame from the public. — If the audiences can only be worked up this winter & some money got in *and* the *General public* — I underline it because she made so much point of it — tho' she might not be willing to pay for a season in London & tour she would be certainly be more likely to contemplate it — her idea is simply to make the Dublin Theatre the nucleus — the factory — the school — for an international Theatre. Irish plays & Ireland she really now cares nothing for — but I quite see she is willing for the Irish plays legendary & otherwise to be played sandwiched in with French ones & others. I don't think the situation is desperate if taken in hand now & worked up gradually. Of course she laughed at me when I suggested that I could work up audiences, yet she really thinks I can do something tho' she wouldn't acknowledge it for worlds. We never mentioned the word countenance & I never mentioned your letter in fact I hardly spoke but we parted excellent friends tho' I had to keep a big curb on myself. The mistake has been not to pay her more attention in the business point of view — answering her letters, consulting her etc. In fact a little tact & diplomacy from Fay but now of course nothing he would or could do would alter things till he takes *apparently* a back seat. She hates not being sent all the details of the Theatre the rehearsals & dates of production etc in short she wants to be treated as a sleeping manager

& not a bank — it is all very trifling but human & very feminine;
Of course you know I think if you had an enterprising clever
American manager who ran the whole thing & got it into ship
shape a man who would put money into it arrange everything &
yet be clever enough to let you all have your way as to the plays &
stage etc it would be so much better. — It is the working of the
machine that is so faulty apparently one thing it is certainly a
mistake to call it "The National" theatre. Everyone I spoke to in
Dublin fell up against that. Surely it would be better to always call it
"The Abbey Theatre" but perhaps this is done only on the posters in
Longford the word National was used if Miss H. had only put her
theatre in London even small as it is there would have been none of
this silly worry about names & Leagues etc. Of course one thing I
cannot quite understand she says you none of you have any ambition
that you all be content to go round Ireland in caravans playing your
plays to a handful of people intead of becoming famous. This
irritates her to death & she is in the mood to like the ordinary play
that makes fame and money as she said about you having refused
"Deirdre" to Mrs P.C. but "he would have made some money". I
did not say anything as it was useless. There is one thing I am sure
you ought to try & work up the theatre and get independent of
Miss H. or try to. She would fling thousands into your lap if she
saw you were becoming independent. — By the way could you give
me any idea of the dates you are playing in Dublin & what &
when you think you will want me as I might fill in time here. I hope
I haven't written too plainly but this is the situation as I see it. — I'm
so glad Lady Gregory's play is getting on. — & let me know what
you think about my idea of an American manager.

                                                    Yours
                                                    F. DARRAGH

From A. E. F. HORNIMAN

                                              Pont-Aven, France
MS National Library of Ireland   26 October 1906

[In opposition to the "patriots", Maud Gonne in particular, Miss
Horniman was upset that seats for 6d were made available. Lady
Gregory's new play was *Hyacinth Halvey*. "Windbag O'Dempsey" is
probably a reference to Boyle's *The Eloquent Dempsey*. The first
issue of *The Arrow*, edited by Yeats, appeared on 20 October.

According to Shaw, *John Bull's Other Island* was refused because it was "beyond the resources of the new Abbey Theatre". Arthur Darley was in charge of music for Abbey productions. Mrs Walton was a character in Boyle's *The Mineral Workers* (produced on 20 October 1906). Ambrose Power played numerous minor roles.]

My dear Demon,

     The weather has been so fine that we lingered awhile on the way here & so I only got your most welcome letter last night. I am very glad indeed that you are so happy about the success on Saturday night. Let us hope that the people turned away will return another night. I wish that you had thought fit to keep the 6^d seats for revivals only, maybe in the distant future when the theatre can be opened nightly circumstances may change. The subscription arrangement I look on as excellent. If anyone new offers of course they can be given extra tickets for the missed Saturdays. If the "corner be turned" we must not drift back again. Let me read Lady Gregory's new play as soon as it is printed please. I am going to write a very polite note to Mrs. McBride to say how sorry I am that the audience behaved in such a manner in any theatre. Why were they such cowards as to stop until the end? They are afraid of the police like Windbag O'Dempsey and his stick! I consider myself to be pitied for having prophesied a fuss with 6^d seats and Mrs. McBride on a Saturday night, my fears made an astral tendency. She knows what "patriotic" manners are like so she knew what to expect; but for my own credit's sake I am sorry that such low behaviour should happen in my theatre. I like the **Arrow** very much, except Messrs. Marks' calm appropriation of my bas-reliefs — but I forgive them. I think that the real reason of our refusal of "John Bull" should be made known as the play is referred to in the paper you sent me. I hate the thought that we should be considered cowardly. You are all *so* delighted to express each others' views and I might get mine in sometimes — those of the valet are mine most assuredly. You would not let me loose in the Arrow and you are quite wise to keep me muzzled. The "at home" programme was a most *common* selection of music chosen to please a vulgar ignorant "patriotic" taste. Mr Darley is an excellent violinist but his worship of archaeological *scraps* has prevented his judgment from being of any value. You are so jealous & ignorant on the subject of an Art beyond words that what you say does not matter. There now! I'm not blaming you for it, I'm very sorry for you indeed, you poor dear tone-deaf Demon!

You must make Henderson understand that *I matter.* I have not had the report about the heating that he promised & except for Miss Darragh's note & the remark in the paper, you might have been frozen for all I knew. I don't think that "Mrs Walton" would be a really "intolerable part" in the hands of an experienced actress, *not* a girl. But the mere attempt will do Miss Allgood good. The better Fay is now the worse I think of his insulting the public at Edinburgh. Power is a nice fellow but I don't think that he will ever be a real actor. Young Walker has it in him but would need a proper master over him. Of course Russell is savage, no wonder considering the title of your next play. He is absolutely a *Philistine*, one of those who fear Art and hate it because of that fear. I think that you should have chosen another title unless you want to defy him & defying Russell is rather like teasing a very woolly sheep. Why do you promise "Shadowy Waters" in the Arrow & mention no date? I have not received my paper with your speech, I'm very glad that you got even one good report.

This is a dear little place in a lovely valley where all the women wear a quaint coif & most a costume & yet there is (bad) electric light in the hotel. I amused myself yesterday at Quimperlé by gossiping with a shopkeeper & a peasant. (I know quite enough queer French for that, you may as well be told). The way in which the Church has pauperised the poor here makes one sorry for them & understand their attitude as to the new law. I heard a priest *lie* wildly on Sunday morning to a large congregation of many women & a few peasant men. After this please send to me chez Mme Pitrois 135 rue d'Entraigues, Tours. Many congratulations to Lady Gregory on her new play. Boyle's play without a dead body of any sort is an alarming novelty at the Abbey. Did you not feel the want terribly?

Now you have got some new good people I hope that you will be able to keep them somehow. If Fay takes to weeping over Miss Allgood you will soon get more excitement in the company.

I'll return to London before you arrive & I'll be very glad to see you again.

Yours
ANNIE

From T. FISHER UNWIN

London

TS Yeats   15 November 1906

[Kegan Paul published *The Wanderings of Oisin and Other Poems* (1889), of which Unwin published a second issue in 1892. The four volumes published by Unwin were *John Sherman and Dhoya* (1891), *The Countess Kathleen* (1892), *The Land of Heart's Desire* (1894), and *Poems* (1895). In the 1890s Yeats had been "prompted by his father" and Edward Garnett to shift some of his publications to Lawrence and Bullen.]

My dear Yeats —

Your letter, as I think you will understand, has caused me considerable surprise and indeed regret. I have never imagined that there would be an ending to our literary and professional connection.

It must be some fifteen years ago since I first became your publisher; but for the little book Kegan Paul published, I might almost call myself your first publisher, and as you will remember, at your request, I took over that little volume for you. Since that I have published the four volumes connected with your name and issued some of them in various editions aferwards, giving them up in a sense and reprinting them in a collected form, and now I note that you wish to transfer them. But after all, that is not quite so easy, neither is it so simple, as practically I hold if not the copyright, I have certain publishing rights in connection with one or more, so it seems to me that I have, shall I say prior rights, if not legal (and I dislike that word), professional rights as your first publisher, and so why not have your other works transferred to the publisher whom you tell me has done well by you and your writings? It would surely be simple to transfer the one or two from the other house to my firm, and I must ask you therefore to consider this suggestion.

When I was your first publisher, the firm of Lawrence & Bullen was not in existence, and I believe that particular firm indeed no longer exists. As for your friend who advised you to go to that house, I think I am right that you were introduced to him first in connection with this firm, and I regret to note that he so ill-advised you with regard to your publications.

Is it not worth your considering the future of your work, and its best interest? So perhaps you will come to see me next time you are in town, when we may arrange this matter to our mutual content.

What a pity it is you did not come to me months or even years ago and discuss this question. As you must know, I have had no chance of seeing you and hardly of corresponding, indeed, I have almost hesitated to write, as in recent months, if not years, I have had so little response.

With kind regards,

Yours sincerely,
T. FISHER UNWIN

From ELIZABETH A. SHARP

London
MS Yeats   9 January 1907

[Sebastopol fell to the allied French and English forces after a siege of nearly a year. The Society referred to may be the Stella Matutina, a Rosicrucian order in which Yeats was an active member in 1907.]

Dear Mr. Yeats

You asked me to give you particulars about Will's birth with a view of having his horoscope made. I have written to his mother, and the following are the particulars she has sent me:

William Sharp was born on Wednesday the 12*th* September 1855. She cannot tell me the exact time, but thinks it was about midday. She writes that bells were ringing and she was told it was because Sebastopol was taken. She thinks it was about 12 o'clock.

12 seems to be a number that has some special significance for my husband's life — as it was the 12th December on which he passed out of this life. Moreover, I went to Iona this summer — to perform a little rite for him myself there — in St. Oran's chapel — and it chanced to be the 12th September, at 12 o'clock. It was pure accident. He had hoped to be buried in Iona — but that was impossible.

Now, would it be possible also to have *my* horosocope cast? I should greatly like it; because I want to see in what way the two horoscopes suggest the touching or our two lives. And to that end may I give you the necessary particulars: — I was born on Saturday the 17th May 1856. Curiously enough, I believe my birthtime was either noon, or early afternoon — but of this I am not quite sure & there is no one now who can tell me — and bells were ringing, & these were the peace rejoicings at the end of the Crimean War.

I am hoping eagerly soon to receive the papers from the Society of which you spoke.

Friendly greetings.

Sincerely yours
ELIZABETH A. SHARP

From AGNES TOBIN

London
MS Yeats   12 February 1907

[A minor poet and playwright, Miss Tobin met Yeats at one of his lectures in San Francisco, her home. She refers to the riots at the Abbey over Synge's *The Playboy of the Western World* (first produced on 16 January) and possibly to the speech Yeats made on 4 February in defence of the play. Ben Iden Payne joined the company as a director in March and became manager in May. The new play was Yeats's *Deirdre* (produced on 24 November 1906 but not then published). Charles Frohman was a New York producer. Arthur Symons's *A Pageant of Elizabethan Poetry* was published in 1906. Miss Tobin had apparently given Yeats a copy of her *Love's Crucifix . . . ,* translated from Petrarch (1902).]

My dear Poet:

I was so very glad to have your letter this morning — to hear of Cathleen ni Houlihan on Saturday, & all. Do let Synge's play drop, now — I hope he will not publish it in America, it would do nothing but harm to him & everybody and everything else. You may well care for nothing but verse! The musicians' lines at the end of Deirdre are as fine as any verse ever written in any language living or dead. I can not but hope this stage manager will take a good deal off your hands — I do grudge your giving so much time to the theatre. However — you would always have to have something to change off onto in the intervals of creative work — and this is allied to your work in a way that makes the transition easy; and also it incites you to work. I hope Synge is better — he is such a dear, charming fellow — do you think he feels at all depressed about all this? I wish it may throw his literary energies in another direction: there are some wonderful emotional and ecstatic lyrical outbursts in both The Shadow of the Glen and The Well — and Riders to the Sea is splendid. I am most anxious to read this new play — but will not lend it or speak of its being in my possession. (Here is, just, a wire from Mr. Frohman — asking me to go to see him at the Savoy at 11 tomorrow. I wrote to him yesterday.) It is Joe — the lawyer — who is coming abroad, with his wife: they sail April 15th for Italy. He has been ordered to rest by the doctors. So I suppose I may go out to Italy about the 25th of April to see him. We will probably be in Europe till September. Dicky (the banker) is most anxious to see Deidre — and writes you are the most beautiful reader of verse in the world (I suppose he must have heard you reading verse at one of your lectures in San Francisco). I am reading verse — but not writing. I have read a good deal of Donne — and a large part of Symons' Elizabethan Pageant. Today — the 12th of February — is a great anniversary in my psychic career — I always keep it with pomp: and looking back through my diaries I see that, curiously enough, your first letter to me (about "Love's Crucifix") reached me on that day. What a tremendous lift it gave me! I suppose you must have written it just after you crossed the Rockies. I wish you were here to tell me what to say to Mr. Frohman if he should want the American rights for Deirdre. I wonder if you will find a good actress, or the makings of one, in the stage manager's wife — it would be strange. You do not say anything about your cold — or the asthma — so I am inclined to think they have both left you: Mrs. Mond asked especially how you were, when I saw her on Sunday, and whether I would take her to another of your Monday evenings. How lovely Campion's songs are! And Lodge — every time I read Fair Rosaline I am more struck by its glories. I am dining at the Protheros' [?] on Sunday.

Greetings of A.T.

From AGNES TOBIN

MS Yeats

London
16 February 1907

[*The Mineral Workers* by William Boyle was produced by the Abbey on 10 October 1906. Fedelm is Seanchan's sweetheart in Yeats's *The King's Threshold*. J. A. O'Rourke played Uncle Bartle in *The Mineral Workers*. Hyde did not write a play entitled *The Lost Saint*. Synge's play is *The Playboy of the Western World*.]

My dear Poet:

I am sorry you are to be so long away — but I think you are right to finish things off for this bout! You *have* worked hard for the theatre the last few weeks. I am afraid Deirdre has gone to the wall meanwhile Mr. Frohman opens in Dublin Easter Monday: at least it is either Holy Saturday or Easter Monday. I should expect him at the Abby on Easter Tuesday and any other evening in Easter week if I were you. When you come to town I will take you to see him and you can talk it over. I am afraid The Building Fund would be too bitter for America — The Mineral Workers struck me as being very interesting to the Irish American mind, though; and William Fay was so well fitted with a part in that. I suppose they will want to call The King's Threshold "Shanahan" — and Baile's Strand "Cuchulain": Frank Fay ought to be great in those two. I should think Miss Allgood was an excellent Fedelm. Keep The Shadowy Waters for the last — it might baffle Frohman. I do hope you will find a Deirdre. It is so splendid that Baile's Strand and The King's Threshold are well within the company's range. I spoke to him of O'Rourke's acting in The Mineral Workers — he was much interested: couldn't you put O'Rourke on in the Lost Saint (is that the name of the play of Hyde's you told me about?)? I am wondering whether you gave Miss Farr rights of recitation on Deirdre: however — it is so hard to get someone in the company or with their style of acting to do Deirdre, that one need not count too much on it — & Frohman is set on having all the acting in the peculiar Abby Theatre genre. At first he said to me: "I suppose eight actors ought to go on the tour" — but after I had described The Mineral Workers he said: "Well, then, if I take fifteen of them over — will that do?" He seemed delighted when I said you had all the real Irish cottage things & the real clothes & all. Have you thought again of using the sound of the waves at some points in Baile's Strand? When the doors are all open at the end & he is fighting the waves, for instance. I was much interested in Synge's play — it is splendid the way he gets the vivid effects of speech & character: but it seems a pity to lavish all that on a thing that has about as much connection with real life as a Chinese mask. There are one or two speeches with lovely lyric effects in them — but it seems to me he deliberately perverts his imagination. It is a curious phenomenon to watch — the way he uses his singular powers. I do hope he is all right again. Your brother's sketch of him is excellent. I shall be here till May — in town — as things now stand.

Greetings of A.T.

From A. H. BULLEN

                                                        London
MS Yeats   14 March 1907

[George Platt Brett was President of the Macmillan Company in New York, Yeats's American publishers. E. J. Oldmeadow, a Nonconformist minister, was editor of *The Dome* and managing director of the Unicorn Press.]

My dear Yeats,
        I have had an amicable talk this afternoon with Fisher Unwin about the limited Library Edition — in eight volumes (to be printed at the Shakespeare Head Press) — of your works. Evidently he wants to "stand in." Tomorrow I see Miss Horniman as I want her to have a financial interest in the venture. If I can induce her to join I will cross to Dublin and arrange for Hone to take a part in the edition for Ireland. Then it will remain to deal with Brett who certainly ought to be willing to handle the book for America.
        Last night I was very sleepy and dull when I was at the Easton Hotel. I have a notion that Lady Gregory asked me to do something for her, but — for the life of me — I can't recall a word of the conversation. I remember that you ate a junk of meat-pie, that I drank a whisky-and-soda, and that we all three exulted over Oldmeadow's downfall. Heaven forbid that Lady Gregory should think of me discourteous; so if you remember what she wanted please let me know and I will attend to it.

                                                        Yours
                                                        A. H. BULLEN

From MAUD GONNE

                                                        [?]
MS Yeats   [April ? 1907]

[Most likely Yeats had sent Maud a copy of a limited edition (30) of *Hyacinth Halvey*, issued by Quinn to preserve American rights. Fernand Labori was the famous trial lawyer who in 1914 successfully defended Henriette Caillaux for the murder of Gaston Calmette, the Director of *Le Figaro*.]

My dear Willie
        All this time I have not written to thank you for sending me *Hyacinth* but I was waiting to have news of my divorce to tell, &

even now I have none. In vain my lawyer tries to get MacBride's lawyer to fix the date for the final hearing. My case is the 20th on the rolls, but as the judge is amenable it could be heard at once without waiting [for] its actual turn, if only the lawyers could agree.

Last Wednesday there was quite a scene in court between my lawyer Cruppi & MacBrides lawyer Labori. Cruppi asked for the case to be heard immediately the judge said he was willing to fix an early date but Labori refused absolutely to allow the affair to be heard before the elections (he is candidate) & they do not come till the 6*th* May. Cruppi insisted but Labori said if they forced the date, he would throw up the case, as he would not plead it till after the elections.

MacBride evidently wants delay, in hopes of winning his libel action against the *Independent* in the mean time, which if by any chance he does succeed in winning would prevent the publication of the trial & verdict in the English & French papers.

My lawyer says there is no hope that the case will be heard now, till the *middle of May*, as when the lawyers dont agree the judge cannot fix a date out of turn.

This waiting is most wearisome [one or more pages missing] absolutely unselfish and patriotic.

What are you writing? It is so long since I have read anything of yours.

I must end this long rambling letter.

> Always your friend
> MAUD GONNE

From AGNES TOBIN

MS Yeats

London
4 April 1907

[The bill at the Abbey for the week of 1–6 April included Winifred M. Letts's *The Eyes of the Blind*, Lady Gregory's *The Poorhouse*, and Yeats's *Deirdre*. Deirdre was played by Mona Limerick (Mrs Ben Iden Payne), whose style was described by Joseph Holloway as "cheap, hysterical". *Phèdre* was completed before 21 April 1908, when Yeats wrote that Mrs Patrick Campbell would play the lead. Yeats liked Miss Tobin's translations from Petrarch and recommended them to Symons and Edmund Gosse, to whom Miss Tobin spoke about the possibility of getting a Civil List pension for Yeats.

Synge's translations of Petrarch's "Sonnets from 'Laura in Death' " were made in 1907. Miss Tobin refers to Alexandre Dumas *père*.]

My dear Poet:

I am grieved about Mr. Frohman — but I hope you are keeping that good bill on all this week, as he is almost certain to slip in again. He told me he meant to go on a night when the company was not prepared specially. If he does not go to you again in Dublin, — well — we must try to get him to come to a London performance. I can imagine his entire bewilderment at a scratch performance of Deirdre! I am going to Bedford tomorrow on a visit — but expect to return to Claridge's Monday afternoon. ("Oakley House — Oakley — Bedford" is the address). Perhaps you could come to dinner at 8 on Monday. Let me know. I saw Miss Jacobs yesterday and told her to send you part of Phèdre she had typed. I have entirely finished the first act — since then — and made a start on the second. It is quite a little education for me. She typed the Casket Sonnets most beautifully — I stiffened the weak places, and took out a glaringly inappropriate line (the 14th of the eighth sonnet): they seem to me to hang together, now — & to be pretty well on a level with each other. Do bring them when you come — but I do not want the Phèdre back. I told her to leave the variants in the Phèdre — as I wanted your advice about them. The Irish dialect versions of Petrarch please me immensely — nothing has pleased my imagination so much for a long time. I am so glad the Synge child is better — the warm weather will help him. I am reading Ange Piloú (Dumas Perè) and enjoying it ever so much. Also going on with Milton. By the way I ran through the Play Boy and made cuts I thought essential — I wonder whether they tally with your's! Perhaps you could bring your Father's sketch of me over — but not if it's a trouble. Please wish your Father & Sisters a happy Easter for me.

                                                        Greetings of A.T.

From HENRY G. O'BRIEN

                                                        London
MS Yeats   13 June 1907

[The Abbey players toured Scotland and England for five weeks in May and June. They did not produce *The Playboy* in Birmingham for fear of further riots, and they received some threatening letters in London while playing at the Great Queen Street Theatre.]

Dear Mr Yeats

I was at Gt Queen St Theatre to-day to try & see you, but was told that you were only there during performances.

I am delighted that you have invaded London with living vital drama, accustomed as we are over here to see fine theatres filled with 'sound and fury signifying nothing'.

I have rarely enjoyed anything better than Wednesday's matinee performance of the 'Hour Glass' & 'The Playboy' (though I would ask you to respect my confidence in the matter, as, being a cleric & in my own diocese my action might involve me in criticism) & I sincerely congratulate you & Mr Synge, the one for bringing tears into my eyes, the other for filling my heart with a sense of humour not unalloyed with truth & underlying sadness. That a morality play such as The 'Hour Glass' may be as potent a factor for illustrating 'simple faith' as many sermons I cannot doubt. I have always maintained that the natural wisdom of the simple uneducated Irish peasant is worth all the knowledge of those classes, to whom knowledge *is* wisdom, and who frequently possess not even a sufficiency of wisdom to render their knowledge of any practical use whatever.

Of Mr Synge's play, I can only say that I consider the action of some of your Dublin audiences inexplicable. I see nothing scandalous in the play, & the moral is sufficiently obvious. What I like about the play is its truth. It is a clean play, such as are not many of the stupid musical comedies to which the prim & 'respectable' have no objection.

One, to whom I talked of 'The Playboy', took exception to the scene 'A Public House'. He was Irish or supposed to be & thought 'we should hide our weaknesses'. I think we may leave the English to do that. Let them call Scene I The Hotel [word indecipherable] & we merely have an aristocratic public house. I prefer Mr Synge's variety & also his play.

I trust, that, time & engagements permitting, I shall see you before you return to Ireland. You will be welcome if you can lunch (we call it dinner) any day up here at 1 o clock sharp. Wishing you & all your Irish Company (for whose acting I have nothing but praise).

Every success & happiness
I remain
Yrs very sincerely
HENRY G. O'BRIEN

From HENRY G. O'BRIEN

MS Yeats

London
6 July 1907

Dear Mr. Yeats

Thank you for your letter of June 29th. I am sorry that I missed seeing you while you were here in London. It never occurred to me somehow to ask for you at the matinee performance of 'The Hourglass' & 'The Playboy', on June 12th, at which I have no doubt you were present. Curiously enough I intended calling on you at Woburn Buildings before the plays had begun, but when I went up there one day it seemed to me that they had been knocking down a good deal of it (the street) & I was consequently doubtful whether I could find you there.

Should you be in the South of Ireland between the 15th of July & the 24th of August I hope that you may be able to see me at Queenstown. The address is Weston, Queenstown.

With all good wishes I remain

Yours Sincerely
HENRY G. O'BRIEN

From A. E. F. HORNIMAN

MS National Library of Ireland

London
7 July 1907

[Horniman writes of Yeats's rooms at Woburn Buildings. One of the unanswered questions about several of Yeats's plays is the extent of Lady Gregory's assistance, especially with peasant dialogue.]

Dear Demon,

There are some moths in your curtains & the books on the top shelves are absolutely filthy. I went upstairs to wash after finding these as my fingers were black. The mattresses are uncovered, the eider-down covers the blankets & that will be *filthy* very soon. The floors are littered with bits of papers, they have not been washed down since you left. I looked in & round the waste-paper basket for paper in which to send this parcel but I found none, only this card, telegram & prescription on the table. The press cutting packet was on the table in the sitting-room. I saw the box marked as containing my letters; I have kept your keys so that I may send anything more which may be required. If not I will return them at once.

I hope that you are going to make it quite clear in the Library Edition that Lady Gregory has given you certain help in peasant dialogue. I felt it only fair to Bullen to tell him what you told me some time ago, that she considers that she has a certain claim on your disposal of your work because of the help she has given you. I know no particulars, not even which plays you referred to. It was about the time when I had said that I would *salvage* what was good from the prospective wreck & she considered that it was a "secret treaty" with me, instead of the plain fact, a mere expression of the desire not to lose good dramatic literature. I have told Mr. Payne to send the pass book & old cheque book to Mr. Henderson. The address books shall follow when the latest ones are copied. Roberts has got a copy of the large London address book, so I need not send you a copy of that. As he is the virtual publisher to the theatre with a monopoly of sales at your performances, he must [not] object to your borrowing it when you require it. I hope that now we have got rid of these worrying affairs that kept causing disagreeables between us, that there will be some peace and quiet. You will find it a rest not to be obliged to write me accounts of the theatrical doings nor to make vain efforts on my behalf. It was a useless task, to try to make the theatre we planned at the beginning. But we were right to try our best. Let me know if there is anything you want me to do for you in London, you know how gladly I will run errands!

Yours
ANNIE

From WILLIAM G. FAY

MS National Library of Ireland

Dublin
[14 August 1907]

[After Maire Nic Shuibhlaigh left the Company in 1905, Sara Allgood played most of the female leads. Florence Darragh (Letitia Marion Dallas) joined the company in 1906 to play leading roles in Yeats's verse plays. Because as a professional she received substantially more salary than others, there was "some degree of heart-burning among the permanent members of the company" (W. G. Fay). Joseph A. O'Rourke and Henderson joined the Company in 1906. Before William Boyle withdrew his plays over *The Playboy* controversy, three were produced: *The Building Fund* (25 April 1905), *The Eloquent Dempsey* (20 Jan 1906), and *The Mineral Workers* (20 October 1907).]

Dear Mr Yeats

I am sorry my bad composition made my letter hard to understand, but I will try again. You asked me in Longford to get Miss Allgood to let Miss Daragh have Dectora. Act 2. Lady Gregory wrote me in Enniscorthy that you wished Miss Allgood to have her choice of Deirdre or Dectora. Act III. You write this morning & say Miss Daragh must have Deirdre. Now what am I to make of it. I don't care a red cent which of them plays either part but is Dectora now finally to be rehearsed by Miss Allgood. Ive got to keep down rows here but I cant if we change about week by week. I dont see any means of comparing Miss Daragh with Miss Allgood but they are certainly not equal in experience. I dont mind a bit how much of Miss Daragh you want its no affair of mine but I will be no use doing any of what we have for something we might possibly get in the future. The bridge across the stage is finished. Is ORourke to go on the pay list at 10/- a week Will you let me have Boyle as soon as possible. Are we to have 6^D seats this Autumn for we could spend it a bit if we are. The Window cleaning people want 8 or 9 shillings a month for keeping the place clean. Will I close with them. There is no chance of doing one night tours with our present strength. Some of the Big Posters of the tour will work up for Galway with slipping.

Is there any word of Henderson. Mr Synge has heard nothing from him.

I am
Faithfully yours
WILL G FAY

From WILLIAM G. FAY

Dublin

MS National Library of Ireland   18 August 1907

[Ambrose Power and Udolphus Wright played minor roles and did odd jobs. Yeats had been working on an adaptation of *Oedipus* some time before. When he returned to Dublin from America in 1904, he "took out of a pigeonhole at the theatre a manuscript translation of *Oedipus* too complicated in its syntax for the stage". This may have been Eglinton's work. Arthur Darley, violinist and composer, no longer played regularly for the Company after the tour of Scotland and England. He was replaced by J. F. Larchet.]

Dear Mr Yeats

Your letter to hand. I have given O Rourke a start and put him on to wardrobe which I think he will look after better than MacDonald. I have closed with Window cleaning can they start Monday. Holidays finished Aug. 13. They have all been here last week rehearsing White Cocade. I am glad to say that Power will be able to come to Galway so the only doubtful case is Wright. I see by your letter you have got my meaning about Miss Algood and the crowd. My objections were not to Miss Daragh but we must get more varied work and keep our best people in good parts for I don't see much possibility of increasing salaries for a good while to come and if we can't pay in money we can in parts. I think the translation of Greek play would help us & I hope we will get the Oedipus as well from Eglinton. The clothes to hand all right and will send P. O. Will you ask Lady Gregory to send me back the list of what I am to find here. I am sorry Boyle had to go back. I am very glad there is a prospect of us getting more poetic work & Romantic, for we have a fine stock of peasant play even at present time. That model for Shadowy Waters of Mr Roberts is 2 inch scale, I take it. Have you thought of the music for next season. Will Darley come on again or had we best look out some new person It none too early if Darley is off to be looking around. Lady Gregory wants to hire some costume for a Masque at Vice Regal Lodge. I am sending them unless you object as we have hired up to this when we knew the people. She is gone on the old cast clothes of Bailes strand. So I mean to hire them to them & then we may well have something out of them if we don't use them ourselves. If you dont like hiring will you please write me by return as they will be round on Monday to settle. Is Galway Booked for 17th Sept. Dont book earlier for we cant get Power any sooner. We had better do Hyacinth I suggest on account of the children for Hourglass and the difficulty of getting them. Let me know by return what plays for tour and if we can get printing in hands.

Yours faithfully
WILLIAM G. FAY

From WILLIAM G. FAY

                                                    Dublin
MS National Library of Ireland   20 August 1907

[Fay suggests travel to Galway on Sunday, 17 September, then to Mullingar on the nineteenth. The judges were American friends of Yeats. Fay probably refers to Arthur Morrison, English novelist, journalist, and dramatist.]

Dear Mr Yeats
    I think the best arrangement of Dates will be Galway 18, 19, travel on 17th Monday, Mullingar 20,21st. If these suit you will you let me know by return. I think its best to stick to one program as we would not serve much by just sending one man back home & the Double printing would be expensive, for we should have to get two sets of bills & programs, I wont put Power into Hyacinth for we wont be able to have him after this for the country. I suggest White Cocade Spreading the News one night Hyacinth Cathleen Building fund second night both towns. Can we get any Music Galway and Mullingar show drop flat without it. I will do something for your friends the Judges if they turn up and let us know when. Will Friday do at eight if not Monday I will give the Spreading the News with Cathleen. Thank for "Morning Post" Its very nice of them. I suppose Morrison. I can get courdory knee breekes for Kathleen here, will I get them I think they will look neater than tweeds. I think we ought to finish the Wardrobe right out now for we never know the minute we may want it Things alway come in a rush so with us. I would like to dress the pieces for our American friends if possible, they look so much better and set [is] the one trouble.
    Please let me know about Dates & Program by post card & I will Book. & post Printing in London.

                                        I am faithfully yours
                                        WILLIAM G. FAY

From WILLIAM G. FAY

                                                    Dublin
MS National Library of Ireland   22 August 1907

[Carter and the Soldier are characters in *The White Cockade*. Udolphus Wright had played Tim Casey in *Spreading the News*. James Bryce was Chief Secretary of Ireland, 1905–7.]

Dear Mr Yeats

More trouble in Ireland. The man I had playing Carter struck yesterday for money he wanted to be paid, he said. I pointed out the fact that he could not speak English and didn't know how to act and asked him to think it over, so this morning he came in & said he couldn't go on as he had a job to go to. Thats Carter off. The genius I had playing the Soldier has not turned up either so theres no chance of getting White Cocade to Galway by the 17 sept. I dont know where the Dickens to look for people. You see it got round town we are paying people, & that we did well on tour, so that every sundowner that turns up expects to be paid, and its perfectly absurd the cheek they have. They cant speak Kings English walk or do a thing One has to begin at the very beginning with each of them & waste the time of our own people Im short even for Spreading the News. Ive no Tim Casy the part Wright used to play. I suppose ORourkes money covers the last Idle cash we had What is to be done. Will I book Mullingar & Athlone, but Athlone has a show on the 17th – 18th so there would not be much left there for us for next week. You see we are at present depend on men that cant get a job at anything else that where the trouble comes in. We want at the very least two more men. Power sent me the enclosed letter could you or Lady Gregory put in a word for him with Brice Chief Secretary he done a lot of work for us, and if he got this job he would be able to help us a good deal more as he would have more spare time Will you let me know what the next move by return I will be ready for the Judges Monday night at 8.15.

I am faithfully yours
WILLIAM G. FAY

From WILLIAM G. FAY

Dublin

MS National Library of Ireland   [25 August 1907]

[Fay refers to Boyle's *The Building Fund*. J. H. Dunne, whose children are referred to, had played minor roles including Carter in *The White Cockade*.]

Dear Mr Yeats

I think your Galway Bill all right only I will put the First night Hyacinth Cathleen & Building Fund so as to make the length of each program the same. It will be necessary to get some sort of music for Galway & Mullingar I think to keep the show up. I am hung up for a man for Spreading the News Dont have a chance of one on Monday so I have not booked until I have a definite caste. I am quite with both you & Lady Gregory about the importance of making every possible effort to make the Galway show a success so there is no use my booking the dates till I can be absolutely sure of a caste for Spreading the News. I have the First act of Boyle in Parts Will start reading it Monday. In reply to Lady Gregorys of Friday Clothes have not turned up yet, I will only get what clothes I can't possibly do without here I will get Tea & do my best to make the visitors comfortable. I intend to give a complete show of both pieces Monday night. It will look so much better. It will be a help to us if Power gets this job he is after. I saw Henderson last night He seems to be a very nice man simple and unaffected with plenty of common sense. I should think he [is] Catholic & Orthodox in his views but that does not concern us. I will try for one of Dunnes children.

    Synge has gone to Kerry.

Yours faithfully
WILLIAM G. FAY

From A. E. F. HORNIMAN

Haute Savoie, France
27 August 1907

MS National Library of Ireland

[Miss Horniman predicts that the passage of Saturn over Yeats's first house (which rules the general focus of life force) "won't be bad", but the sesquiquadrate (an evil aspect) of Jupiter and the sun "look bad". The Yeats sisters broke with Miss Evelyn Gleeson in 1908, moved between June and July to new premises, and changed the name of the Industries from Dun Emer to Cuala. Mrs Cora Brown-Potter, one of several people for whom the Abbey occasionally held matinée performances, was an American actress and manager. Before the word "blue" Miss Horniman drew the sign of Scorpio, usually associated with water and creativity. "The Unicorn from the Stars" is a translation of *Monoceros de Astris*, a title associated with one of the degrees in the Golden Dawn.]

My dear Demon,

    I would gladly have fetched you any books or sent you my own astrology. I only sent back the keys when there was no more time to hear from you.

That transit of ♄ in your first won't be as bad as it would be if he were ill-dignified there but the ⊔ ♃ & ☉ look bad for your prosperity & fame. You must be very determined not to take any fresh serious course of action under those aspects. I cannot help being anxious about you, you ought to be doing your greatest work now. Don't let any idea of duty to persons come in the way of this. Worrying over the Abbey Theatre and the Dun Emer Press is putting side-issues in their wrong places. You cannot possibly find & write enough books for your sisters, they must get hold of material themselves sooner or later. I don't blame you for starting them, but they must run their own business in time. You are not valued enough by your own people, either your relations or your fellow country-men. I shall be so glad when you return to London in the early Autumn; I want to see you again, *yourself* & *myself*, not two people worried to death about difficulties neither can remove even with the best will in the World. I shall be in Manchester from the middle of September onwards for some weeks. The general public seem much interested in the scheme and it is a great nuisance that we can only get the Midland Theatre by scraps & will be difficult & expensive to evict the man who has the building. I want for a permanency, even if I buy the place out-right. I will send you a circular as soon as they are ready.

Miss Owen seems to be enjoying herself, but naturally she finds Mrs. Brown-Potter a trial. I wish that I had been there to help sail that boat. You would love the lake here, it is generally ♍ blue, pale like a discoloured turquoise & the mountains are grey at the top & green at the foot. We are going to Chamonix for a day or two & shall return here next week but I expect to leave here about Sept 6th or 7th at latest for London.

I had some long cuttings from the agency about Cork & Waterford. There will be always a difficulty in first visits at a bad time of the year. If you cover expenses it is something. "The Unicorn from the Stars" is a splendid title, it gives one a feeling of the marvellous & the unexpected. This lovely place & the rest are doing me much good.

I have never shewn you the water-bag make of a goat-skin I bought for you in Tunis. It is an ugly thing but interesting. Remind me of it when we meet. Do bear in mind that I *beg* you to avoid any new course of action at present, at any rate until you have talked about it to me.

Dear Friend —   Yours
                                                  ANNIE

From WILLIAM G. FAY

                                         Dublin
MS National Library of Ireland   28 August 1907

[Father O'Donovan was an activist priest. Yeats referred to him as "my friend" in his New York address (on 18 February 1904) in celebration of the birth of Robert Emmet.]

Dear Mr Yeats
    The Americans came last night and seemed very well pleased with the show Pixie Smith Father ODonovan & your father & two sisters, we had about 20 people all together I was under the impression that you had engaged Henderson definitely and I gathered from him that he had given notice to his present employers. I have not got a man for Tim Casey yet so I need not say I have not booked Galway up to date. I am advertising again to see if it will do any good. Cant get the box of clothes from Sheehans of Gort from the Railway company Have fit up scenery well in hands.
                                         faithfully yours
                                         WILLIAM G. FAY

From ELIZABETH A. SHARP

                                         Perthshire, Scotland
MS Yeats   19 September 1907

Dear Mr. Yeats
    The Year of Will's birth was 1855. I am so interested in this matter of his horoscope.
    I go to Edinburgh to – 22 Ormidale Terrace, Murray Field – & remain next week in order to be present at the Pan-Celtic Congress. After that I return to London.
    Please give my kind remembrances to Lady Gregory.
                                         Sincerely yours
                                         ELIZABETH A. SHARP

From ELIZABETH A. SHARP

                                         London
MS Yeats   [late September 1907]

[Apparently Yeats's lecture to the Franco-Scottish Society in the Aberdeen Centre focused on Sharp's "extraordinarily primitive mind" and his "secondary personality". Yeats may have been in Scotland to attend the Pan-Celtic Congress mentioned in Mrs Sharp's letter of 19 September.]

Dear Mr. Yeats

I have just heard from an old friend an item regarding my husband's birth that is valuable in regard to his horoscope.

That is, that he was born about *two o'clock*, on Friday the 12th. September.

I am interested to see the account of the Franco-Scottish meeting in Aberdeen. I wish I had been there to hear your address. I hear you read a poem of Fiona Macleod's, which rejoices me.

Very Sincerely Yours
ELIZABETH A. SHARP

From A. E. F. HORNIMAN

London

MS Yeats   3 November 1907

[Mrs Patrick Campbell acquired rights for five years to Yeats's *Deirdre*. The reference to "Macdonald" is probably a mistake for Thomas MacDonagh, whose *When the Dawn Is Come* was produced by the Abbey on 15 October 1908. Mrs Campbell did not play *Deirdre* in Dublin until 9 November 1908, several months after the Fays had resigned (on 13 January 1908). After their departure three plays by "Norreys Connell" (Conal O'Riordan) were produced by the Abbey. *The Piper* (produced 13–14 February 1908) aroused considerable controversy. Yeats explained the play at both productions. The portrait of Yeats by Antonio Mancini is the frontispiece to Volume V of *The Collected Works* (1908).]

My dear Demon,

I have not told you much about the Manchester affair because I don't see why your time should be taken up with details about what you consider to be "an error at judgement". The Gaiety is one of the well-known theatres, in a splendid position & it holds over 1000 people. Everyone is glad to hear that I am buying it & that I intend if possible to arrange for all the seats to be booked. The date on which

I shall take possession is not yet settled, it may be in six weeks or not until the end of July next. I think it is a sad waste of time for you to try & make yourself into a technically good stage manager; all the more that you will have to work with unwilling material & neglect the literary tasks which you can carry out as no one else living can do. But what are my words against the wooing of the vampire Kathleen ni Houlihan!

That Mrs Pat Campbell made such an offer (in blissful ignorance of Macdonald's powers in poetical drama & Frank Fay's insanity) and that you are most naturally delighted with it are merely details. I believe that she admires your poetical powers & very likely she has taken a fancy to you too although you are much too old for a woman of forty who might well go in for someone young. The root matter is whether Willie Fay will let the Directors & the Company consent to allow an Englishwoman to play at the Abbey & whether his permission (if he grant it) be genuine or not. This is the whole gist of it all, but you will only be angry with me for putting it so clearly. But I will not see the rest of your life wasted without raising my voice even if it be useless. You *must* know that Fay would not permit a second company of actors at the Abbey, they would need to be paid & some would not be Irish & they could not be kept together to do proper work amongst the present company. You have not the discipline amongst the present people which is absolutely necessary — as long as things are going on at the Abbey like this your time is being wasted. I am only writing what Masefield or Arthur Symons would say to you if they knew the circumstances. I am not going to interfere ever again in your Abbey theatrical affairs — except to remember the dates for the subsidy & to see after the building affairs. That is what *you* really wish. Thank you very much for your long letter. I go to Manchester on Tuesday for a week at least. Later on I shall go to Glasgow I think for a little. I shall indeed be glad to see you in London, *my* dear old friend; but you must bear in mind that your wish that I should trouble you less will be fulfilled. You will have no less kindness from me, but I will not waste the rest of my life on a Lost Cause. This should be a great relief to your mind, to know that you need never fear any more interference from me. I saw Norris Connell last night, he wrote & asked for an interview. I told him the bare fact you told me, that "Fay did not like his play" & how that your passing it & my liking it were of no avail. The man lives by his pen so it was only just that I should tell him the truth. Naturally I told him that I have no more connection with the Abbey beyond the subsidy & the building itself. Can you send me a photograph of the Mancini portrait?

Yours
ANNIE.

From A. E. F. HORNIMAN

London

MS National Library of Ireland   27 February 1908

["Norreys Connell", one of the new writers for the season of 1908, later became the Abbey's stage manager.]

My dear Demon,

I told you that I had explained my pecuniary circumstances to Mr. Connell & he said that that settled the matter. He has now written to me what he would have proposed if I had been better off. I have tried to make him understand that I feel a great sense of responsibility about money & that I could manage to go on as I do now *if I thought it right* but I don't.

It is of no use to worry you with old tales but I hate doing anything behind people's backs. So I tell you that I've shown him the subsidy letter & that after the last visit to London to Lady Gregory so that he may clearly understand my attitude. Evidently he has never grasped the idea that I wanted to make the nucleus of an *Art* theatre, not for your work in particular, but a theatre where *such* work would be well done and other good work too of all kinds. "Mr Yeats' ideas" never for one moment struck me as a scheme for personal aggrandisement, but as a phrase meaning something much wider. Why the same sum as the subsidy spent each year on a week of matinées of your work at a good London theatre done *decently* would do more for your reputation & as there would be *some* receipts, the expense would be less. Don't bother about answering this letter, it is only to impress on you that *I* never imagined for a moment that you were practically exploiting me. (Mr Connell did *not* imply that at all). You are a great deal too stupid. I laughed at one of the Irish papers saying that you "discovered" me. Several times I've had a little difficulty in saying that *I* suggested the theatre & then the subsidy to you, not you to me, because it was so obvious to me; but I have said it all the same.

I hope that you are well now.

Yours
ANNIE

From JOHN SINGER SARGENT

MS Berg Collection,   London
New York Public Library   23 March [1908]

[Sargent is speaking of the chalk drawing he did for *The Collected Works*, which Yeats liked so well that he used it as the frontispiece for Volume I. John Quinn, who purchased the "beautiful thing", had received it by 20 December 1908. Sargent's oil portrait of Sir Hugh Lane is now in the National Gallery of Ireland.]

Dear Mr Yeats

I have just received a letter from certain forwarding agents, Pitt & Scott, asking me to attend to some American Custom House formalities in order to get the drawing I did of you into America. They say they sent it over last August for "Mr Wellson". It seems to me as very likely that the thing in question is a photograph and not the original drawing that I am writing to you to make sure before replying to Messrs Pitt & Scott.

There is another point on which I have more than once thought of writing to you, ever since I painted that bust of Mr Hugh Lane. The feeling that it is rather coarse to betray such vagueness as mine in business matters has deterred me. The fact is I have sometimes wondered whether I have ever been paid for that bust of Mr Lane, as I do not find any entry to that effect in a book in which I usually keep such records. It is very possible that I was paid and that I neglected to write it down, but I am quite uncertain; as I am, for that matter, as to the price agreed upon. I remember that you were interested in the presentation of that sketch to Mr Lane, so you will probably know who acted as treasurer in the matter. This person would be sure to know whether the payment has taken place, and I would be glad to have my own most unbusinesslike vagueness disputed.

Hoping to hear from you speedily with regard to the Custom House matter.

                                    Yours sincerely
                                    JOHN S. SARGENT

From JAMES RICHARD WALLACE
Manchester

MS Yeats   8 May 1908

[We cannot identify the friend born in 1884 whose horoscope Yeats had requested. Yeats preserved the "Progressed Horoscopes" for 1907 through 1917 calculated "as at 27 Dec." for each year. Yeats also preserved a "Supplement to No 1 *Modern Astrology*" entitled "Short and Simple Glossary of Astrological Terms". It defines "Transits" as "the passing of the planets over places or points in the horoscopes by daily motion", "Speculum" as "a table of the aspects in the horoscope", "Part of Fortune" as "a point in the horoscope where the rays of the Sun and Moon converge", and "Cusp" as "the beginning of any [astrological] house". Alan Leo was the editor of *Modern Astrology* and the author of *Practical Astrology* (1902?) and numerous popular books and manuals on astrology. "Sepharial" was the pseudonym of Walter Gorn Old, author of *The New Manual of Astrology* (1898).]

Dear Sir,

I regret I cannot send you the Primary Directions this evening yet. They are calculated (I told you they are very numerous), but the tabulation (arranging them in consecutive order by thair dates), & the fair copy, cannot be completed until *to-morrow*, when *you may rest assured I will send them to you.*

On *Monday*, I will write out the nativity of your friend born 1884.

I now enclose your Secondary Directions, Transits, & Progressed horoscopes from Jan. 1907 to June 1917 — 10½ years. These are most fully & completely made out. Directions are noted in red ink. "R." means that the aspect is in "Radix." Those which have no mark are actual aspects formed after birth. I think the whole will be quite clear to you. As to Transits, "pr." ☉, ☽ , &c. means a Transit over the *progressed* place. I give the *dates* of ♂ transits as nearly as I can fix them, in the coming years.

I return Speculum & Map which you sent.

I enclose a fresh copy of your Horoscope made out in my style, with Speculum subjoined, I think you will like this kind of map. For *form's* sake, I have inserted the Pars Fortunae, correctly computed. It is not expressed in Longitude, in a Nativity — it is a purely mundane point.

It is found thus:

Oblique Asc. of Asct.	332° 16'
Less Ob. Asc. ☉	46. 55
	285° 21'
Plus R A. ☽	320. 38
Deducting the circle (360°) gives	245° 59'

This is the R.A. of ⊕, so it is inside 10th cusp. Its S.A is that of ☽, but as they are in different hemispheres, S.A. is ☽'s diurnal Semi-arc.

As to Speculum, — I do not hold with giving *fractions of a minute*. This only causes unnecessary bother, and *is of no earthly use*. If the fraction is over half a minute, call it 1'; if under take no notice of it. For Declinations, however, if one has access to Nautical Almanac, it is worth while to give them to °, ', & ", as you then can get the Semi-arcs more exact.

You said you would have your natus rectified, when you got certain dates which you required. Mr. Leo has said, 2 or 3 times, I am the best man he knows at rectifying a horoscope. I may also say it was mainly I who convinced him of the truth & value of Primary Direction. Years ago, he was *most averse* to them. He has also got his eyes somewhat opened to the fallacy of the "Pre-natal Epoch" theory. The evasion and trickery to which "Sepharial" has resorted in trying to establish this theory (of which, after all, he is not the author) have been disgraceful; & I say so very plainly: I had ample proof of this.

I will feel very grateful to you if you will take the trouble to remit me tomorrow (Saturday) *for the enclosed work*. The fee is 15/., wh. I think you will not complain of, when you see how carefully the work is done. It took a good deal of time, as you will understand. *Believe me, I am in great need of the money*. I have had a very harassing spring, partly through a Court Summons. I am far from comfortable here, & must leave soon for cheaper apartments. When you get conclusion of work (the 7/6 map &c.) in beginning of week, you will let me know if you wish more done.

I am, Dear Sir,
Yours very truly,
J. R. WALLACE

Wd. you please send a Postal Order, as I have some difficulty in cashing a cheque.

From A. E. F. HORNIMAN

London

MS National Library of Ireland   14 May 1908

[Sheridan's *The Scheming Lieutenant* was produced on 29 May. Whitney and Moore were the solicitors for the Abbey. Mrs Old was Yeats's housekeeper at Woburn Buildings.]

Most polite Demon!

Greetings! Is it Influenza or Conscience that has made you so civil? 1 Tinkler key — 1 bundle mixed keys & — 1 unusual instrument are being sent to you. Your own keys are retained for a day or two in case of further need. One dozen astrological forms & three penny stamps enclosed — the latter to replace some I took from your rooms to-day.

I am much relieved to hear that you think that Mr Synge will survive the operation. He will be very weak for a long time though & I suppose that will put the theatre business on your shoulders unless Lady Gregory comes forward. The Sheridan play is new to me, it will take much careful rehearsal.

The Sargent picture is excellent, it makes you look very young but with more vigour than you had in youth. Many thanks for sending it.

I paid the Abbey rates & taxes yesterday & I suppose that the furniture bill will soon arrive. Dr. Moore has sent in his bill for the past three years, to be paid at my convenience, so it can wait for a few weeks. I hope that these extras are at an end now as they have taken far more than I ever got from lets.

Why on earth are bits of mostly fur kept carefully in your drawers, I opened them in search of the keys. Your under-garments will get moth-eaten & then I'll have to annoy Mrs. Old again with naphthaline. I suppose that they have tumbled off your fur rug.

I brought back an empty stylus and left two in good repair in the basket on the table under the Bavarian candlestick. You have grown much tidier now-a-days.

Yours

ANNIE

From MAUD GONNE

                                                      Paris
MS Yeats   26 June [1908]

[Yeats enclosed this fragment in an envelope marked "P I A L letter
of June 26" which he pasted in a notebook given to him by Maud.
George Russell's *Deirdre* and Yeats's *Cathleen ni Houlihan* were first
produced on 2 April 1902.]

Friend of mine
      It was sad you had to leave paris so soon — there is so much I
wanted to talk to you about & so much we had not time for — Next
time you come you must arrange to have a little more time to spare.
      I was so tired last night when I got home I could not do much,
but several times I felt your thought with me quite distinctly.
      I am thinking it would not be right for you to give up your
London life completely yet — There are elements in it which you still
need — The theatre is the millstone from which you must try to get
free, or at least partially free. I understand how you feel about the
responsibility towards the players who depend on you, — it is that
recognition of responsibility which I always admire in you & which is
such a rare quality in our country but for the sake of Ireland, you
must keep your writing before all else — A great poet or a great
writer, can give nobler & more precious gifts to his country than the
greatest philanthropist ever can give — Your own writing, above all,
your poetry must be your first consideration, any thing that takes
you from it — or makes it less intense is wrong & must be shaken off.
      You remember how for the *sake of Ireland*, I hated you in
politics, even in the politics I believed in, because I always felt it
took you from your writing & cheated Ireland of a greater gift than
we could give her — & the theatre is just as bad, or worse for it brings
you among jealousies & petty quarrels & little animosities which you
as a great writer should be above & apart from — It is because you
vaguely feel this, that you are exasperated & often very unjust to our
people — It is this exasperation that has made you take up old class
prejudices which are unworthy of you, & makes you say cruel things
which *sound* ungenerous — though you are never ungenerous really. I
hate hearing you speak of Russell's Deirdre as you do — of course
Russell cannot write as you do, but all the same Russell is an artist &
has a very noble mind, & his Deirdre did not hurt your Kathleen
when they were first played together long ago. In painting your

father might say hard things about Russells technique, but in his lecture in America he spoke of what he saw great & beautiful in Russells painting — it is not like you to speak like that of an artist & a great mystic.

Forgive me Willie for writing all this which may make you angry. I ought to have *said* it but I was so taken up by this thought when you were here that I had not time — every thing else seemed too unimportant to waste the short time we had together in discussing & indeed even now I know these outer things are of little importance, but even in little things I dont want there to be the least jar between us. I know on many things we think differently but only when you spoke of those two things I felt a slight surprise & disappointment, as though it was not you yourself who was speaking —

I think a most wonderful thing has happened — the most wonderful I have met with in life. If we are only strong enough to hold the doors open I think we shall obtain knowledge & life we have never dreamed of.

The meaning of things are becoming very clear to me, I shall work it all [remainder lost]

From MAUD GONNE

Paris

MS Yeats   26 July [1908]

[This letter was also enclosed in an envelope and pasted in the notebook given to Yeats by Maud. On 29 July, the day he received this letter, Yeats recorded that he had made evocation "on the night of 25" and "sought union with PIAL" (Per Ignem Ad Lucem, her motto in the Golden Dawn, which she had left years before). The play referred to was probably *The Player Queen*. Blake's illustration with the caption "The Soul hovering over the Body reluctantly parting from Life" is in Robert Blair's *The Grave* (1808).]

Willie,

It is not in a week but in a day that I am writing to you. I had such a wonderful experience last night that I must know at once if it affected you & how? for above all I don't want to do any thing which will take you from your work, or make working more arduous.— That play is going to be a wonderful thing & must come first — nothing must interfere with it —

Last night all my household had retired at a quarter to 11 and I thought I would go to you astrally. It was not working hours for you & I thought by going to you I might even be able to leave with you some of my vitality & energy which would make working less of a toil next day — I had seen the day before when waking from sleep a curious some what Egyptian form floating over me (like in the picture of Blake the soul leaving the body) — It was dressed in moth like garments & had curious wings edged with gold in which it could fold itself up — I had thought it was myself, a body in which I could go out into the astral — at a quarter to 11 last night I put on this body & thought strongly of you & desired to go to you. We went some where in space I dont know where — I was conscious of starlight & of hearing the sea below us. You had taken the form I think of a great serpent, but I am not quite sure. I only saw your face distinctly & as I looked into your eyes (as I did the day in Paris you asked me what I was thinking of) & your lips touched mine. We melted into one another till we formed only *one being, a being greater than ourselves* who felt all & knew all with double intensity — the clock striking 11 broke the spell & as we separated it felt as if life was being drawn away from me through my chest with almost physical pain. I went again twice, each time it was the same — each time I was brought back by some slight noise in the house. Then I went upstairs to bed & I dreamed of you confused dreams of ordinary life. We were in Italy together (I think this was from some word in your letter which I had read again before sleeping). We were quite happy, & we talked of this wonderful spiritual vision I have described — you said it would tend to increase physical desire — This troubles me a little — for there was nothing physical in that union — Material union is but a pale shadow compared to it — write to me quickly & tell me if you know anything of this & what you think of it — & if I may come to you again like this. I shall not until I hear from you. My thought with you always

MAUD GONNE

From JAMES RICHARD WALLACE

MS Yeats

Manchester
31 July 1908

["Ephemeris" is "a Table for each day, giving the latitude and longtitude of the planets". The most popular *Ephemeris* for many years was prepared by a series of men using the pseudonym of "Raphael". Yeats preserved a copy in which he underlined in red the date of his birth, 13 June 1865.

The "1866 case" refers to Maud Gonne (b. 21 December 1866). Wallace says that he is rectifying by Saturn ("soul at the nadir of matter") in opposition to *medium coeli* or mid-heaven. For birth cause, it is the sun ("infinite potentiality") in opposition to Uranus ("self-potency entirely uninhibited"), and the semi-square (45°, "an evil aspect") of Saturn ("soul at the nadir of matter"), and being parallel conjunction. In such a case there could be no happy marriage even if Jupiter ("soul on the ascendant of matter") should be in the Seventh House (for which the keyword is "partnership"). In this astrological position "the native at his best is the perfect partner in a real reciprocity of interest". Her loss of popularity is due to the Sun being in opposition to the Moon. We are unable to identify the "1884" case. Sir Ralph Shirley, for whom Wallace worked occasionally, was editor of *The Occult Review* and managing director of William Rider and Son, publisher of occult books.]

Dear Mr. Yates,

I forgot, yesterday, to say I got my case so far arranged for a payment, & an order for 10/ a month — first 10/ is due next week.

To-day there is more trouble here. Life in this house is nearly misery. I have only had 4/ this week from London & Mrs. R. refuses to cook anything further for me till she gets more money. I told her I was on work, as she saw, but cd. not get money just yet. She said she "knew nothing about my work — she wanted money." She can neither read nor write — she was born in Russia. It was a bad day for me when I came here.

I must appeal to you to save me from sinking, for I am in misery. *Please wire me 20/ to-morrow, or send me an order.* If you wire it, sent it to "Elizabeth St." If you post it, leave name & P.O. unfilled, for Mchr. P.O. will be closed all Monday, but I could get it changed in a shop on Sunday (Nearly all shops are open here on ☉ day).

I will send you, if you like, in *Security, a set of 30 years' Ephs.,* until I finish off yr. work, & square up with you.

I have written "Raphael" that I can now undertake the work of *1910* Ephemeris. Last winter I was not well enough to go on with 1909, as I told you before.

I am almost sure my Rectif^n of yr. natus is right, but *wish* *your own opinion, before altering all the primary arcs, & writing out judgment.* The secondaries will not be practically altered.

1866 case I am rectifying by ♄ to ☍ M.C. I can see no other reasonable explanation for her period of trouble. Of course, for *birth* cause, it is ☉ applying to ☍♅, & ∠♄, & being Par. ☋. There never was, or will be, happy marriage for a woman in such a case, even if ♃ be in ♐. Her loss of popularity is, of course, ☉☍☽.

1884. No, I do not think Asc. ☌♃ con. are for marriage. I am writing it out as for M. C. △♆ zod. for event.

I wish you to understand that, after I finish all your work, I must advertise a bit.

Mr. Leo (Mr. Shirley does *not* like L. — did you see any of the astrologers when you were in London?) has repeatedly promised me *constant* work, & objects to my advertising. But his work is *not* constant, & in summer falls off tremendously. In Sept. — *their* holiday time — I generally get a lot.

In end 1905, his work had been so bad that I advertised, and was likely to do well; but Mr. L. seemed to object, & got me to stop it.

Now if a man promises you regular work, he sh^d give it, or give you a *regular weekly wage*, whatever the work might vary. That is what I want.

Then "Raphael" meant me to prepare new "Tables of Houses" not for every exact degree, but for some great town in nearly every degree. That w^d have been practically very useful.

His long illness & seclusion (I don't think he is *much* better) has knocked all these plans on the head.

Do help me this time, Mr. Yeats; & I will endeavour never to trouble you again for any loan, & will faithfully work off all my present indebtedness.

My health is much better if it were not for such want of sleep this summer, through mental anxiety. Your natus shows you a friend to me (& with ♃ on yr 11 cusp, *you* have naturally many friends).

Do please, for Heaven's sake, assist me by return. You will never regret it.

Yours very truly,
J. R. WALLACE

From CHARLES RICKETTS

London

MS Yeats [November 1908]

[Mrs Patrick Campbell played the role of Deirdre in London on 27 November. Charles Shannon's portrait of Yeats (the frontispiece for Volume III of *The Collected Works*) was sold to John Quinn.]

My dear Yeats,

I intended congratulating you on your play after the performance, but saw your back vanishing down a stairs when the time came. I like it immensely, not so much as Baily's Strand but very much indeed. If our Time had a sense for Tragedy and if we had actors capable of understanding it and with the gift to interpret it, Deirdree would be famous instead of a literary curiosity for a matinee. I do not think it forceful enough, here & there, notably at the start, and any latent indecision was of course emphasized by the abominable performance. The chorus of musicians which should act as a musical chorus or accompaniment which is admirable in conception in its relation to the action and climax, drove me to distraction by its lack of intelligence beauty or decision in its interpretation. Mrs Campbell was fine when she rose from the chess board, and in the major part of the scene with the King, but her entrance was deplorable. Personally I believe that the play is thin at that moment or somewhere there abouts. As a Saxon I failed to grasp the full value of the chess playing episode, that is, I was unfamiliar with the situation or legend which you conjure up, and therefore unprepared to give it its importance. Of course all that part was shamefully acted, Naisi was ridiculous and offensive in his every movement and intonation. The play becomes admirable with the entrance of the King. I believe the dreadful interpretations you have always met with (and to which you seem quite blind) have spoilt your chances, so far, as a playwright. I have always liked your sense of construction, your sense of the stage. Where I am hostile is to a certain vagueness of texture for which you receive praise and in which I detect a sort of hesitation and a bias towards rhetoric of a kind.

Yours ever,

C. RICKETTS

P.S. Shannon was hugely impressed and now tells me to ask you what he is to do with the picture. It is here.

From MRS. ROBERT W. FELKIN

London

MS Yeats   15 November 1908

[Mrs Ethel Felkin (Quaero Lucem) was the clairvoyant wife of Dr Robert W. Felkin (Finem Respice), Chief of the Stella Matutina, an offspring of the Order of the Golden Dawn. SR (Sacramentum Regis) was the Order motto of Arthur Edward Waite. In "The Cat and the Moon" Yeats relates the "changing eyes" of Minnaloushe "to the changing moon".]

Care V. H. Frater,

Thanks much for your letter which greatly interested us. I think that for yourself you are quite right in regards to the star and symbol since, as you will see on looking at the diagram of the ✡ you are allotted to ☿ . My impression therefore is that each of us should chiefly follow the star to which we are attributed though interchanging and mingling to a certain extent. My own symbol seems preeminently the Chalice. I suspect also that we ought as far as we can to seek the correspondences to our own planet throughout nature both on the material and astral planes. Your alternative symbol would obviously be the Lamp or the Kerux, Anubis, your animal the dog, your planet Mercury, your metal Alchemic Mercury, and so on, each having some special message for you. My animal is the cat — whose dilating pupils correspond to the waxing and waning moon: my flower is the night-blooming ceres or evening primrose, my metal silver. You and S.R. must to a great extent be the guardians and teachers, F. R. the link between the spiritual and material, myself the receptive and reflective meeting-place of the other more positive points. In regard to working with planetary forces you would of course project the Zodiac around you as you do in consecrating a Talisman or Implement, placing yourself in the position of the planet to be acted on. For this purpose it is well to have a set of cards with the Signs of the Zodiac painted on them. I can show you a very simple set I made for myself a little while ago, the big ones are troublesome to make though more imposing when done.

Let us know when you are in town so that we may have a meeting of the Group if possible. Have you received any definite teaching from the Meditation so far? I can get easily up to the top of the Mountain now but have got nothing further as yet. I generally find myself beside a large bush with grey-green leaves. There is a guide waiting for me but I cannot yet consciously follow him.

Greetings and thanks from us both.

Fraternally yours,
Q.L. (MRS. FELKIN)

From SARA ALLGOOD

MS Berg Collection,   Belfast
New York Public Library   3 December 1908

[Allgood had apparently been in London, probably to appear in a series of productions, beginning on 27 November, given by Mrs Campbell. F. R. Benson and his wife played the leads in *Diarmuid and Grania* (21 October 1901).]

Dear Mr. Yeats

I arrived quite safe, had a splendid crossing, they did bad business the first two days but there was a better house last night, and both plays were splendidly recieved, I got a great reception and some splendid notices this morning. I have just got a letter from, F. R. Benson, who wants me for the month of February next year 1909 also for the Stratford Festival commencing April 19*th* 1909 for 3 weeks. Can you let me off? I do hope you will see your way, as I am sure it would be a great thing for me, also for the Company as well.

Please let me know by return of post, as Mr. Benson asked for an early reply, and I cannot do anything until I hear from you.

Yours Sincerely
SARA ALLGOOD

From CLAUDE DUMAS

                                         Liverpool
MS Yeats   18 December 1908

[The lady is Maud Gonne, the boy her son Sean. The sun in the semi-square of Uranus is ominous. Both Maud and Yeats had her horoscope cast in 1908: she going to the famous Ely Star in Paris, Yeats to J. R. Wallace as well as Dumas. He asks Yeats for money by postal order.]

Dear Sir,

Thank you very much for your kind & appreciative letter. Am now enclosing herewith the horoscope of Lady (21. Dec. 66) & consider it most interesting. It is curious how the ☉∠♅ in the boy's horoscope you mention, coincides with the mother's fears. I think ♅ in Natal 12th. rather critical in this respect.

I will get on with the other horoscope & send it on to you early as possible to Paris – meanwhile you might please send the p.o. for the *two horoscopes* if convenient by return of post. I might then get it early in next week & would be much obliged if you can do this.

Thanking you in anticipation.

Very faithfully yours
C. DUMAS

Should like to know at future time how the forecast in this present horoscope works out. It is my own private system which I wish to test in the present case. I have never known it fail – when birth time is correct.

From GEORGE BERNARD SHAW

London

MS British Library   [*ca.* 1908–10]

[Antonio Cippico, who lectured for a time at the University of London, became Yeats's theatrical agent for the continent. An ardent fascist, Cippico was a senator from 1923.]

My dear Yeats,

I find that at the theatre last night I quite forgot an engagement which will oblige me to leave home at half past five this evening and keep me away until midnight. Can you come to lunch with your sister at about half past one? Cippico, whom you perhaps know (he translates Shakespear into the Italian) is bringing a compatriot of his who wants to interview me in a general sort of way; but we can manage to have a few minutes to ourselves after luncheon. If you are engaged for lunch, can you look in afterwards any time up to 3. After that I must go out; and though I shall be here from 5 to half past, I am threatened with a [indecipherable] visit at that hour. Come to lunch if you can. Send a line by the bearer to my wife, as I am just off to rehearsal and shall not be back until lunch.

Yours ever,
[GEORGE BERNARD SHAW]

From: GEORGE BERNARD SHAW

London

MS British Library   [*ca.* 1909—10]

[When Shaw lived at Hindhead, a remote corner of Surrey, in 1898—99, he joined Grant Allen (whose home was a "model of domesticity") and other neighbours in a play-reading society. W. Kingsley Tarpey's *Windmills* was produced by the Stage Society in June 1901.]

My dear Yeats,

I dont know whether you were a friend of Grant Allen's. I was; and one of his difficulties was that his son, Gerry Grant Allen, would not take an interest in anything except the theatre. I dont mean the drama: I mean literally the boards and the canvas and the switchboard and the boxoffice and the dressingrooms and the inhabitants thereof. He is now a theatrical manager but he cannot get anything to manage. He managed Tarpey for the season, and, as might be expected, incurred his lifelong enmity. He now wants to manage a theatre company for you; but he believes that you are under the hands of Tarpey, and would receive any application from him with disfavor. He therefore asks me to obtain access for him to you, as he believes you are about to send round a company with your plays. I promised I would write to you and ask you to see him if he writes to you for an appointment. This promise I accordingly redeem. He is a clever, energetic, young ruffian, fearfully spoilt by his father, but in such a fashion that it is very hard to say whether his father's treatment was the spoiling or the making of him. For instance, he is not above his business; and as he might turn out useful on one occasion or another as your operations develop, you might as well have a look at him for five minutes.

Yours ever,

[GEORGE BERNARD SHAW]

From JOHN QUINN

TS Manuscript Division,   New York

New York Public Library   16 April 1909

[White was a clerk in Quinn's office. Frederick James Gregg, former friend of Yeats at Erasmus Smith High School, Dublin, worked on the New York *Evening Sun*. JBY'S letter, "John Synge: Some

Recollections by an Irish Painter", appeared in the *Evening Sun* for 3 April. Swinburne died on 10 April. James Gibbons Huneker, literary critic and writer on the New York *Morning Sun*, dedicated a book of essays to Quinn: *Ivory Apes and Peacocks* (1915). Francis Hackett wrote for the Chicago *Evening Post*. John Devoy, Irish-American revolutionary, was editor of *The Gaelic American* and author of *Recollections of an Irish Rebel* (1929). The "New Gallery" was the Municipal Gallery, Dublin. Synge's *Poems and Translations* with a preface by Yeats was published in July by Cuala; a limited edition was published in New York by Quinn; Thomes B. Mosher was a widely known piratical publisher. Synge's fianćee was Molly Allgood. Symons had a mental breakdown in 1908. The one-volume edition of Synge's plays was not published; his unfinished *Deirdre of the Sorrows* was published by Cuala in 1910. The quotation from George Borrow appeared in Chapter XV of *Lavengro* (1851).]

My dear Yeats:

You may imagine what a shock the news of Synge's death was to me. Mr. White got a clipping from a Dublin paper on the 30th or 31st and we thought that Synge died on the 24th. I at once called up Gregg and told him about it, and I told Gregg I would send him the clipping. I started to dictate a note enclosing the clipping, and then went on and with four or five interruptions by office boys and callers and telephone messages, I dictated a letter to Gregg. Gregg published it without my name with a little judicious editing. I didn't know it was going to appear and I had no chance to revise it. That evening I got your father to agree to write a letter to the Evening Sun. He came to my office the next morning and dictated it, and it was published that afternoon. I send you with this two copies of each edition of the paper. I think your father's letter is very good.

In the death of a man like Swinburne, seventy-two years of age, a man who had delivered his message or done his work, there can be regret but not the keen sorrow that there is in the death of a man of Synge's age. He was just a year younger than I am. I was born in 1870; he, it seems, in 1871. Your sister Lily sent a copy of The Manchester Guardian containing a good notice of Synge and a splendid editorial notice. I have sent it to Gregg. Gregg intends to write an editorial article for the Evening Sun. James Huneker is also going to write an article on Synge. Francis Hackett wrote a half column in the Chicago Evening Post. John Devoy wrote a half a column in the Gaelic American, still talking philology and discussing questions of pronunciation in various counties and claiming that The Playboy misrepresented Irishman. But it was written with a friendly intention.

I cabled to Lady Gregory that I hoped a mask had been taken of Synge and that I should be glad to join in the project of having a bust made in marble or bronze and put in the New Gallery or in the Theatre. I hope that something of that sort will be done. I should be willing to contribute £20 or £25 to it.

When I cabled I didn't know that a mask had not been taken. Since that time your father has shown me a letter from your sister to him stating that you tried to have a mask taken but the family didn't care to have it done. I am sorry that you didn't persevere. I think the right kind of urging would have brought it, but I have a pencil drawing of Synge by your father and two smaller ones by him, and from photographs and from the painting by your father in the New Gallery in Dublin I should think a sculptor could make a good bust. Synge had a magnificent head and it is a great pity a death mask was not taken.

I hope that something will come of this. I could get some others here to join in the fund.

A second thing: I assume that you will write about Synge, perhaps an introduction to the volume of poems which your sisters are printing. I shall be obliged if you will write to your sisters and tell them that I will have the poems copyrighted here if they send me an advance copy or a copy in press sheets with your introduction. If this is not done Mosher in Portland or some other pirate is sure to re-publish them and the least that can be done for Synge and for the girl he left behind is to save them, and I shall be glad to copyright them in a little edition. I hope you won't overlook this. It wouldn't delay the publication by your sisters over a week. I can have the book printed within a week or two weeks at the outside after I get the copy from them, including the copy of your introduction, if you are going to write an introduction to the book, as your sister Lily wrote your father you might do.

If he left a will, the copyright should be taken out in the name of his executor. If he made you his literary executor it could be taken out in your name. Please let me know about this.

I can imagine that Synge's death was a great shock to you after the calamity that has overtaken poor Arthur Symons.

If you think Mrs. Symons will accept it, I shall be glad to send a gift to her. Would she feel offended if I sent it, or had I better send it to you, or is it needed? I read a part of your letter about Symons to James Huneker. Huneker was a personal friend and a great admirer of Symons and was very sorry to hear of his break-up. (I read only part of it to Huneker; he didn't see the letter.) I didn't quite understand your allusion to the de Goncourt novel or the phrase "the desolate ignorance of the nursery." Some time when you write put on a separate slip what you mean and I will tear up the slip.

Your father is in good health and has been lecturing. He has lectured on art at two or three places, on the Irish Literary Revival, and on Ireland, and in a note which I had from him this morning he states that he expects to continue to lecture. I daresay he will stay here until the beginning of the hot weather.

I was shocked to hear of Lady Gregory's illness. I didn't know she was ill, but I was relieved at the same time to hear that she was better. I don't think I would ever feel like going to Ireland if anything happened to her.

I had helped Roberts to make the arrangements for the publication of Synge's plays here in one volume with an introduction by you. I hope it will come off now. It is a pity that it wasn't done in Synge's lifetime. In the last letter I had from Synge he asked me to overlook the contract with the American publishers. I told him that I would safeguard his interests.

Do by all means arrange something about the bust and also about the copyrighting of his poems here.

Do you know whether he finished his Deirdre play? Or is it in such shape that it can be published?

When one is in the early 20's life seems to stretch a great distance before one. Then in ten or fifteen years more when one gets to be your or my age and one's friends begin to go and one begins to realize that one is in the 39's or early 40's, the thought of the slight hold that we have on life keeps coming over one. This thought never terrifies me — never frightens me. Sometimes I think of it as a relief. All we can do is to do our work, write as well as we can, work as well as we can, give a lift to a friend where we can, do as little harm as we can, see that nobody is worse off or has suffered by our existence, and try to play the part of a man. That is what Synge did, and that is why we can always sincerely respect his memory.

When you come to read what I dictated in my letter to Gregg, don't criticize it from the point of view of style but remember that I dictated it in about ten minutes with no thought of publication. The Borrow quotation I thought was very apt:

"There's a wind on the heath, brother. Life is sweet.
Who would wish to die?"

After all, Synge is better off and made a better end than poor
Symons is making. What news of Symons? Write me when you are in
the mood.

With kind regards, I am,

Sincerely yours,
JOHN QUINN

From JOHN BUTLER YEATS

New York

MS Yeats   21 May 1909

[Mitchell's attack on Yeats and the Abbey appeared in *Sinn Féin* (8
May 1909). The blackguard at Ely Place was George Moore. Charles
Johnston and Yeats were classmates at Erasmus Smith High School
in Dublin and founders (with others) of the Dublin Hermetic Society
(16 June 1885). Mrs Johnston was the niece of Madam Blavatsky.
The letter contains pen sketches of Moore and AE.]

My dear Willie,

Have you seen the article by Susan Mitchell in *Sinn Fein*? It is
very bad and low and treacherous. Fortunately it is so flagrantly
lying as to defeat in some degree its own wicked, wantonly wicked
purpose. One should lie with discretion.

Susan has a rich and generous personality, and one of her
charms is that she has no opinions, leaving them to the other sex.
Unfortunately, having no opinions means that she has no principles,
and so she falls a victim to George Russell's spiteful purposes. George
Russell is general utility man to the big elderly blackguard who
lives in Ely Place. This article is an overflow from that cesspool.

At the same time we must learn from our adversaries. You have
offended Russell's vanity, I fancy, more than once, and though there
is a Real Russell, which is magnanimous, one must not forget that
Russell is a prophet and the centre of a circle, and therefore intensely
self-appreciative. Nothing surprises me so much over here as the way
in which people make allowances for human nature and all its
infirmities. As I put it, here the conscience, by its nature so flexible,
so anxious for information, so full of speculative doubts and fancies,

is the *upperdog and the LAW the underdog*. In England it is just the opposite, and hence the brutality and unyielding stupidity of England. Hence also its smoothness. At least it is smooth to people who do not walk with wary and sensitive feet. Perhaps you have been too English in your methods. I hope this article won't do the theatre very much harm. For a time it will hearten the blackguards. I am sorry Lady Gregory is away, but I suppose she will be back before anything happens. She is a woman and therefore disinterested, and wise because disinterested, and she has a man's force. Indeed with the wisdom added she has more than any man's force.

Mrs. Charles Johnston tells me Russell made some very unfair attacks on Charlie and she recognized his style in Susan's article. (This was said in private, and I suppose *confidentially. Therefore* perhaps it ought to be kept to yourself.) She says there is a real fine Russell, but that of late it has become submerged. I don't profess to give her words. Both Johnstons are very indignant with him on their own account, their ideas of personal dignity and behavior making it, I imagine, impossible that they should make reprisals.

It is all very disagreeable, but the better the cause the surer it is to meet this kind of enemy, baseness coming to the top. George Moore came over by the Devil's aid to stand in the background and stimulate the baseness. These two conspirators have now got a woman in front to do their dirty work. If they wrote articles they would have to write the truth — but a woman has the privilege of her sex, and a charming woman never seems so charming to her friends as when on their behalf she is lying — and, my God, she has lied with a brazen face. John Quinn, to whom I showed the article, read it most carefully, and then said, "That article is dishonest. That girl should not have written it." After a while he added, "Dublin is like a large family, none of them married, none of them with occupation or woes or children, and so they pick at each other, while all the time they love each other."

The only cure is Home Rule, when they will forget themselves in the interest of larger questions, as we do here. I think this explains that Irish treachery which so much shocks our friends.

The article is of course treacherous. It is not opposition. It is all striking below the belt. An Editor here to whom I showed it said it could not be published here in *any paper, "there would be such an outcry."* He said this *before I had told him anything and before he knew about the lies.* It was the tone and style of the article that had thus impressed him.

I hope you will go on with the battle. If you do, such articles as this will *end* by helping you enormously. Good causes progress by the violence of their opponents. After a while the decent people who want to see intellect paramount in Dublin (that is your cause, is it not?) will rally to your side. Russell thinks G Moore a great man because, being from the North, he admires noblemen and he thinks Moore a sort of real nobleman, and because he is a successful writer of novels. He also admires Moore because Moore really has a poor opinion of Russell. Russell must either boss or be bossed. And then Russell is lonely. He has no friends, and he is exasperated against things, and so he likes to wade into the black puddle of the Moore cesspool, and to throw mud or get others to do it.

I think it would help you to publish broadcast that article of Susan's. You should quite largely reprint it in your next *Samhain* perhaps.

As I said before I hope you will go on with the battle. I suppose it is a question of money, and therefore it is perhaps impossible. But it is awful to think that Ruffianism, whether George Moore's cynical kind, or Russell's slyer sort, should triumph.

To come to my own fortunes here — I wish I was a few years younger. Never was my intellect and my tongue so free as it is here — *provided you are not vulgar*, you may say and do anything. The absence of tradition is more a blessing than a curse. Intuition has a freer play. A nice woman is not afraid to show how nice she is.

Mrs. Charles Johnston says the women here are extraordinarily free but never do anything wrong. *That is absolutely true.* They will talk about any subject, but they are all Dianas. I believe George Moore wants to come here. I fancy there would be some sport, and we should have some Homeric laughter.

Yrs Affectly
J. B. YEATS

From JOHN BUTLER YEATS

New York
9 June 1909

MS Yeats

[Yeats was a candidate for but failed to get a lectureship in literature at the new University College in Dublin. Frederick J. Gregg was a schoolmate of Yeats at the Erasmus Smith High School. William Mackay Laffan was the publisher of the New York *Sun* and founder

of the *Evening Sun*; Mrs May Hartley was the author of *Flitters,
Tatters, and the Counsellor* (1879). AE worked in several capacities
for the Irish Agricultural Organisation Society, founded by Sir
Horace Plunkett in 1894. JBY probably refers to C. M. Doughty,
whose sacred drama *Adam Cast Forth* had been published in 1908.
The Vagabonds was a men's club in New York. In his lecture (early
1906) on "Watts and the Method of Art", JBY had maintained that
"Art . . . seems to say . . . : 'Seek temptation; run to meet it; we are
here to be tempted'." The witty barrister was Thomas F. Delehanty,
who was prominent in Democratic politics.]

My dear Willie,

I am disappointed at your not getting the Lectureship; I think
had you got it I should have been tempted to go home. I think I
could have got home free of charge. Quinn suggests to me that I
should go home with him. I am very anxious to go home, but not at
present. Just now I am very hopeful. People here are very
appreciative. They *like pictures and portraits*. It is not pretense with
them, and I find I can please them. The people I am among are the
most intelligent in New York, and it follows without saying that
therefore they are not the richest, so I have to work for little money.
However, next week I shall be among richer people. I am to do a girl
whose sisters are all married to French noblemen. It is to be a pastel
and if it succeeds anything may happen.

I have heard not much further about that article in *Sinn Fein*,
except that Susan is very penitent. Of course she is. Such a thing was
quite alien to her – but it is not alien to her *to be put up* to doing
things.

Do you know the kind of paper "The Sun" is? I have been
taking it all along, as Quinn says it is the best edited paper in New
York. I have got tired of it, finding its tone *cynical and trivial*. It is
edited and written by Protestant Irishmen, Gregg, Charlie Fitzgerald,
the editor of the Morning *Sun* being someone, a Protestant from
Ulster, and its chief Director Laffin, brother to Mrs. Hartley
(authoress of "Flitters, Tatters and the Counsellor"), and therefore,
though Catholic, a man punctuated with the Dublin Protestant spirit.
He is a friend of Dr. Fitzgerald's.

So that this particular brand of cynicism is that with which we
are all so familiar in Dublin in Merrion Square and such haunts of the
well-to-do, and among barristers and Irish officials. It is the real
enemy. It has sterilized thought, and it is what makes George Russell
so depressing and so disappointing.

I think your mystics often regard the world as a poor sort of place, and from this disbelief in the higher possibilities of life on their little planet they get an exaggerated value for its lower possibilities. For that reason Doughton and George Russell are at once mystics and materialists. They are mystics, cynics, and materialists. I think G Russell has gradually become one of the most discouraging men I ever met. He would cure all the ills of Ireland sometimes with a dose of George Moore and always with a dose of Plunkett, and as to Literature it has no value for him except as a vehicle for mystical doctrine. If he had his way he would set up a priesthood and a church, and be as anxious for the material prosperity of his devotees as other churches are — and for the same reason.

At a luncheon party lately given by the Vagabonds (of which I am honorary member, the first and only one) I startled them all at the end of a long debate about theatre and Literature and their ethical purpose by saying that the summum bonum was not virtue nor pleasure or happiness — but *growth* — and that it was the cosmic movement towards growth and development working in the conscious mind that produced Literature, Art, Music, &c. In light of this principle, temptation becomes as motivation — and nothing is wrong except what contradicts our nature.

Of course I mean our *whole nature* — man's whole orchestra must be brought to the performance, not merely the big drum of animal energy, but all the instruments — flutes and violins and clarions and wailing violins — notes of desire and reflection and apprehension and hope. Of course this is all very vague, but the doctrine looks *in the right direction*.

In my lecture on Watts, do you remember I said we are all here to be tempted? Lust and spite are obviously violations of nature. Love and anger are often our strongest and completest fulfillment. I said in my speech that it followed from this principle that artists are the real leaders of mankind, and that when a clash occurred between the artist and the moralist, the moralist must give way, because the artist in his work embodies human desire.

The ecclesiastics and moralists would build the palace for man to live in and leave the artist some side chapel, making it as small and noisome as possible. But no, it is we who must build and who do build man's dwelling.

The end of Literature is to stimulate human nature, and we enjoy ourselves at the theatre only when we find ourselves growing and because we have been given growing weather.

The most potent instinct we have got is this instinct for growth. It is as strong in age as in youth, and the ground of all hopes, taking all kinds of shapes — and one reason why I like America is that here more than anywhere else growth is *recognized* at its true importance. It is the *real spirit of America*. Every man, woman, and child has got it, and like plants shut up in an enclosure they will *break the windows*, so that they get to know the kind of air and light which suits them. That is the explanation of American restlessness. Among plants have you not noticed what a wild spirit of adventure and curious experiment? It is the same with humans.

I dined with Quinn last night at Belmont. With him was a witty barrister named Delehanty. I tried to explain to him the difference to me between living in Dublin and living in New York. "Ah! I see," said Delehanty. "In Dublin it is hopeless insolvency. Here it is hopeful insolvency." Rather neat, I think, and quite true.

There are very nice people here, and it is not all difficult to find them. I like their mental activity and I like their naiveté. They are as naive as children or men of genius. No one can say that of Dublin folk.

> Yours Affectionately
> J. B. YEATS

N. B. In writing to you I am always a good deal distracted and disconcerted by the fear that you won't read my letters carefully — but this letter is important.

From SARA ALLGOOD

MS Berg Collection,   Dublin
New York Public Library   11 July 1909

[This letter and the two following refer to a recital by Miss Allgood at a London programme organized by Lady Alfred Lyttelton, wife of the Commander-in-Chief of the British Army in Ireland. Miss Allgoods's appearance, according to Miss Horniman, violated the "no politics" agreement she had made with the directors. Yeats noted in his Journal that "Miss Allgoods accepted an invitation to sing at a concert . . . without consulting me".]

Dear Mr. Yeats.

I have just come home, and got your letter. In the interests of the Theatre I shall write the letter dictated by you, but personally I consider it most humiliating that I should be compelled to do so. Of course this will be a *new* clause which should be in my contract. I hear Norreys Connell has resigned, is this a fact? I thank Lady Gregory of her kind letter, which came in the nick of time as I was frightfully depressed and upset over the attitude of Miss Horniman. I shall be here all next week, or if I make arrangements to go for a short holiday I shall let you know. Give my regard to Lady Gregory.

Goodbye
Yours sincerely
SARA ALLGOOD

P.S. Mrs Campbell was delighted when I told her you had attacked her play the "player Queen" I mean.

From SARA ALLGOOD

MS Berg Collection	Dublin
New York Public Library	11 July 1909

Dear Mr. Yeats. On reading your letter a second time I felt rather mystified, so I have written one to Miss Horniman which I enclose for your approval. I have also written an agreement, re, recitations to the Directors. I dont feel justified in saying to Miss Horniman that "I am sorry I did not inform her before I accepted the offer in London that is in question," so Ive left that out as no matter what happened I should never apply to her for permission to do anything I wanted to do or otherwise. I dont feel bound to her, nor am I. Mrs Campbell did not show me the letter she only *told* me of it so Ive altered that part slightly.

I am indeed very sorry that this is causing you such annoyance. I had no idea I was doing wrong and poor Mrs. Campbell thought she was doing me a good turn because you must remember I went in her place she had originally been asked but was too busy.

I would like to talk this over with you sometime when we meet, and I sincerely hope all these apologies to Miss H. will appease her. the Hon Mrs. Lyttleton has written also.

Goodbye
Yours Sincerely
SARA ALLGOOD

From SARA ALLGOOD

MS Berg Collection,   Dublin
New York Public Library   11 July 1909

Dear Mr. Yeats. I am in reciept of your letter. "I agree not to give any recitations or performances without permission of the Directors while I am under contract to them."

Yours Sincerely
SARA ALLGOOD

From A. E. F. HORNIMAN

                                             London
MS Yeats   10 December 1909

[Horniman was attempting to get released from her commitment to subsidize the Abbey through 1910. She asked Yeats and Lady Gregory to purchase her interest for £1428. On 10 December Yeats wrote to Lady Gregory that he had seen "Miss Horniman yesterday" and that "she was very cross because we had not submitted to her our second statement" (*L* 544). A note across the top of Horniman's letter suggests that Yeats forwarded it to Lady Gregory: "I replied to this very much as you did. I said how could we accept for a company that did not yet exist. Her answer came by 'express' this morning."]

Dear Managing Director,
        As it could only have been Shaw or Lady Gregory who saw no necessity for me to know the exact wording of the appeal I have written to them both. I must have my conditions formally accepted in writing by both Directors before the appeal be issued. The conditions as to rents, rates, taxes, insurance etcetra have been explained to you very often & they are quite simple. Without this I might find myself involved very seriously in regard to these payments. What you & Lady Gregory's reasons may be I do not know & I do not ask. But an offer which is not even discussed but the benefits taken & the conditions ignored cannot stand. The extra payment to Fay of which I arranged the conditions with you & then found that they were not being carried out by Lady Gregory is a case in point. You may be as annoyed as you like about this but you know as well as possible that I have every right to demand a formal acceptance of the conditions from the Directors to whom I offer

them. If you or Lady Gregory refuse them, that means resignation from office for the refuser or refusal by both of my offer. In that case I shall dispose of the Abbey as best I can after Xmas 1910.

Yours sincerely

A. E. F. HORNIMAN

From A. E. F. HORNIMAN

London

MS Yeats 13 December 1909

[Horniman refers to the 1909 *Samhain*, which was privately issued in three states in 1909–10. As with the previous letter to Horniman, Yeats added a note and forwarded this letter to Lady Gregory: "The unlucky statement which seems to have caused all this was something like this. She demanded appeal of which some one must have told her. I said we were in a great hurry & some one said that as the part about our offer was in substance unchanged it was not necessary to delay things by sending it to you! I had thought to turn her suspicion on to the unknown.

You had better send this letter back to me.

God knows what she means about Fay. She wrote me some days ago about some correspondence years ago with Fred Ryan. WBY."]

Dear Managing Director,

The serious mis-statement regarding "leases" in that appeal must not be published nor distributed in any form whatsoever.

I am awaiting an answer to the letter posted to Coole last Friday. If Lady Gregory sends me no response direct, I must conclude that my offer is refused.

If Samhain be already printed the expense of suppressing the whole edition should be born by the person who prevented me from seeing a proof. If my offer be accepted a full & detailed statement with figures must be printed on the appeal in a form either approved of or (preferably) signed by me.

Future letters to me on this subject must be signed by both Directors.

Yours Sincerely

A. E. F. HORNIMAN

From GORDON CRAIG

MS Yeats
                                                    Florence
                                                    [?late 1909]

[Craig adopted "John Semar" (a character in Javanese shadow plays) as a pseudonym for the editor of *The Mask*. The regular issue of *Samhain* planned for 1909 never appeared. The tale of the dead man and the vagabond is Synge's *In the Shadow of the Glen*.]

Dear Yeats.

I might as well ask you why in heaven you write to me on a typewriting machine. Besides I did not write to you as John Semar — Is "Samhain" dead then? But you might try a reply to the questions sent you by the "*Mask*" editor even though you have not seen Sicilians. They are wonderful & my dear poet, they are nearest approached by your Irish players.

I no longer concern myself with the problems of the modern theatre as I have found a further problem more worthy spilling ones souls blood for, but if I were to speak of the old dead I should speak most lovingly of that little group in the Pot of Broth & the tale of the dead man who rose up & chatted it over with the vagabond — In their wonderful way they still *compel* me to glance back at them — and the Sicilians who surpass them by aiming lower, also cause me to stand stock still on my road & look lovingly at their retreating figures — ah they are all so sweet so beautiful & dear — with their babyways & their mothers madness in them —

In Europe I often speak of you — saying how in Ireland the only theatre of England dwells — blaming you & lauding you & your boys at the same time & leaving at the end of the talk the feeling in the Poles — Russians — Finns — Italians — & the rest that you are a courageous & lovely lot. You ought to make part of our circle.

I go to Warsaw soon to do some work & then to Moscow & Berlin — after that possibly to england — but ——. or Ireland ——? but ——.

No I am not patriotic & I cannot feel attracted home — I need & must have affection & enthusiastic followers & you all of you want to lead — without knowing where.

Well — bless you —

                                                    EGC

I had lost your address —

From GORDON CRAIG

London

TS Yeats 25 January 1910

[Craig discussed the case for the model he had built in a letter of 18 January. His mother was the famous actress Dame Ellen Alice Terry.

James Carew (actually Usselman) had become Miss Terry's third husband in 1907. Yeats did "reward" Craig with an essay called "The Tragic Theatre", published in *The Mask* (Octber 1910). Somewhat altered versions were reprinted in Yeats's *Plays for an Irish Theatre* (1911) and *The Cutting of an Agate* (1912).]

My dear Yeats.

Very good, the case can be kept within the dimensions you want. I daresay it will get even into the Office door, and all shall be as you want.

Now about the conditions. Will you please not show the scene in Dublin before the end of July, and before using it in England, will you communicate with my mother, for what rights there are in England, she must possess. If you propose to take it to America or anywhere else out of Ireland, except England, where it is more or less my mother's property, I must ask you first to communicate with me, for I shall probably make arrangements in other countries later on and care must be taken to infringe these foreign rights, or I shall be getting into trouble.

When you write to my mother I think it would be politic on your part to address yourself to Mr. Carew. So much for the conditions.

Perhaps later on you will find it possible to more reward me by writing something about it that can be published in Florence and elsewhere, and a tiny line in your programme would also flatter me very much.

I will send you full details about the working of these screens, etc., when I come to the end of my work here, for every day I discover new things about them. It will be to your advantage to have them as small as you can bear them, for the higher you go the thicker wood you have to use and the heavier they become, and in my opinion 12 ft. to 14 ft. high is as high as is desirable.

By the time you have built your new National Theatre I shall have a better thing for you which shall be as high as you like.

Your little model is coming out very nicely, and you must be

prepared to give a good deal of patience and faith to the making of
the other screens when you come to make them. They are full of
many difficulties, but if your carpenter follows my directions he will
forego them. In a few months I shall know even more about them
than I do now for I shall have been once more to Russia and shall
have learnt much from their craftsmen.

I leave for Italy in a couple of days — Write me when the model
arrives — to Florence
Arena Goldoni

Yours
GORDON CRAIG

From GORDON CRAIG

Moscow
MS Yeats   April 1910

[Craig was in Moscow to plan the staging of *Hamlet* produced by
Konstantin Stanislavsky at the Art Theatre. The pictures for Bullen
were four designs by Craig for *Plays for an Irish Theatre*. Edward
John Trelawney, author of the popular but not always reliable
Recollections of the Last Days of Shelley and Byron (1858) and
Records of Shelley, Byron and the Author (1878), was fascinated by
Shelley's silent coming and going.]

My dear Yeats.

I shall not be able to write to you clearly about the scene until I
get back to Florence — for Hamlet is overwhelming — Ophelia was
never so drowned as I shall be ... What I should send you are
directions to help your carpenters etc. and to you some notes of any
hidden bothers & traps to be avoided. You must send me some
pictures too —never mind how bad the photos are ... I shall be able
to see —

Your shallow stage — praise heaven for its shallowness. This
"depth" here will help to sink me.

If I were you I'd make my stage *shallower* not deeper ... it is a
condition of stage to be feared but faced & great things can come of
it I believe.

Yes, I must send you some hints about the costumes. I am
having a hundred experiments with these this very week — they are
not easy.

Notes about light too, if I can get useful ones down on paper. That's very good about the shaddows! I am having Fortinbras whole army this way too. . I hope it can become rhythmic – the movement – but – .

Very good about the pictures for Bullen if you arrange something.

Scenes & costume

Have you yet found a way to get your actors on the stage almost without us knowing how they came – keeping them *quite still* (quite!) & removing them as mysteriously. Trelawney I think writing of Shelley describes this way of vanishing & appearing – "where is he" – ?

– "he comes & goes like a spirit no one knows when or where"

I am hopelessly hunted at present by little circumstances or would give myself up to consider a particular play – (one of yours for instance) – without movement of any kind.

A hundred greetings

I hope to write you a useful letter from Florence

GORDON CRAIG

From JOHN DRINKWATER

MS Berg Collection,   Birmingham
New York Public Library   1 May 1910

[Poet, actor, dramatist, and critic, Drinkwater became general manager of the Birmingham Repertory Theatre, which began with amateur productions by a company known as the Pilgrim Players. Yeats visited Maud Gonne in May at her home near Calvados in Normandy.]

My dear Mr. Yeats,

Many thanks for your letter. I can assure you that all our people feel very greatly honoured by your visitation.

I have made enquiries and find that they could, with one or two possible exceptions, get housed by friends, so that our only expense would be train fares, with one or two incidental items. These would amount to something under £20 – probably about £16 altogether. If our performances could be arranged for Friday and Saturday, it would be a great convenience to some of our men who might find it difficult to get away in the middle of the week. They are all very keen, and want to begin rehearsals at once. Will you let me know as soon as possible whether the performances can be arranged, as we should wish to leave nothing undone that would justify your kindness?

Would it be possible for the Company to have a couple of tickets each to give to their friends who put them up? I don't know whether this request is irregular, but I venture it on the ground that the saving in lodging bills would be very considerable.

Good wishes for your Normandy holiday. Your visit was a great treat to us, and your commendation of the Pilgrim was most encouraging.

My wife sends her kindest regards.

Very Sincerely Yours
JOHN DRINKWATER

Our company would number just 20, and there would be a 'staff' of 3.

From LENNOX ROBINSON

MS Berg Collection,   Dublin
New York Public Library   [13 May 1910]

[Horniman was incensed at the failure of the Abbey to close on Saturday, 7 May, after the death of King Edward VII late on Friday night. Yeats was in Normandy, and Lady Gregory at Coole. When Robinson wired to ask "What am I to do?" her reply, "Should close through courtesy", came too late to stop the matinée. Robinson also chose to present the evening programme, and Miss Horniman demanded his dismissal. Padraic Colums's *Thomas Muskerry* was produced that weekend. Seaghan Barlow was scene-painter and carpenter for many years. John F. Larchet, director of music, was apparently preparing background music for Yeats's *The Green Helmet*. Robinson's *Harvest* was presented on Thursday, 19 May. Maire O'Neill (actually Molly Allgood) played leading roles in the Abbey for many years. Sydney J. Morgan played minor roles and doubled as prompter.]

Dear Mr Yeats

You have heard from Lady Gregory all about this fuss with Miss Horniman. Her letter and our explanation appeared in all the papers, here last night and this morning. I hope this will be the end of it. I suppose I should have closed down on Sat. but without hearing from Lady Gregory I didn't like to. Colum's play was certainly a success. There have been good notices in 'Leader' and 'T.C.D.' There has also been a correspondence in 'Independent.' I am sorry you won't be here to see my play but you will see it, I suppose in London. They are rehersing very keenly — of course we were rushed for time but I think it will be quite presentable by Thursday. The new scene is nearly finished and Shaun painted the blue back-cloth to-day. I only got the music for the 'Helmet' to-day. Larchet has been so slow about it so it may not get a good performance next week, but it will be good practice for London. We can discuss Miss O'Neills salary in Cambridge and Morgan wants money for prompting.

Yours sincerely
S. L. ROBINSON

From GORDON CRAIG

Florence

TS Yeats   18 May 1910

[The well-known actress Gertrude Kingston opened the Little Theatre (London) on 11 October 1910. See headnote to letter of 25 January 1910 for information about Yeats's article.]

My dear Yeats,

I have been carrying about your letters with me intending to answer them, and when one goes on intending nothing ever comes of it but a finer intention, sometimes too fine to destroy.

I have got back to Florence somehow or other and feel in the very worst mood for being practical because one wants a large staff to begin.

Yes, if you could come up to Moscow that would be delightful. Several people are coming up and I will let you know exactly when the date is fixed.

I saw Gertrude Kingston before I left England. I doubt if I shall be able to do anything for her. My experience in Moscow spoils me pretty well for anything in England except two millions and elbow-room.

It would be nice to get the volume of your plays which I shall enjoy rereading. I have not heard anything from Bullen.

Can you let *The Mask* have the introduction by the middle of August so that they can get it properly printed, proofs sent to you, etc? and may they quote the few lines you write about *The Mask* in your letter of the 25th?

In Moscow some of the screens are 15 feet high and some are 24 feet high, which begins to be rather stupendous.

I must write to you something about the costumes soon and make an effort to do the drawings, but at present it is too much of an effort and I think the results would be bad.

Some of these days when your theatre has got a lot of money to spare you must invite me over for a month and we will talk of nothing else but ordinary technical things to do on the stage & make experiments there & then with the machine; but you must give me the devil of a time or I shall get terribly depressed.

Is there anything on earth more depressing than to contemplate the modern theatre?

> Yours,
> GORDON CRAIG

From A. E. F. HORNIMAN

MS National Library of Ireland

London
18 May 1910

Dear Director,

On Tuesday 9th at night I received the returns which gave only circumstantial evidence as to the opening on Saturday. I wired next morning to Coole, Henderson & Manager. "Opening last Saturday was disgraceful. Performance on day of funeral would stop subsidy automatically."

Letters were received by me on May 11th in reply to my telegrams. These called forth wires to Henderson & Coole. "Subsidy ceases now unless Directors & Robinson express regret in Dublin press that decent example was not followed."

Having by my first wire intimated my attitude & given twenty-four hours margin to the Directors & management to take action themselves, I wrote to the Irish press & the Stage & Era.

The remarks tacked on to the ordinary paragraph in advance may be read as a regret that the opening was accidental, a regret that it was not deliberate. A telegram to me on Friday night when every theatre manager was expecting to close immediately would have been the right thing.

I did not follow my impulse on Saturday morning to wire a message, fearing that it would cause bad feeling & so *prevent* closing because of *my* request.

I have never had any information from the Directors that Robinson was Manager & I must hold them responsible for the agent they selected to leave in charge. My course of action leaves it possible for the Patent to be renewed, otherwise the affair would have been used to oppose the petition successfully & I should have appeared to condone the action. The injury was done by the person who opened the Abbey & who forgot the Patent. I expected your blame knowing that I did not deserve it. The Directors can save the situation but they cannot expect to re-new the Patent & to keep on Robinson too.

Yours sincerely
A. E. F. HORNIMAN

From GORDON CRAIG

Apennine Mountians
10 July 1910

MS Yeats

[T. Stanley Chappell was Chairman of the board of Chappell & Co. Ltd, London music publishers, concert agents, and piano manufacturers. *Hamlet* was not produced in Moscow until 8 January 1912. Craig quarrelled over the production and did not return for further work.]

My dear Yeats.

I have Deirdre & Green Helmet & thank you. And that proposed Opera – Chappell – is an interesting idea. Only in Opera are notes to the music – & who's going to rise to writing *that*. It all depends on this & whether I have the time I should want to give to the work. It seems to me that it would be folly to do anything that was wanted in a hurry. I would want to give six months to it at least, and even then unless I stage managed the other operas as well I should be unable to get our wishes through the stupid barrier of the *other* stage manager.

It is always so.

But perhaps Chappell are going to propose to me that I take the whole stage management of the season. That is what they will do if they are sensible. & if the musician *is* a musician London can expect to see something like an opera when "The Countess Kathleen" comes before them. What fun ... the idea is exciting. Why not advise Chappell to invite me over for a month in August to discuss the whole scheme?

Letters are useless. I went to Moscow by invitation & we talked & talked & after 3 weeks a glimmer of light was seen by both parties! Ecce! My only fear is that the Chappell people may not understand the difficulties & will go to some "old stager" for enlightenment who will advice them "to do as was done last time." If you come to Moscow I'll meet you & help you through with the language. I know "thank you" "very good" "very bad" — & they'll also understand when I say in good English "This is Yeats of the Irish National Theatre". The slope of a stage doesn't matter much for my scene though flat stages are desirable. In 10 years there will be very few sloping stages I fancy.

Yours
GORDON CRAIG

I shall probably come to England after "Hamlet" has been produced & prepare the next Moscow play in London — so that I can see something more of the exact position of things.

At this distance the London Theatre seems to be nothing — but I want a closer view to see if one dare waste time on it.

E. G. C.

From EDMUND GOSSE

MS Berg Collection,   London
New York Public Library   13 August 1910

[Gosse was largely responsible for getting the Civil List pension of £150 for Yeats. Herbert H. Asquith was Prime Minister, George V was King.]

My dear Yeats

I was very truly rejoiced at the result of the affair, which indeed was settled by the Prime Minister in an immediate reply to my letter to him. But I was forbidden to tell you, — until the King had given his consent. Now all is right, and I hope it will help you to enjoy life, and continue to write beautiful things, long after I have passed away.

> Believe me always sincerely yours
> EDMUND GOSSE

From GORDON CRAIG

Florence

MS Yeats   6 September 1910

[After the Moscow production in December, Seaghan Barlow and Joseph Holloway had considerable difficulty adapting Craig's screens to the Abbey stage.]

My dear Yeats.

I am so glad that the costume note is useful. I will send the proscenium note in a day or two.

Bad news arrives from Russia that Stanislavsky has typhoid fever. It will take 5 or 7 weeks for him to recover. Hamlet is postponed for a couple of months at any rate.

I could well come to Ireland now for a fortnight, only I am so wretchedly poor that you'd have to pay my fares to & fro & give me some hutch to sleep in.

Keep the news about Stanislavsky to yourself please.

Your carpenters excitement over the screens has done me more good than a doctor could. Tell him so, & say that I hope the handling of the screens will prove easy to him & that if he evolves some special method for opening & closing them rapidly & smoothly & safely & will let me know about it. When I left them in Moscow they had commenced a kind of "screen drill" — but I have not seen results.

Im so glad to hear that your "Deirdre" is capturing their hearts in Cork . . how much good the right success of ones plans does one.

I wont forget the notes about the painting.

> Yours
> GORDON CRAIG.

From JOHN O'MAY

Kuala Kangsar, Malay States

MS Yeats   23 November 1910

[O'May misquotes from "The Twisting of the Rope and Hanrahan the Red": " 'Look,' he cried, 'at the serpent dance, the dance made by the wise Druids'." Also misquoted slightly is the excerpt O'May enclosed from "The White People", in *The House of Souls* (1906) by Arthur Machen. The passage is about "an old game called 'Troy Town,' in which one had to dance, and wind in and out on a pattern in the grass. . . ." O'May's "Playing the Wer-Beast: A Malay Game" appeared in *Folklore* (September 1910). It was followed by a supplementary letter, "Playing the Wer-Beast", in June 1911. Mrs Annie Besant, prominent theosophist, was editor of *Lucifer* and President of the Society from 1907 to 1933. Sabine Baring-Gould was the author of *Curious Myths of the Middle Ages* (1866–8). Yeats's discussion of "the others" appeared in "The Prisoners of the Gods", *The Nineteenth Century* (January 1898). O'May had seen "Rosa Alchemica" in *The Secret Rose*. Roth's *The Natives of Sarawak and British North Borneo* (2 vols.) was published in 1896.]

Dear Sir,

I have just been reading your "The Secret Rose" and was struck by a reference to "the serpent dance, made by the wise Druids" (p. 148, 1897 Ed.). I wonder if I am right in connecting this with a passage in Arthur Machen's "A House of Souls," of which I enclose a copy? And if so, whether I may so far presume on your good nature as to ask where, if anywhere, I can get to know more about it. I am keenly interested in the point because this is the only parallel I know of to a most extraordinary game which is played by Malay boys all over the Peninsula, and which consists in turning a boy, as they say, into a musang — a kind of civet-cat. One of my chief interests is the gleaning of ancient ideas, beliefs and methods of magic among the Malays, and this is quite the strangest thing I have met. As it had never been described before, I sent in an account of it to "Folklore," in which it will appear in, I think, the December issue. Briefly, the subject is hypnotised by a prolonged swaying of his body and the monotonous chanting of certain rhymes; when his feet feel cold or he is no longer ticklish, the process is complete, and "the spirit of the musangs" has taken possession of him. (I should hesitate to say that the Malays, like Mrs. Besant, believe in collective animal-souls: for I have met no other trace of such an idea). Then his companions rush off, imitating the clucking of fowls, animals which are the natural prey of the musang. The subject starts up and pursues, and it goes ill with any whom he catches, for he bites and tears as a musang tears the body of a fowl. He uses only nails and teeth, and a blow in the face does not in the least stop him. He is said to catch and devour genuine fowls, as the maniacs whom Baring Gould describes in his monograph on werewolves used, in France and elsewhere, to slaughter and consume the flesh of domestic cattle. He also climbs to the summits of trees as an ordinary musang would, and leaps from branch to branch in a quite marvellous way — performing feats impossible to his waking self in the manner which marks somnambulism, hypnosis, intoxication and other abnormal states. His natural soul is recalled by the sound of his name, and this, I am told, should be done within an hour or so, or he turns wholly into a musang, body and all.

Constantly one finds the closest resemblances between what are called, for want of a less offensive word, the superstitions of the Malays and those of Europe, and that not only in the great universal ideas such as witchcraft and its methods, or the were-animal (here it is a tiger) but also in details in which one could hardly expect coincidence on general grounds and can scarcely suppose there has been any communication, however indirect. I believe the "voice folk" of the Malays are purely native, yet, they are quite singularly like "the others" which you once described in the "Nineteenth Century," and, I suppose, in the "Irish Fairy Tales" I ordered a while ago; and like European fairies in general. Yet the elves of Iceland and other Northern nations are too old, I think, to have come from India or the East. There remains, of course, the hypothesis that they are literally real, but that I do not at present believe at all. Mysticism in various forms has interested me much, but only as a spectator. I have not the soul of an artist, and yet I feel towards these things in some degree the attitude which you suggest at the beginning of "Rosa Alchemica."

Dancing, by the way, is not unknown to the Malay races as a method of developing the ecstatic state (H. Ling Roth, Natives of Sarawak I 279).

I have no excuse whatever for troubling you with my query, but if you can and will guide me to further knowledge of the serpent dance, or of Celtic magic in general, I shall be very greatly obliged. And if there should be any matters in which you would like to know what is done and thought at this end of the world, I should be more than happy to assist you to the best of my power.

I am, Sir,
Sincerely Yours,
JOHN O'MAY

From GORDON CRAIG

                                        Florence
MS Yeats   29 November 1910

[In *Plays for an Irish Theatre* (1911) Yeats included Craig's sketch of the masked Fool for *The Hour-Glass*. Craig refers to Charles Frohman's productions in the Duke of York's Theatre. Otto Brahm founded the Freie Bühne; Max Reinhardt was well known for highly stylized productions which dwarfed the actor.]

My dear Yeats.

I'll be over before long & we can do something about the masks then — at this distance it doesn't seem safe or practical.

It would be folly to play with so serious a part of the theatre — & until I can get to work upon the mask itself its best to leave it quietly alone. After I had sent you that 1st fools mask I wondered if I had done right — & in regard to that I beg you to send me the *actual mask your people make* before using it on the stage. By all means add the Hour Glass Fool into your book — by all means & I'll try & design a Blindmans mask — but not for actual use on stage *till I can make the thing itself, & show the actors how to use it.*

Don't let them mess up your Kings Threshold in Berlin. Germany is impossible & consciousless — would howl & daub the thing as Frohman does. Wait! & go over with your own company. When you want to go — when you are ready — I'll send you to the right persons — but avoid Reinhardt & Brahm* as you would avoid vulgarity.

I am most absurdly BUSY with a lot of little things having to be done, or I would have answered you at once.

Bullen has sent me no proofs to see. I hope he send *brown* ink proofs! not *black*. I am very keen to see them.

                                        Yours
                                        GORDON CRAIG

* two directors who fleece you & score with your skin.

From A. E. F. HORNIMAN

Manchester

MS National Library of Ireland   11 January 1911

Dear Sir,

As the Directors have now possession of the Abbey I must protest against bills being sent on to me like the enclosed. Unless the £1000 due to me be paid before Jan 23rd, when I shall return here from London, I must consult my lawyer as to taking proceedings against the Directors. They have possession of my property & have not paid for it. Any quibble as to my not paying the subsidy would injure them in the public eye. They accepted my condition as to no politics at the Abbey & broke this condition on May 7th. They made no application for the subsidy, they made no public protest against my letter to the press, they did not protest at the remarks reported at the application for the renewal of the Patent & that £400 was not in the Accountant's statement in December as a debt. This would I believe be called "consent" by the law & at any rate unless I am paid there will be a scandal of the Directors' own making which will damage the future of the Abbey.

Yours truly

A. E. F. HORNIMAN

From GORDON CRAIG

Paris

MS Yeats   [? February 1911]

[Yeats won his "Manchester fight" with Miss Horniman over the payment of her subsidy to the Abbey. The French edition of *The Mask* was not published. The "Moses play" was Lady Gregory's *The Deliverer* (produced on 12 January 1911). Craig had returned £100 to Sir Herbert Beerbohm Tree who had sent the money for designs for *Macbeth* but had suggested alterations Craig would not accept.]

My dear Yeats.

Thank you for your letter from Woburn Buildings about screens.

1st. Manchester fight. Let Mask know whenever you want anything put in about your fight there. Send the paragraph or article & if in time it goes in.

2nd. *"The Mask"* comes out in French — from Paris offices in about a month. So send duplicate of anything you want put in.

3rd. I shall set up the scene as you have it for Moses play & have a look at it.

Thank you for leading article Irish Times — I have seen nothing in the English papers — was anything said — I escaped from Tree by the back wall — I left the tails of my coat in his mouth — the tails alone were worth £100 — he has the cheque.

These wonderful people about the "Mask" of Fool I *will* write soon. Don't use it just yet for every reason. I can't write here & now on so important a subject because I am in a room littered with mss & proof sheets of "Le Masque."

Thank you for "On Baile's Strand." I'll read that after work hours. I look forward to delicious moments & to carry away its perfume which shall stay around me ever after. I saw my first performance of Moliere yesterday at Comedie Francaise. The ease of it all is very mighty — "Les Femmes Ridicules"

Scene: You say "at last one composes like a painter." That expresses very much but could one not say "like a stage manager" or to compromise a little "like an architect" — For one must just take care of that "very knowing overflowing easygoing" desire to break loose into grouping like a painter — a Daumier or a Rembrandt — & must must must first find the law: The audience should be driven out of the theatre by the just grouping — To appease the audience by shaddows & highlights — by profiles of easy apprehension — NO —

I'm wanting to read a lecture delivered by Mr John Grey on "The Modern Actor." Have you it & if so would you lend it me.

Yours
GORDON CRAIG

From GORDON CRAIG

MS Yeats

Paris
March 1911

[Craig quotes from the Blind Man's speech, the last in the play.]

My dear Yeats.

I have the pictures all ready to send off to Bullen but they have not gone off yet because I have been busy — bothered by many thousand *little* difficulties — etc etc etc. You know the situation —

Added to that I am singlehanded for the time being – & "Masque" beginning to make its appearance – These things happen – I see from the Daily Mail that England is beginning to understand that foreign imitation goods are not as valuable as is supposed –

Well – All this to explain I am not asleep nor have forgotten these things – But what I wanted to write you about was something different – Having no time or strength yesterday to go on with my labours & wanting the only refreshment, I took out your "On Baile's Strand" to read.

For the 1st time – for I couldn't read it before – in middle of work & worries – And I cannot tell you at all the refreshment it has given me. Of all your works that I have read it seems to me the largest – most most splendid – a great play – I was carried along by its waves & thrown exhilarated upon the beach & the noise of the back wash is it so called – that soft noise of the water departing from the embrace with the land – sang on in my ears for long after – even now I hear it

"The ovens will be full – we will put our handsss into the ovensss –

Ah it is a great & wonderful play & stands high up above all the Irish plays. Someday I must persuade people I know to come & offer themselves to your theatre & its service. I think only fine actors can interpret such a play – men with finest strength in them – that which gives up so as to create – Its men you want, that first of all. No other play of yours that I have read is the force & the tenderness so closely joined – the two are almost one – its lovely.

CRAIG.

From JOHN O'MAY

Kuala Kangsar, Malay States

MS Yeats   6 April 1911

[Yeats preserved an offprint of O'May's article about the Wer-Beast. W. W. Skeat's *Malay Magic* was published in 1900. Dr Hereward Carrington, the author of *Hindu Magic* (1909) and many books on spiritualism, was a prominent member of the SPR. Completed and published after the death of its distinguished author, Frederic W. H. Myers, *Human Personality and Its Survival after Death* (1903) was

well known to Yeats and is in fact still highly regarded, especially in
the SPR, of which Myers was a founding member (in 1882) and
President (in 1900). H. F. Hall's *The Soul of a People* (1898) was "a
study of the life and belief of the Burmese". O'May was searching for
Yeat's *Irish Fairy Tales* (1892). Lady Gregory's *Visions and Beliefs in
the West of Ireland* with two essays and notes by Yeats did not
appear until 1920.]

Dear Mr Yeats,
    Your letter has given me enormous pleasure. It is, I think,
remarkable that a man so busy as you are, and busy with such
important things, should find time to write to a stranger as you have
done.
    My account of *main hantu musang* (the first attempt at a
description of the whole thing) was printed in "Folk Lore" last
September, and I sent you an off print (through Messrs Lawrence &
Jellicoe) which should have reached you in December. If it lost its
way I hope you will let me know, as I should like to send you
another.
    What you tell me of the power some Irish people have been
believed to possess of taking the form of a serpent is exciting – it
brings one close to the actual person who did whatever really was
done. In this country one can frequently get *near* the wonder-
worker, but I have not be able hitherto to *see* him perform his
marvels. Few men are credited with special powers, and when one
hears of a *pawang* with unusual gifts he always appears either to be
dead or to have left the district. I have had descriptions from eye
witnesses of various feats of telekinesis. In one case an old pawang
was seen to make his betel boa slide along the floor towards his hand.
In another a conical fishing trap of basketwork set on end rocked
violently from side to side, untouched, and four men could not stop
it – the is obviously like the turning tables and riotous furniture of
European seances (Sekat describes the same thing, *Malay Magic*
p 468). Another man would set a couple of coconut scrapers fighting
furiously with prodigious din – and the scratches they made on the
walls were visible next day. (A scraper is a sort of stool usually made
roughly in the shape of a cat, from one end of which rises an iron rod
ending in a toothed circle of iron: you sit astride the wooden body
and rub the inside of a half coconut on the teeth.) Another kept
some jointed dolls of very light wood or pith dancing together before
a number of people for a considerable time. In this threads might be

used, as in many European tricks. A Javanese who, if he is to be believed, had fasted completely during five years of retirement as a hermit in a mountain cave near here, once laid a small dagger on the top of the funnel of an unlighted lamp placed upon a table, and it revolved slowly while no one touched it or stood near it.

These things Malays tell me they have seen. Other feats they have heard of. Second sight and clairvoyance are attributed to (Muhammadan) saints, of whom a good many are now alive in the country. They are mostly foreigners — Javanese, Arabs, etc.

The whole idea of magical power inherent in a man's self, as distinct from control over spirits, is not, I believe Malay at all but imported from India through Java, and the Malays have not developed it much. The Peninsula is not a good region for studying that sort of thing.

The hypnotising of audiences, the explanation you mention, is an uncomfortably elastic solution, but I suppose there is no doubt that it is in some cases the right one. One hears of latecomers at Indian performances whom the juggler had not seen and who simply saw nothing of the feats presented to the other people around. As for merely material miracles, when one considers how totally in-explicable seem many of the things done by conjurers in London — how slate-writing was reproduced, for instance — one concludes that the only possible course is to ignore them altogether. There is a little book on *Hindu Magic* by H. Carrington which explains the mango-tree trick among others. The mango seed is large, and the mango-leaf is peculiar in that after being rolled up it can be opened out without showing any traces; Mr. Carrington says the whole "tree" is in the leaf to begin with and opened out bit by bit under the cloth.

Is not your experience, when you imagined your arm as in a sling and it was so seen by another person, covered by telepathy? The most sceptical cannot doubt that telepathy is a fact. And not only is mental communication sometimes easy and fairly common between people who are united by close ties — intimate friends, sisters, and so on — but it sometimes occurs in a capricious and apparently accidental manner. It explains an enormous lot. The impression which remains in my mind from what I have read on spiritism, of which the most important part was F. W. H. Myers's wonderful book on *Human Personality*, is that the subliminal consciousness — whatever that may mean, but it certainly means something important — and telepathy cover most of the genuine evidence, and as for what remains, one is certainly justified in allowing a wide margin for our ignorance of the nature and working of the human mind. These two ideas of a subconscious self and telepathy explain so very much which otherwise must have seemed to point unmistakeably to spiritual agency that it seems exceedingly likely that whatever activities still seem non-human will yet be otherwise accounted for. My own nearest approach to a ghostly experience is described in the enclosed cutting, which perhaps you will kindly send back (at your convenience — taking the phrase literally: I have no reason to want it quickly), as I have not another copy. In Fielding Hall's "Soul of a People," (p. 251) there is an account of what I take to be the same thing. Such phenomena are quite common.

Your juxtaposition of obsession with the assumption of a character gave me the thrill that accompanies a really new idea. And your conception of "a power which can work either inward and cause an obsession, which may be either animal or human; or outward, and cause an apparent change of shape" raises all the curiosity there is in me. I have been accustomed to regard obsession, whether among the religions of the past in Europe or in asylums or among Malays — an interesting temporary case occurred here last week — as due to "divided personality," another idea which Myers elaborated and popularised in his "Human Personality." But I am not mad enough to imagine I know that you are wrong, and I am on the inexperienced side of that age of thirty after which cynics say that a fundamental change of a man's point of view is impossible.

Your book of Irish Fairy Tales did not reach me. It was ordered from a list of second hand books, and what they sent me was a ghastly attempt to make children learn natural history about wasps and spiders by translating it into fairy stories. Meantime the other book was sold. I shall be on the watch for your and Lady Gregory's work on Fairy Beliefs, and I trust it will see the light.

The note on civit-cat-possession in "Folk-Lore" was my first attempt to publish anything concerning Malay beliefs. Material is always coming in, and I don't feel ready to write much. But new and unpublished material "burns a hole in one's pocket" and I have used some of my notes in making a comparison between Malay and European beliefs. This took the form of a series of newspaper articles, and I am sending you off prints, as parts of them might interest you. They are not ambitious, but can claim to be original work, for statements about local things come from my own collection except where acknowledgment is implied and for the

European side I abstained rather from using the obvious sources. I have references for all I have taken from printed matter; and if there should be any point among those mentioned on which you would wish to have more information which, living among the Malays, I might be able to give, I should be more than happy to do what I can toward supplying it. The reference to you in No. I is to your article in "The Nineteenth Century" January 1898. IX & X are on Malay Fairies, which I believe have never been dealt with before. You needn't read these things if you find them dull—obviously. I hope I have not already bored you. If you were to put yourself out, from politeness, to answer this letter when you were not really inclined to do so or were over busy, the matter would lie heavy on my conscience.

I am

Very Sincerely Yours
JOHN O'MAY

From GORDON CRAIG

Alassio, Italy
MS Yeats   1 May 1911

[Edward J. M. D. Plunkett, Lord Dunsany, wrote several plays for the Abbey at Yeats's request. The stage carpenter was Barlow. Craig insisted that his mother, Ellen Terry, should approve the use of his screens by the Abbey Company at the Royal Court Theatre. Craig refers to the school of acting established at the Abbey by Nugent Monck, the organizer of the Norwich players. Craig's school, in the Arena Goldini, Florence, opened in 1913 and closed with the outbreak of the First World War. The reference to *The Countess Cathleen* may be related to the plans for the greatly revised version produced at the Abbey for the first time on 14 December 1911.]

My dear Yeats.

Your two letters in one cover. I don't understand a word of what you write about Dunsany. Who is he — & why do you write me of him — It sounds a nice name anyhow — and what will *he* do to my screens — grace or disgrace them? The thought that his work (if he's a carpenter) should go into my screens is pleasant enough — but Lord, he might be something else — & one never knows —

In your other letter you tell me you got your stage carpenter to make some gold doors go into my screens. Good God — is it possible

I omitted to leave exit & entrance ways in my patent. If I did so I must certainly put it right — but please Mister Yeats your carpenter mustn't. *He mustn't add or take away anything whatsoever*, but if any fault is found in said screens *I will always be glad to do what I can to rectify it.*

By the way has the Court Theatre a flat stage? — & have you written to Miss Terry about England & the screens — ? Let me know will you. We mustn't have any complications about the use of the invention — I anticipate a manager in London using it before long — & of course frontiers have to be respected over such a thing as this — Still if you want sufficiently to take the thing to London arrangements better be made at once — but *at present* no one has the right to use it there but my mother. You will remember I wrote to you about that point a very long time ago. If you finally do arrange to use the screens in London you could perfectly well use them for "Kings Threshold" with a couple of rehearsals. I remember seeing the performance & the thing adapts itself exactly to your requirements. I could in two rehearsals without upsetting your past work adapt my screens exactly to the scene necessary. I should also suggest *one* simple change of light which would I believe prove valuable.

It is interesting to hear that you have now a school of acting. I think it is a very good move — without a school one cannot learn — it is for this reason that I am determined to get a school for the study of the art of the Theatre — there is so much one must learn — I dare say I shall be the only pupil in the place & the 20 others will do the teaching — & what they teach me I will execute & it shall go hard but I will better the instruction.

You go to London you say to meet the musician who is to set Countess Cathleen to music — Is that the Opera you wrote me I must stage: Did the people there agree to that condition — ? I am eager to know — I suppose it must be so for I think you said you would not agree to anything else. Its most awfully kind of you & as soon as I hear from you I shall get to work.

Yours
GORDON CRAIG

From SARA ALLGOOD

MS Berg Collection,   Stratford-upon-Avon
New York Public Library   30 May 1911

My dear W.B.

I was delighted to get your letter, and I was overjoyed at the good news it contained. I feel sure Success has come to us, and come to stay.

I have been rather upset and depressed since last night because the Specialist was here again last night, and he said it would not be possible for me to go to work until about the 11*th*. I am very disappointed, as I know how difficult my absence makes things for the Co, and I had been looking forward so much to being quite able to start work next Monday, but Dr. Hemetson explained that if I go [into] a relapse now it would mean perhaps months of ill health. I am enclosing a certificate from the Specialist Dr. Hemetson, and also one from Dr. Thomson, which will explain better than I can, and will you please send them also to Lady Gregory.

It has distressed me beyond words that I cant join the Co next wek, but I am sure you will understand, that "tho' the spirit is willing the flesh is weak." Goodbye.

Yours Sincerely
SALLY ALLGOOD

From JOHN BUTLER YEATS

                                        New York
MS Yeats   21 March 1912

[The gift book, *Plays for an Irish Theatre*, was published in December 1911. Arthur Sinclair and Sara Allgood (Widow Quin in *The Playboy*) were prominent Abbey players. JBY attended the performances in New York when the Abbey Company toured America from September 1911 to March 1912. Yeats had written to his father that Edmund Gosse has "the timidity of the sedentary man" (*L* 567). Lily was at his side when George Pollexfen died in September 1910.]

My dear Willie

Many thanks for the book. I have only just got it and read *On Baile's Strand* and looked through the Preface. I hope soon to read all carefully as possible.

I am very glad to hear you have good prospects as regards new actors and actresses. I don't think Miss Allgood quite a success in such parts as Cathleen ni Houlihan, though she is of course very much improved, no longer so declamatory, so oratorical. Sinclair is splendid, and the others are all as good as possible, but you *do* want someone for the principal part in your plays, someone if not with beauty at any rate with dignity, and the physical gifts that go with dignity. Sarah Allgood has activity and intelligence and lots of other things. In the Widow Quin she is everything.

We have been having Summer weather — such a delight after the long weary winter, and now it is gone and winter is back again, and I am sitting shivering beside the radiator from which no heat is coming. All from force of habit I sit beside it. Outside everything is covered with snow, and I have a sneezing cold. What you say of Gosse is interesting. We may be alarmed. The men of leisure and easy living — the sybaritist element — gone out of life, what will become of the pleasantest part of literature? A man is an ascetic for the sake of a blissful moment or two of a sybaritist existence — Milton for instance. What did you think of my phrase "self exaggerated"? I think, however, it should have been "self-obsessed." It would apply to Milton both when he wrote so nobly about himself, his [word indecipherable], and his misfortunes, and when he treated his wives and his daughters so ignobly. And George Pollexfen, being self-obsessed, died so calmly and *solidly* during those six weeks when Lily stayed with him, during which time as far as I can find out he never spoke of anyone but himself, regarding Lily merely as an adjunct to his comfort. Wordsworth was another self-obsessed man — in fact, many great men, including George Moore — but not Shakespeare, who was much too interested in other people to be so very much interested in himself. Self-obsessed people get more than their share of respect and attention. We really like them, and selfish people we fear and dislike and despise as far as we dare. We smile at a self-obsessed man but we do not despise him or distrust him — and a reason for our liking him is that he makes us smile.

Yrs Affectly
J. B. YEATS

From R. L. ALLEN

Dublin

TS Yeats   1 June 1912

[Allen was headmaster of Homan-Allen College on Harcourt Street. Yeats noted that he answered the letter.]

Dear Sir,

I have read more and heard more about you than about any man in Ireland today. Here is a potted play which I heard from Patsy Sheridan of Knockbeg, Collooney many years ago.

Minor Magic

Act I. Mrs. Higgins has had a goose stolen and the problem is *Find the thief.*

Act II. Richard Tighs the schoolmaster my predecessor in that office is a dabbler in occult science and he sets his wits to work.

Act III. Scene in R. T's parlour. The church key is got and the wands are placed over a verse in Ruth I think, the ring is left exposed and the whole thing is tightly bound up. Tighs and Sheridan place their index fingers in the ring of the key and it and the Bible hangs over a basin of water.

Act IV. "Tommy Nolan stole the goose." No response. Same formula is repeated with different names. No response until the right name (the name of the thief) is mentioned.

ACT V. Then the whole apparatus (Bible and key) begins to vibrate violently until it releases itself from the men's fingers and falls into the basin of water.

Many a time Sheridan (a labouring man) related the above story to me.

Many small superstitions — for want of a better word I call them such, still linger about the Co. Sligo — e.g. Taking the butter, rat-billeting, etc., but the adepts have mostly all passed away and the practices were frowned on by the church.

Yours faithfully,

R. L. ALLEN

From JOHN BUTLER YEATS

New York

MS Yeats   8 June 1912

[John Pentland Mahaffy, whose portrait was painted by JBY, was Provost of Trinity College, Dublin.]

My dear Willie

I would make a distinction between opinions and convictions and beliefs. Opinions may be described as ideas to which men are attached polemically. They are snatched up in the heat of controversy for the purpose of defense or offense and abound in cities where men live together in such close contact that they become infected by mutual personal likings and dislikings craving expression. Convictions are ideas sought and maintained in the spirit of truth, yet these are limited to the sphere of the reason and the ethical will, and are the discoveries of enlightened and earnest-minded men.

Belief is in another category. Belief is neither offensive nor defensive. And involuntary Poets, which include the saints, possess it. John Knox was never a believer in the high sense of the word. With him opinions grew into convictions and there stopped. There was too much noise and tumult in that formidable man for belief to have a chance. Belief is Protean and can take many definite shapes, yet itself remains apart — a serenity, a great inner assurance. It is like the harvest when it waits ripening in the heat and silence of the long summer days, and when the harvest is full the harvesters will come. Where there are many believers the poets will multiply. I was asked the other day scornfully if there was any poetry in a Yorkshire peasant, and I answered, "He and all his silent like are as full of poetry as the oak tree is of murmurs." Some day there will be good husbandry. The harvest of their silence will be reaped by the inarticulate poets.

George Russell is a true believer and for that reason a true poet, though his note be as monotonous as the woodpecker's, of whose monotony we do not easily tire. For all that it is a monotony. Like the wood-dove he lives partially in an Eutopia of his own, where there are no problems for the intellect. He is the reverse of Browning. Mahaffy told me he could not read him. When Russell faces intellectual problems he writes with extraordinary force and charm, but he has not learned how to be a poet in that difficult world. I have always wondered why.

Yours affectionately
JOHN BUTLER YEATS

P.S. Obviously Russell's intellectual world is debating and striving and polemical. That is why to write poetry he must keep within the narrow world of mystical dreams — his poems like Turner's skies.

From WILLIAM ROTHENSTEIN

MS Yeats

Hampstead
11 July 1912

[Rothenstein, who invited Tagore to London, introduced him to Yeats on 28 June. This letter refers to a dinner given for Tagore at the Trocadero Restaurant in London on 10 July. Tagore's *Gitanjali* (1912), a selection of the poems mentioned, was dedicated to Rothenstein and contained an introduction by Yeats dated September 1912. The frontispiece is a reproduction of one of six drawings Rothenstein made of Tagore that summer.]

My dear Yeats —

let me congratulate you on your noble occupancy of the chair last night. Your opening speech was a great & generous song of praise which must, coming from a poet to a poet, have filled our friends heart. It seemed to me that the whole spirit of the evening was touched by it, for I have I think never been present at a dinner where the minds of the diners were less bent on a thousand things & more centered upon the object & subject of the occasion. We must arrange to meet one day next week to go over the poems. Will you lunch & then sit & work afterwards? I think that will be better than waiting for the evening — Tagore is an early rester.

Yours always
W.R.

From HARRIET MONROE

TS University of Chicago Library

Chicago
15 August 1912

[Yeats had been in Chicago in February 1904 and had lectured at Hull House, the famous social settlement founded in 1889 by Jane Addams. Yeats contributed five poems to the December 1912 issue of Monroe's *Poetry* (Chicago).]

Dear Sir:

When you were in Chicago I had the pleasure of meeting you, though you may not remember. At any rate we have many friends in common, including Miss Jane Addams and other Hull House residents.

I trust that you may be interested in this project for the relief of the muse. It will be a great pleasure and honor if you are willing to testify to that interest by sending us a poem or a group of poems for early publication. Indeed, I can think of no contribution which would delight me more.

   We are not very rich, but I hope that I may be able to meet any rate which you think is just; at least I shall do my best and tell you promptly what we can do.

Yours sincerely,
HARRIET MONROE

From WILLIAM ROTHENSTEIN

Stroud, Gloucestershire

MS Yeats   18 August 1912

[*Gitanjali* was published by the India Society in a limited edition of 750 copies. The popular edition was published by Macmillan in 1913. Roy may be Basanta Kumar Roy, author of *Rabindranath Tagore: The Man and His Poetry* (1916). Launcelot Alfred Crammer-Byng was editor of the John Murray 'Wisdom of the East' series. The young German is probably Bernhard Tauchnitz, who published *A Selection from the Poetry of W. B. Yeats* in 1913.]

My dear Yeats —

   Until yesterday Tagore had been anxiously hoping for your arrival. I believe if you had written that you could not join us here he would have come to you in London. He is very keen that the book should be out while he is still in England. Did you get the typed copies of the rest of the poems? I hope we may count on you to get the introduction done by the end of the month. With regard to a publisher, I should of course be most willing to consider your own advice, & put it before The India Society. Our idea is to publish 750 copies ourselves, to give 100 copies to Tagore for his own use, & 200 copies to the members of the Society as the publication of·the year, & to give 250 copies to Hatchards or Luzac for public circulation — the rest we store for future members of the Society. We propose to print the book simply but nobly; & make it a very perfect volume. *Then we propose to offer the book to a publisher*, in order that he may issue a larger & more popular Edition, together with other works of Tagore which he & others are working on, in a cheaper form. We think that the small number which will be available to the public will do no harm to a larger edition: which we feel certain will be called for, & which will then be produced with all the prestige which the reviews will give it. I personally feel certain that the book is going to take its place among the books of the world, & that the noble christening the India Society will give it will be welcome to those of us who care for a more intimate edition of a great work. Tagore is busy here translating plays, & poems he has written for children, of which four you will remember are among the other poems, & Sakumar Roy is doing his best with some of the longer poems. My idea is that we shall arrange with a publisher (Murray I believe is already willing through Cranmer Byng to produce several volumes of translations. I feel with you that nothing of the kind has appeared in Europe during the last few generations, & the more I read the more am I stirred by the beauty & clearness of Tagore's vision. I wish you could have joined us here, for the poet is at his best away from too many people, & we have had a most blessed time here – never I think have I got so *frequently* in touch with a man's soul as here. What the poems are he is. For years I have believed this to be a necessary relation between the artist & the work of art, & have suffered greatly both in my own struggles & because it has been difficult for me to accept much that is admired by many good men. When I first met Rabindranath it was like a personal reward, & the renewal of intimacy has been one of the prizes of life. Above all, the poems have nothing in them which any man must feel it necessary to reject, as is the case with so much of the great mystical poetry of the world, where here & there are stated things which offend that perfect balance of visions which great art must show. We are here until the 28th when we return to Hampstead. With warm greetings from us all.

Yrs always
W.R.

What about the young German? You might when you write let me know if he may count on your permission to publish.

From WILLIAM ROTHENSTEIN

Stroud, Gloucestershire

MS Yeats   24 August 1912

[Tagore's "school for children and disciples" was at Bolpur. For Yeats's reply see *L* 569–70].

My dear Yeats —

We were sorry to hear you had been laid up — we both of us missed your visit. I read your letter to Radindranath & he cared very much for what you said of him. He has been most prolific here — he has translated 22 new poems on children, making 26 in all for a volume of children's verses, & also 3 plays, each one of which is remarkable. I propose, when they are typed, getting him to send copies up to you & Lady Gregory. Every thing he does he makes so complete & round that it becomes significant viewed from *every* side. I believe that the actual beauty of his language prevents Bengali people realising how great a thinker he is — we who can only imagine the beauty of the Bengali original seize on every hint of wisdom & beauty of vision that he gives us throughout his work, & clothe the beautiful naked form according to the riches & charity of our own hearts. I hope, now that you have absorbed the spirit of the poems so completely, that it will not be difficult for you to write a short & emphatic introduction. Nothing is more convincing than absolute praise; nothing is more delightful than to be able to give it — it is not want of generosity in us artists, but want of the transparent sincerity we look for in the work of our contemporaries that again & again prevents us from praising as we would wish — & I hold you fortunate in once more being able to speak in noble terms of a friend's work. I think that a great deal of hostility is thwarted love — our natures grow bitter & fierce when they cannot pass through their natural channels, & finding a barrier, overflow in anger. Directly they find their course again, shame comes to us at once. Tagore is very anxious that the introduction should be done as soon as you can get down to it — I think he is very eager for the book to appear this autumn, while he is with us all. He is the simplest & most modest of men, yet he is quite touchingly keen to have the book in print.

I am glad you approve of the Murray plan — will you perhaps write him & I will see him on my return. There is a rich mine, & if Murray has the courage, there might easily be three or four volumes — the India Society book would of course be one of them. R.N.T. would like, he tells me, to entrust his literary interests to you & to myself, as well as the financial side of the works. He would very much care to have them bring in as much as possible, as he dedicates all the profits of his writings to his school. By the bye — you spoke of Thomas à Kempis — don't you think that there is some kind of parallel between his religious lyrics & Dante's sonnets in the Vita Nuova? There is the same garment of love clothing a deep conception of life & death; he is more religious in the manner of Dante I think than in that of Thomas à Kempis, who is more of a Christian mystic in so far as he advocates obedience to Church authority, to saints & to prophets, while Tagore never touches this side of life at all, believing that Gods breath will come if man but put his lips to the flute with the faith & a mind emptied of "self," without the intermediary of man living or dead.

We return to Hampstead next week. Please commend me to Lady Gregory.

> Yours always —
> W.R.

You still say nothing of the young German!

From RABINDRANATH TAGORE

MS Yeats

London
2 September 1912

[Tagore was in America from the autumn of 1912 till the spring of 1913, when he returned to England. *The Autobiography of Maharshi Devendranath Tagore*, trans. Satyendranath Tagore and Indira Devi, was published in 1909.]

Dear Mr Yeats

It has been such a great joy to me to think that things that I wrote in a tongue not known to you should at last fall in your hands and that you should accept them with so much enjoyment and love. When, in spite of all obstacles, something seemed to impel me to come to this country I never dreamt that it was for this that I was taking my voyage. What my soul offered to her master in the solitude of an obscure corner of the world must be brought before the altar of man where hearts come together and tongues mingle like the right and the left palms of hands joined in the act of adoration. My heart fills with gratitude and I write to you this letter to say that appreciation from a man like you comes to me not only as a reward for my lifelong devotion to literature but as a token that my songs have been acceptable to Him, and He has led me over the sea to this country to speak to me His approval of my works through your precious friendship.

We intend to leave England in the beginning of November. I do hope I shall be able to see you before that, and, if possible, to have a sight of my translations published with your introduction.

I hope you will kindly accept from me a copy of the English translation of my father's Auto-Biography which I left with Mr Rothenstein to be sent to your address.

Very sincerely yours
RABINDRANATH TAGORE

From ROBERT W. FELKIN

London
TS Yeats   15 September 1912

[During June and July Dr Felkin (Finem Respice) and his wife (Quaero Lucem) had gone to Germany to consult Dr Rudolph Steiner, founder of the Anthroposophical Society, from whom they received Grades or Degrees in the Order. Dr William Wynn Westcott (Sapere Aude) claimed that he had received letters from Fräulein Anna Sprengel (Sapiens Dominabitur Astris) authorizing the founding of the Isis-Urania Temple in London. MacGregor Mathers (Deo Duce Comite Ferro) accused Westcott of forging the letters. The rituals of the Golden Dawn were based upon the Cypher Manuscripts discovered by Rev. A. F. A. Woodford in a London bookstall in 1884.]

PRIVATE.

Care V. H. Frater,
We do not leave till October the 10th: so that I hope that we shall see you before we start. We had a very interesting time in Germany & got several Grades.
I also found out that "S.A." did indeed get the letters from Frl: A Sprengel so he did not forge them as D.D.C.F. said. I have made an affidavit to this effect.
The Cypher M.S. however were not of real German origin i.e. they were notes of Ceremonies which had been written by an Englishman in English in an old Cypher.
I was too much engaged in getting grades & things that I could not go into the Astrology for you this time I will do so when I go over again.
I am sorry that you cannot come on the 21st: but BE SURE & LET US KNOW SOON WHEN YOU CAN COME.

Fraternally yours,
F.R.

From JOHN BUTLER YEATS

New York

MS Yeats   5 October 1912

[JBY admired the poetry of James N. Johnston, an Irish-born poet living in Buffalo. The painter John Sloan and his wife Anna ("Dolly") were among JBY's closest friends, though he disapproved of their socialism and pacifism. JBY illustrated this letter with a pen sketch of the three legs representing the Isle of Man.]

My dear Willie,

I have found your letter — in my pocket, whereat you will smile, as do I. I will send to Johnston what you say of him. Still write to the old fellow.

I was at a Socialist political meeting — 15,000 people *all paying for their seats* — (mine cost 3/s), the last unprecedented in political meetings here in NY. I enjoyed it with my intellect and judgment. It was revealing, an amazing instance of the blank dullness of American methods. It is my belief that Americans will never run their own politics. The Bosses are here to remain, only they will become expert with recognized positions and definite salaries. We have got rid of Parnellism, our attempt at the Boss. Of course if America broke up into small independent nations, local politics the only politics, it would be different.

The speaking at the Socialist meeting was no good. Nobody cares for the science of political thinking. At an Orange meeting every sentence is a variety of the words, "To Hell with the Pope." At this meeting the same function was performed by the words, "To Hell with Capital." So I sat, bored, deafened, but enlightened.

I said to Sloan, "Why do you shout so much, you yourself the worst among them?" He replied, "We came here to shout."

In America is no intellectual life in anything. Everything is movement and a mood of motion. The three legs which represent the Isle of Man should be adopted by America. It would suit them better than the eagle.

Of course on America and guessing as to what it will do I am the merest amateur, but Roosevelt himself is no better. The wisest of us can only guess. God Almighty only knows, or his representative here on Earth, Demos.

I have been reading lives of Goethe, big books, also his

conversation. It is an epoch for me. Hope you will soon write and tell me your plans.

Yrs affectly

J. B. YEATS

From FLORENCE FARR EMERY

Colombo, Ceylon

MS Yeats   26 October 1912

[The Hon. Mr P. Ramanathan was the founder of the Ramanathan College for Hindu girls which Mrs Emery was Principal of from its opening in January 1913 until her death in 1917. Sydney Olivier, first Baron of Ramsden, was a founder of the Fabian Society and an English colonial administrator. *The New Age*, edited by Alfred Richard Orage, was a London weekly review.]

My dear W. B. Yeats.

I thought of you yesterday because I came across a metaphor in the translation of a book you may be able to find in the British Museum. It is badly translated but full of wisdom. It is The Yoga Vashishtha Maháramayyana of Valmiki, Volume IV page 314.

"The seeds of our notions play at random in the broad sky of the mind (antar kamna = inner cause) some of them of like nature some all various ===== many are bound together and many unknown to each other by nature both in feeling and thought. As inert seeds they moulder & moisten in the same heap." The whole passage suggests to me that the seeds of our dreams are the seeds unknown to each other and the seeds of waking life are those in which a number of seeds grown in the same pod as it were are united by the unripeness of their state & produce the delusion in common which one feels is so difficult to account for. Ramanathan of course explains that delusion only consists in our reversal of truth. We consider the solid things to be changeless and the unseen self to be changable instead of the reverse.

Well — I don't know how to begin to tell you about everything that is happening. I am living here in a bungalow in the Cinnamon gardens surrounded by extraordinarily tall cocoanut palms. The garden is a series of lawns with tropical flowers growing as in the hot house at Kew the colour is a kind of grey light different in everything from the rich golden light of Egypt but at the same time much more bright. Beautiful creatures walk about the streets like exquisite mahogany statues come to life; everyone, even the crooked and old, has the air of being an extraordinary work of art.

Mr and Mrs Ramanathan (the English wife) and her little daughter aged 5 live down stairs. The eldest son and his wife & girl child in the left-wing and the second unmarried son at the back next the servants quarters, the father of the first wife who died & his 2 children somewhere else. I have the upper story (which seems to be a sort of guest house) to myself. There is a bedroom in which I sleep an empty bedroom full of pictures & stacks of things that are to go to the Jaffna College when it is ready and long enclosed verandahs in which I write walk meditate and read. I have coffee at 7:30 a currey meal at about 1 tea at 3 another currey meal at 8. At the currey meals Ramanathan appears, & we have great talks about the nature of the soul. At 2 every day I learn Tamil with his secretary for an hour. They have a victoria & a motor car one does nothing for oneself. It is a great adventure to walk in the garden. Servants waiting round every corner to do all one wishes. One never may go outside the gate except in a conveyance of some sort. The life is really rather like that of a royal personage. I interviewed the Minister of Education with Ramanathan the other day. I see Sidney Olivier is to be the next governor. I know him (an old friend of Shaw's) he has been in Jamaica lately.

Ramanathan is starting a nationalist newspaper in March & a private printing press. The newspaper will have the advantage of appealing to all the richest people in the island: unlike *The New Age* which could never get anyone to advertise in it. I shall probably settle in Jaffna at the end of the year. The roof is not on yet. The address of the college will be Ramanathan College (for Hindu girls) Channakam Ceylon. It is five miles from the town of Jaffna in an estate of 25 acres. Built round a courtyard 148 ft. by 147 ft.

I had a fortnight in Cairo beginning about 18 September. Ever since that date I have been constantly perspiring and now I have reached Ceylon & live on vegetable curreys I find that one simply seems to exude spice. All ones clothes have become drenched with a spice laden cloud over & over again. Today is the first unclouded day. It always (at this time of year) pours in torrents for about 6 hours. Yesterday it didn't & today the ground is hard as a brick. It is red for about 6 inches from the surface as I saw when a Brahmin came & blessed the foundation stone laying of a house to be built in a corner of the garden.

Yours ever

FLORENCE EMERY

From A. H. BULLEN

MS Yeats

Stratford-upon-Avon
27 October 1912

[Even the "Preface" was not new, as it had appeared in *The Mask*. Chapman and Hall (London) had taken 250 copies of *The Collected Works. Stories of Red Hanrahan: The Secret Rose: Rosa Alchemica* appeared in March 1913. G. P. Putnam, not Bullen, published the "Irish Folklore" book (*Visions and Beliefs in the West of Ireland*, 1920).]

My dear Yeats,

In the course of this week I shall be sending Mr. A. P. Watt a statement of the sales of your books since I last reported to him.

I doubt whether any publisher could have done better with the "Plays for an Irish Theatre" (as only the Preface was new); but the sales of the Collected Edition have been disappointing.

I printed of the Collected Edition 1060 copies — allowing 60 for gratis, review, and spoiled copies — and according to my stockkeeper I have (though I must verify the figures more closely) 460 sets in quires and 21 bound sets. I put down this poor result to three causes:—

(1) The Macmillan Company of New York refused to take the book in bulk themselves & would not let another publisher handle it. Quinn kindly drew up a lengthy legal opinion in which he showed clearly that the Macmillan company ran no risk whatever of endangering their American copyrights by taking up my edition; but Brett remained higheadedly obdurate.

(2) This is a delicate matter, but I must refer to it. When the Collected Edition began to come out, certain people (both in the Press and in literary circles) were exalting Synge at your expense. The older critics were not gulled; nor those young men who still kept their fine enthusiasm. But the "unbaked and doughty youth" — semi-educated reviewers who have no real standard of comparison — proclaimed Synge to be the master-spirit of the Irish movement. It was absurd; and a leading bookseller lately wrote to me that the "Synge 'boom' is now nearly over."

(3) Chapman & Hall turned out to be very inefficient allies. My sales would have been larger if I had not bought back copies from them, and handed over to them — for their encouragement — orders that I would have been glad to execute myself. Only two days ago I

had a letter from them to say that they intended to dispose of their unsold stock for what it would fetch; and I wrote at once to ask what their cash-price would be to me for repurchasing it.

The task with this Collected Edition is at present hard: Unwin's scheme would make it infinitely harder and is an intolerable proposal (the second paragraph of his letter — enclosed — is indeed insulting). As a matter of fact all your books are kept in "readable and handy" form, with the exception of the "Secret Rose & Red Hanrahan," which is up in type and can be issued at any moment.

I shall call on Mr. Watt in a day or two and have a talk with him; and I should much like to talk with you when it is possible.

— What became of that projected volume of "Irish Folklore" which you & Lady Gregory were to do together? It is the sort of book that I could handle with advantage.

Yours

A. H. BULLEN

P.S. I sent Gordon Craig his drawings some weeks ago. He promised to send his cheque in receipt of them, but it has not come! Those drawings rather hindered than furthered the sales of Plays for an Irish Theatre.

From JAMES H. COUSINS

Dublin

TS Yeats   5 December 1912

[Alfred Vout Peters, well-known clairvoyant and trance medium, became famous through the accounts of his communications with the dead son of Sir Oliver Lodge recorded in *Raymond* (1916). Cousins made a sketch of the ring with elongated diamond in the margin.]

Dear Mr. Yeats,

I received your contribution to the Peters visit, for which I was obliged. It enabled me to pay him a decent amount for his work in addition to his travelling expenses.

I trust you will be able some time soon to make a report of your deductions, and I shall be happy to add my observations, or help to strengthen your own in any way I can.

I had an interesting test in Belfast on Sunday last. I was speaking for the Spiritualists in a public hall, and during the course of my address I used a phrase which came into my head. It was germane to my topic, but quite unanticipated, and formed no part of my notes or my thought in preparation, and had not occurred to me since I first heard it used. That is the first point. The second point is that, as Mrs. Cousins sat in the audience, she felt the presence of her sister, Mrs. Pielou, who said: "I can hear through your mind all that Jim is saying, and I am going to try and impress something on him." Almost immediately I used the phrase referred to, and Mrs. Cousins recognised it as one used by her sister, and took it as a fulfilment of the effort to impress me. I, of course did not know this till the end. The third point is that, at the end of the meeting, a lady who had never met my wife before, but who knew she was Mrs. Cousins, came over to her and told her that, being a clairvoyant, she had seen both beside and on the platform, and her in the seat, a lady somewhat like her, but taller and darker. The clairvoyant knew nothing of Mrs. Pielou, and the description is correct although very broad. At the evening meeting the lady told me that she forgot in the morning to say that the figure showed her a letter 'A'. I did not care to ask her directly if in the meantime she had heard the name. At night she said the figure was again with me on the platform and held over my head a gold circle into which was inserted through the top part of the ring an elongated diamond. I know of no connection. The person indicated has been apparently active, as she spoke thro' Peters, and has written thro' Mrs. C., but I would not think of her actively as a source of inspiration on the metaphysical side of things as she was not subtle in mind. The curious thing about the phrase used by me, as apparently a result of her suggestion, is that is was not used by her in earth life, but was said by her thro' Peters a year ago. It was, "I did not think it was so easy to die." I had never thought of it since, until it occurred to me on the platform.

When you are in town, I shall be glad if you will come out for tea and an evening's chat, or at any time convenient after school. There are other experiences which I would like to tell you.

Yours faithfully,
JAMES H. COUSINS

From GORDON CRAIG

Florence, Italy

MS Yeats   [? 1913]

[Harold Edward Monro, who met Craig in Florence, edited *Poetry and Drama* at The Poetry Bookshop. Craig bought a large collection of marionettes in 1913 and published *Drama for Fools*, a series of plays for marionettes, in 1916.]

PRIVATE

My dear Yeats

I have had a letter from Harold Monro who edits a shop in Holburn telling me that you and Sturge Moore are *"the originators of the idea"* operating one of the 1st London parodies of the wonderous & difficult art of the marionette —

Monro used to come to see me & the last time he came from some instinctive feeling that I was in the presence of a man utterly weak & yet determined to do or die — & as he asked me to help in something or other I talked of you — knowing that you were generally in London & that if he followed your best advice he couldn't go wrong — nor harm any of us or our dreams.

But now he seems not only to have gone wrong — but also to put the blame upon you .. or rather to use you to spiritualize & make holy his damnable deeds.

London loves to piddle & see everyone else piddling provided everyone else will piddle all over beauty & sanity & other dear things.

I detest these London brutes, & now they're going to piddle on the loveliest dream I ever dreamt. Can't you persuade them to keep their hands & their water from these descendents of the Idols. My dear Yeats — if you knew how I get at hearing the smug & filthy proposal. Do me this service — keep them from making COMMON what must be kept out of shops — & the pickers & stealers of these brutes.

Who can love Venus after seeing her parody in a music hall. Who would love the *Idols* I am now & here trying to recreate when a Book shop has dirtied the whole idea —

Yours

E.G.C.

I see that Monro also says that you told him you spoke to me on this subject of marionettes but that I was naturally too engrossed in my own undertakings. What all that rigamarole may mean I am at a loss to guess.

From ROBERT W. FELKIN

TS Yeats

Havelock North, New Zealand
1 January 1913

[Neville Meakin (Ex Oriente Lux), who had been chosen to succeed
Felkin as Chief of the Amoun Temple in London, died unexpectedly
in 1912. The Rev. J. C. Fitzgerald (Deus Meus Deus), of the Anglican
House of the Resurrection in Mirfield, Yorkshire, was a member of
the Amoun Temple. Felkin founded the Smaragdum Thalasses
Temple in New Zealand.]

Dear Mr Yeats,

Your letter has only just come & you do not seem to have had
the long letter I posted to you the day we left.

I had expected Mr Meakin to have told you much but he died so
very suddenly that I have to write you.

The Revd: Father FitzGerald. C.R. House of the Resurrection
Mirfield Yorks. is the address but remember he is often away so you
cannot count on a reply by return post sometimes. You can give me
his address as he will not have forgotten the matter if she recalls it to
him but I will try & write to him anyway you can at once as I may
not catch the post today.

We are all well & hope to be back in April.

I must not write more as your letter only came just before the
post leaves.

Every good wish for 1913 I wrote to you twice already with
general matters of interest.

Yours always,
R. W. FELKIN

From FLORENCE FARR EMERY

MS Yeats

Jaffna, Ceylon
7 January 1913

My dear W. B. Yeats —

You might get someone to "paper up" a copy of Tagore's poems
for our library here, if you feel benevolent.

The building is supposed to be ready on 20th Janry I cant say
what the college will be like but you'd delight in this place. They
postponed the opening day because public opinion demanded that
no important work should be commenced when the ☽ was in

conjunction with the Pliedies (the 7 stars in Taurus). Also the music is planned out like a Dutch garden. You choose your mode your rhythm & your time & then you may not use any notes that are not in that mode. Otherwise you can sing as you please. You cannot change the key but you may change the note you stop on. I think you would be excited about the verse if you could hear it with the proper pronunciation. This is one couplet.

> Nō my nengé, nōmy nengé
> Roon pulatta mernda sherēlei neringil

It means

> "Hurts my heart – hurts my heart"
> "Where grass grows & fades the sweet smelling neringil.
>
> (The rest of the translation is)
> "To the eye sweet blossoming flower-thorny fruit brings
> forth
> "Sweet doings once beloved-sweet doings not now
> "Hurts my heart."
> Kadkiniya mălăr puttŭ mudpăyundangŏ
> Tniyaseÿta Kadelei in ná cheyil
> Nōmy nengé

Tamil means Sweet. Jaffna means the land of the lute player. A man is specially engaged at the college to tell stories with songs in them to the children. He plays the violin holding it between his chest & his knees. He twangs a long stringed instrument in such a way as to make it buzz all the time.

3 of them sit on the ground looking like figures out of a Beardsly drawing. The violinist & the man who plays the elaborate drum (made of stone parchment & wood animal vegetable & mineral) which he plays with fingers & wrists. The violinist & he gaze into each others eyes when they are working up their final runs and thumps as if they were lovers producing their progeny in immediate ecstasy.

I am [in] the thick of politics here & am having a really interesting life at last.

> Yours ever sincerely
> FLORENCE EMERY

From HUGH LANE

MS Berg Collection,   London
New York Public Library   [after 20 January 1913]

[At a special meeting on 20 January the Dublin Corporation passed a resolution in favour of erecting a Municipal Art Gallery over the Liffey River to house Lane's collection of "Continental Pictures".]

My dear Yeats
        Thank you very much for your letter & the enclosure (which I return). It was so interesting that I read it to a few friends at the Arts Club. The mansion house meeting was fairly satisfactory. They agreed to the *Metal Bridge* site. I decided that this was much better, than a building attached to an existing Bridge. It will be getting rid of the principal eyesore of Dublin, & in its place we will have a stone bridge with a beautiful building on it. All the members of the Corporation that I have seen — also the Irish Times & Freemans Journal — are for it. We will have some opposition from the enemies of the Gallery, but if we can get about £9000 more we can count on its going through. I don't wonder at Aunt Augusta being confused, no one in Dublin seemed to know how much was wanted — I find that the estimate for £11,000 was only for the metal foundation of a bridge, though I had been given to understand that it was to cover the whole cost. However if £5000 can be collected (now) I will go ahead. If you have nothing better to do will you take pot luck on Sunday at 8, a P.C. will do.

                                        Yours
                                        HUGH LANE

From A. H. BULLEN

                                        Stratford-upon-Avon
MS Yeats   6 and 10 February 1913

[The proposed revised edition of *The Collected Works* was not published. *The Celtic Twilight* was reissued in 1912, *Ideas of Good and Evil* in 1914. See *L* 575–7 for Yeats's reply.]

My dear Yeats,
        At the first reading of your letters on the proposed changes in the Collected Edition I became puzzled and bewildered; but, as I thought the soaking rains and chilly East winds might have dulled my

wits, I let the matter stand over for a few days. Meanwhile I had received the revised version of *The Countess Cathleen* and *The Land of Heart's Desire* in their very latest state; and I can well understand that for stage-purposes these last abridged versions are the best.

Your proposals for vol. IX are perfectly clear; but I think it would be well to put the four rewritten plays in smaller type at the end of the volume.

It is the proposed changes in vols. II & IV that trouble me; and I must think how the various difficulties are to be surmounted. At present I am inclined to think that the extra matter had better be thrown (in small type) into Appendices – which can be given in loose wrappers to the purchasers of bound sets, old purchasers & new. When the present bound stock is exhausted the new appendices could be bound up in their proper places with the old quires.

When Brett comes over I must see him and try to offer him some inducement for letting me export sets to America.

When you were last in Stratford we talked about re-issuing the Red Hanrahan stories, Secret Rose & Rosa Alchemica (from the text – all of them – of the Collected Edition) to range with the Celtic Twilight & Ideas of Good & Evil. These selections from vols V & VII are now up in type and will make a very good volume.

10. ii. 13

This is a makeshift sort of a letter. I put it aside, in the hope that some ideas would come to me – but they haven't come yet. On the 14th. I have to give a lecture at Birmingham (& I hate lecturing, but couldn't get out of it): when that is over I'll see what can possibly be done with vols II & IV.

The enclosed letter should have been sent earlier. I am registering this note as I am not sure where you are now & the American letter may have money in it.

Yours
A. H. BULLEN

From A. H. BULLEN

London
MS Yeats
26 February 1913

[*A Selection from the Love Poetry of W. B. Yeats* was published by Cuala on 25 July. Miss E. M. Lister, a relative of Bullen, was an assistant at the Shakespeare Head Press.]

My dear Yeats,

    By all means let your sister issue the collection of Love Poems. Miss Lister has often suggested that it would be well to have something of the kind to sell at the Shakespeare Head Press (not for the booksellers), as she thinks she could dispose of a good many copies in the course of each season. So you might have two little anthologies going.

    I think I begin to see a way out of the trouble with the Collected Edition, and I should like to discuss it with you – for I think you will readily agree. When I had almost despaired of finding a satisfactory solution of the difficulties, a bright idea suddenly – a few minutes ago – suggested itself; a scheme for turning the dead stock into live cash, and for making the changes you want to be made.

    Can you lunch with me here tomorrow, one o'clock sharp, when I will explain? Telegraph form enclosed. "Yes, Yeats" will mean you're coming. If you are engaged, telegraph "Engaged" – but name a time when I can see you at your rooms tomorrow (though I hope you'll be able to lunch here in this quaint old inn). I want to return to Stratford-on-Avon by the 4.45 train tomorrow afternoon.

Yours
A. H. BULLEN

From WILLIAM THOMAS HORTON

MS Yeats

London
3 March 1913

[Horton and Miss Locke "lived together platonically", according to Yeats, from this time until her death on 19 June 1916. "A Legend of Life" (consisting of nine drawings and a story) by Horton appeared in *The Occult Review* (Dec 1912), edited by Ralph Shirley. The man seated in the armchair and "wearing spectacles" was surely Yeats. "The dark thin man" may have been St John Ervine, with whom Yeats, Rupert Brooke ("the beautiful youth"), and Edward Marsh had dined on 2 March.]

1 Enclosure

My dear Yeats,

    I am sorry to say the lady I mentioned, Miss A. Audrey Locke, is down with influenza here at Tunbridge Wells where she is on a visit & where I have run down for the day. Under the circumstances I think it advisable to put off the meeting & dinner you so kindly invited us to until *after* Easter. Perhaps you will kindly name a day, if I do not hear from you I will write again. We are very disappointed but hope our meeting is only put off for a few weeks.

Allow me to thank you for the really delightful time you gave me yesterday evening, everything was so genial & warm & full of good fellowship — I most thoroughly enjoyed it all. I will get Shirley to send you "The Occult Review" Xmas Number, containing a Legend of Life & drawings by me. It may interest you.

In meantime I shall arrange a few extracts from the material I mentioned last night to discuss when we three meet after Easter.

> Yours sincerely,
> WILLIAM T. HORTON

To the man in big, low armchair & wearing spectacles.
"Go on, you will succeed."
To the dark thin man — a friend of the above —
"You wonder & at times are puzzled & under a cloud.
Go on, persevere, rugged spirit, & you shall attain."
To the beautiful youth — Mr. Brook, I think.
"In your reverence & worship of another forget not the reverence & worship you owe equally to your own highest Self & its manifestations, & *its manifestations*."
To Ezra Pound —
"You'll do, only climb higher, ever higher & then forget *the* burdens."

> Good wishes to all
> from
> your little brother
> WILLIAM T. HORTON

From ROBERT BRIDGES

MS Bridges

Chilswell, near Oxford
20 April 1913

[Tagore's *Gitanjali* was published in a limited edition for the India Society late in 1912. In the introduction Yeats had explained that "Four-fifths of our energy is spent in the quarrel with bad taste, whether in our own minds or in the minds of others." The literary scholar William John Courthope and the writer Edmund Gosse were, like Yeats, members of the Academic Committee of the Royal

Society of Literature. Their meeting probably concerned the award of
the Polignac Prize. Walter Raleigh was Professor of English Literature
at Oxford.]

My dear Yeats

Binyon brought us Tagore's poems with your lovely preface.
What a delight it was! O most blessed one! there is no one but you
who could write so. He told me that it was coming out in a cheap
edition – and he promised to give you a message from me, the
practical part of which was that I want you to alter one word in your
masterpiece. It is the expression "four fifths" or "five sixths", or
something of that fractional quality. He did not see the point, but
you will.

It led me to wondering what fractions could be admitted into
that consummate style. A half is of course all right; and perhaps 2/3,
because 3 is the mystic subdivision of all things, and 2/3 might be
called "two parts". But after that one falls into conversational
meaninglessness.

Last time I had the happiness of seeing you, you were sitting
in Committee with Messrs Courthope, Gosse and others, and were so
much interested that I could not speak with you!

Will you never come & see us again? You are not always
attended, I take it, by your company of players. Term begins today,
and there are sympathetic souls who wd be rejoiced to meet you:
above all Walter Raleigh – and my house is retired on a hill, & has a
large room, library and music room, where you cd do what you
liked. Really you wd not do badly – I, though I am getting very old,
am still alive. I can't however think of anything to attract you, unless
honest flattery can draw. Anyhow it's better than London Committees with Gosse and Co.

Really I write this lest Binyon shd not have told you about that
4/5. It came to me as a discord. But if you don't feel it, there is a
chance that I may be wrong: but I don't think so.

So come and see us this Spring before the hyacinths are over.
The Spring is very beautiful in our woods. We are quite in the
country, but can walk across fields & ferry to Oxford in 40 minutes.

Yours in poetic devotion
ROBERT BRIDGES

Don't feel obliged to write a letter. – a postcard, or 4/5 of a postcard
wd tell me you will come.

From JOHN BUTLER YEATS

New York

MS Yeats   27 May 1913

[Daniel Cohalan's troubles with the law were widely publicized in the New York newspapers. His accuser was John A. Connolly. John Quinn spent five weeks defending Cohalan, who was cleared by the State Legislature in July. JBY refers to the Charles Johnstons. For more about JBY's articles, see letter dated 10 February 1914.]

My dear Willie,

This will amuse you. A French woman lodging here told me my fortune from cards in queer broken English. She said, "You have a son coming here who will be a very great success." She said also that I am "all among strangers, not much heart." The second true and I hope the first. I am *busier* here than ever I was before, that is, I have a busier hope, and to be busy is the greater part of life – but if not actually busy I am not the happiest of mortals, particularly since my dog was killed.

Next Saturday I dine at the annual Whitman dinner, a guest of John Quinn's (by the way full of heart for all his friends). I will make a speech. It will be a mixed joy. Hundreds of people the most remote from art and literature come to these dinners – all mad – in an amicable sort of way. Only if a fire-brand is thrown among them in the shape of a blood-and-thunder speech the amicability vanishes. Of course they interpret Whitman literally, as a few years ago they did the Bible – the same lunacy in another form.

What with Socialism and the I.W.W. (International Workers of the World) and the rage against graft, looking about for victims in high places, life is not a pleasant place here in N York, except for the people who like to give and receive bloody noses. Quinn's friend Cohalan is in trouble, the papers calling upon him to resign his position as Judge of the Supreme Court, or else successfully meet certain charges of getting 55 per cent on contracts obtained by him for a favored individual, a former friend named Connolly, who now makes the charge in some vendetta between them. I suppose Cohalan is guilty, but only guilty as every other Tammany man was guilty. It is a great private calamity though it be a public good. Cohalan is a good honest man who helped everyone, friends as well as relatives. He has six children and has just lost his wife, and is very pious, piety and uxoriousness combining to make him long for death when he hopes to meet his wife — a primitive man as is always your pious Catholic. A pious Protestant is never primitive, but very much up-to-date. For him the rewards of piety are in this world.

I am in the midst of annoyances. I had contracts for four articles, one of them handed in, so that I daily expected my 75 dollars, and another partly written. And now the magazine is sold and everything cancelled. I said something to the editor about legal obligations, but he only replied that no one cares anything about law in N York, which is the naked truth. The article handed in is on "Personality." The Editor thinks very highly of it and feels sure that the new Editor will accept it — the first a friend of both the Johnstons and a real lover of literature, the other a pushing Philistine. So it looks badly.

Yours affectionately
J. B. YEATS

From WILLIAM THOMAS HORTON

London

MS Yeats   19 June 1913

[Apparently, Yeats had told Horton and Miss Locke about his experiments in automatic writing with Elizabeth Radcliffe (the "wonderful friend"?).]

My dear Yeats

I enclose promised copy.

We appreciate deeply your relation to us of all those wonderful experiences, they are most illuminating and encouraging.

I wonder whether you'd care to come & see me some afternoon convenient to all? We could have tea &, if you could manage it, stay to supper which would be of fruits as our friend & I are practically fruitarians.

I very foolishly left my knife on your table last night. I will call for it some day soon when your housekeeper will perhaps kindly return it to me.

Allow me to thank you most heartily for yesterday's most delightful evening.

Yours,
W. T. HORTON

Am looking forward to blindfold experiment & to report progress in automatic writing.

I want to tell you that yesterday has left a feeling of great strength & calm & self effacement. We both felt very strongly this feeling of self effacement about you yesterday, as though when speaking at times you were lifted up into the Higher Self & there we all three understood one another more & realized more fully our union with all men in the Universal.

Thank God it was so, for it was good to be there.

Just before adding this to my letter I saw Christ, surrounded by flowers, looking down with steadfast gaze & with Him came the feeling of strength, calmness & utter selflessness & also a great satisfaction & elation.

Evidently our meeting has brought about more things than we realize at present.

We both send all good to you & your wonderful friend.

W T H

From AMY AUDREY LOCKE

London

MS Yeats   30 June 1913

[Horton and Miss Locke had spent the evening of 29 June at Yeats's flat. Unfortunately, only a part of their experiment is preserved.]

Dear Mr. Yeats.

Early this morning I dreamt of a chart that was suspended before me with several items on it that concerned you. All I could remember, however, was the second, namely: — "The fight is between 4 & 9; see that it is 9." This evening Mr. Horton & I tried the Planchette with a question as to the other items. We received the enclosed which I have copied out for you.

If there is anything in it you will be able to interpret it and only you, — so I send it in case it has any bearing on the difficulties you spoke of last night. If not, then no matter. Don't trouble to answer this. Thank you so much for your hospitality of last night. I only wish that our experiment had been rewarded, even with one word of sense.

Yours sincerely
AUDREY LOCKE

June 30, 1913   ⎧W.T.H.⎫
                                           ⎨A.A.L.⎬

(1) The first is that in the contest with the psychic elements in the storm of spirit, there is brought into play a material force corresponding with the ethereal force. This is the force to be guarded against and if conquered on the material plane [*no other pages*]

From EVA FOWLER

                                                    Brasted, Kent
MS Yeats   21 July [1913]

[Mrs Fowler, who was a friend of Olivia and Dorothy Shakespear, Ezra Pound, and many London artists and writers, may have introduced Elizabeth Radcliffe (B in this letter) to Yeats. Over a period of several months, chiefly in the summer of 1913, Yeats observed the automatic writing of Miss Radcliffe which he analysed in a long manuscript essay (completed on 8 October 1913): "Preliminary Examination of the Script of ER". Harold Hartley was a sceptical friend whom Yeats hoped to convince by his essay and the now-lost Appendices. The spirit of Thomas Emerson, a London policeman who committed suicide in 1850, communicated through Miss Radcliffe. Yeats sought information about him from Scotland Yard. Although signed "ER & EF" the letter was written by Mrs Fowler.]

Dear Mr Yeats,

I am *so* glad about these things. Not from my own point of view – because I am so certain nothing could shake me or make any difference – but for B's sake. Someday I want you if you have time to write me a little note about the theories & the proofs you have so I can show it to Harold Hartley – He would not believe me – for he thinks I am just carried away like the rest of the women. I'm sure you'll find the policeman if you have every one else. I showed the letter B. got the other day (a copy) to a friend who knew my sister well & all her little tricks of expression – and all about her life and character. She would not believe me when I told her how it had come, but said it must be a letter I had had! So real it is. I did not show it to you as it would not have been of any use to you as proof and it was very private. It came as you know after the warning to you. We have not tried to do any more – I thought it better to let her rest as a very great deal had come. (If you had copied it — you would think so).

I have now got some wonderful things from Africa but I cannot tell you about them or show them to you or anyone — but they are so extraordinary I wish I could. I don't know the medium — they were sent me by some one else. I shall be consumed till I hear from you again. You will let me have the papers back with the questions when you can wont you. Our greetings to you

ER & EF

You left your ink and enclosed letter.

From EVA FOWLER

MS Yeats

Brasted, Kent
21 August [1913]

[Because less could be found concerning Thomas Emerson, it was more convincing that Miss Radcliffe should have communicated details about him than about John Mirehouse, concerning whom Yeats found information "in Burke's Landed Gentry". The system of asking the trance medium prepared questions which she answered in automatic writing was used extensively by W. B. and George Yeats for *A Vision*. Yeats had been "making a Pilgrimage" to Winchelsea in the belief that he could "make communication more easy" with "Peter the Malacite", who had appeared in his experiments.]

Dear Mr. Yeats.

It is most satisfactory about Thomas Emerson — a much better test than Mirehouse, for unbelievers might think she could have come across his tomb somewhere long ago, and forgotten it — but indeed she could not have come across T.E. & the circumstances. She sent me your letter on. I shall be glad of the papers when you have a chance of adding your questions to which they were answers. I can't get on with what I want to do, until I have them. I had thought of making a book for you too — like B's & mine — with *all* the writing in it & drawing but if you don't particularly want it — do tell me — because you know it takes a good long time. My idea in her book is to leave blank pages so the questions — and also the solutions to as many of the problems as we succeed in solving can be written on them. I shall have time alone in September — so if you could possibly let me have your questions by the end of this month I should be very grateful. Perhaps we should have some of the Greek & Latin translations by then. I mean to get at the meaning of those symbols too — sometimes I feel as if I had just got some of them and before I can write it down the idea goes. It has happened time & again. I can't think what interferes. The other night I saw that eye drawing ⬭⟿ the one open — the other shut — all in gold which flamed and with it a flaming-glowing gold cord which twisted itself into circles — knots — double & single & triple — sailors knots — what they call true-lovers knots and also the eye ♫ of a hook & eye. there were other deisgns too which I could not remember in detail in the morning. B. came down for the day on the 15th but we hadn't time to talk of anything that interested us as there were others here — but she told me of a curious dream she had had three nights running with a slight change each time. Perhaps you can throw some light on it.

She was walking with me and someone else over a moor and we came to a little lake in the heather — I stood on the bank with the other person — and watched her while she jumped onto a tussock of thick grass a little distance from the shore. On it she saw a nest with three silver eggs in it — and then a huge — I think silver grey bird alighted on her breast with its wings folded tip to tip. The next night the bird's wings were half open — the third stretched as wide as her arms could stretch with the tip of a very strong feather going into her palms and holding the arms out.

I wish we could get some days here together again, but I fear that wont be possible as she goes to Dartmoor. I hope however to go north with her the end of September for a little motor tour — but that is not the same as being quietly here. However I am quite convinced that when the time is ready we shall come together again.

If you are in London in September and want a week-end of air — just let us know.

> All greetings
> Very very sincerely
> EVA FOWLER

Let me have the drawing of the cross. I've had some very interesting papers which came from South Africa — and I wish I could have sent them on to you — but they were sent me in strictest confidence and I could not. If ever they are published they ought to convince the most sceptical. Did you find out anything at Winchelsea?

From EVA FOWLER

Brasted, Kent

MS Yeats   21 September [1913]

[Yeats was not satisfied with the information he was able to find about Peter the Malachite, a spirit who appeared several times during the months of the sittings with Miss Radcliffe. Like Sister Mary Helen Ellis, Peter probably first appeared at one of the seances conducted by Mrs Etta Wreidt, the famous American medium who visited England several times between 1911 and 1919. Mrs Fowler's niece was Eva Focke. John Mason Neale wrote *A History of the Holy Eastern Church*, 5 vols. (1847–73).]

Dear Mr. Yeats.

Your letter came this morning and I must just get this line off to you before I leave, as I don't think I should have any chance to write at any rate till we get to Bamborough, and I don't know just when that will be. We are due on Loch Loug the seventh of October. I do not know how long we shall be getting to John o'Groats – but anyway if there is a chance of our stopping anywhere for three days I will wire you a couple of days before. It would not be worth your making what would be a very long and tiresome journey, unless we can get a clear three days. This is a crazy expedition – or at least it seems so to everyone but Bessie and me – I am like you, and I begin to imagine a meaning in everything, and find myself wondering if there is one in this. I will write anywhere about Sister Mary Ellis if you will only tell me where you wish me to write. I will also ask Father O'Connor to make enquiries. I don't mind telling him why as I have often spoken to him about these things & even went down to his house to try to locate a troubling ghost for him. I got no satisfaction at all from six different volumes of Dr. Neale. The other book they sent me from the L[ondon] Li[brary] was in Latin. There was mention of the Melchites who were Catholics – but the record only goes to about 700 or thereabouts. I could find no Peter connected with the "Holy Eastern Church" in 1400 any time. I shall have to look at later records when I return to town, and above all find out if these Melchites continued as a sect in the Greek Church. I haven't the original script and Bessie does not come till seven to-morrow & we leave very early the next morning – besides her house is shut up and she stays with us. I am however quite certain it is written Malachite. It is one of those auditory errors of yours. The Arabs would pronounce Melek, which means King, and from which the name was given, as if it were Malak — not a flat a — but one almost au — and a little thick — If you should get on the track of any books I will go to the museum when I get back home. I saw the first mention of Melchites in the dictionary of religions. I have no doubt at all we shall find him. If I had not been afraid of boring you, and also very much afraid I was jumping at conclusions I could have sent you a lot of impressions about the various script as I was copying them. I know I very often "jump true" but then I am also quite capable of missing, so I never like to say anything. If you write send the letter to 26 Gilbert St. I don't know just when we should get it — but when I see a day ahead I shall wire for letters to be forwarded.

Certainly those papers grow more and more interesting, and I am certain we shall get at something.

She sent me a little scrap the other day, and she tells me she is bringing one or two others — but that they seem "very incoherent." I write it on the other sheet — All greetings.

Yours v. sincerely
EVA FOWLER

By the way there were knocks in the cabinet one night — when I was alone here. My little neice has sent me an account of Anna Luise Karsch's life. I have asked her to find out about her "wisdom" and "saintliness."

From T. M. JORDEN

MS Yeats

Athenry, Galway
2 December 1913

[In his lecture about "Ghosts and Dreams" to the Dublin branch of the SPR on 31 October, Yeats referred to his experiments with Miss Radcliffe.]

Dear Sir

An advertisement appeared in the Irish Weekly independent on the 22nd Nov. a book which is to contain and interpret the latest results of Continental and British investigations on the subject of gosts and as the paper stated you have not confined yourself to mental phenomena, with recent experiments in London with a girl Medium. I was just thinking you might be able to assist me in a matter which Im greatly interested in, as Im a great believer in

Sorcery, and when I seen the advertisement it struck me that you might be a sorcerer or a magician, for the last two years I have made several enquires through the press for the address of a sorcerer or sorceress, but up to now I have not been successful. And Im sure if you are not one yourself you might be good enough to send me the address of one if you have got the like, and whatever your demand will be I will return same when I get a reply from you. The subject that I am interested in at present I believe that no one can give me any information about it except a sorcerer. I expect between yourself and Miss Medium you will be able to tell me the few questions I want. I inclose a penny stamp for reply I will tell you in my next letter the questions I want to know.

Your Well Wisher and friend
T. M. JORDEN

From HARRIET MONROE

Chicago

TS University of Chicago Library   [after 8 December 1913]

[Yeats received the award for "The Grey Rock", *Poetry* (Apr 1913), but the announcement of the prize did not appear until the November issue. The typescript of this letter is a rough draft upon which Ezra Pound, then foreign correspondent of *Poetry*, commented that "the thing should have been done with decent deliberation", then added: "I don't see how Yeats could possibly go on contributing after yr. letter".]

Dear Mr Yeats.

You may have seen our announcement of an award of £50 for the best poem sent us during the year.

This is, I think, the first award of this sort given in America. The first attempt to treat the poet as well as the Painter is treated. An attempt to show appreciation of the finest work in contradistinction to the commercial variety.

In offering this award to you, we add more dignity to the custom, and we hope that you will consider the spirit, rather than the substance of the act.

HARRIET MONROE

From KATHARINE TYNAN HINKSON

                                        Shankill, Co. Dublin
MS Yeats   17 December 1913

[In the "Introductory" essay to *The Wild Harp* (1913) Mrs Hinkson wrote: "W. B. Yeats brought a new soul into Irish poetry". Her new volume was *Irish Poems* (1913). Although Yeats wrote to Mrs Hinkson that she had been a little indiscreet in quoting from his letters without permission in *Twenty-Five Years: Reminiscences* (1913), Pamela Hinkson informs us of a letter to her mother from Alice Meynell reporting that Yeats "has said . . . K. T. knew he would not mind her using his letters". Mrs Meynell's poem was published as "Sonnet" in *Poems* (1893) and as "Your Own Fair Youth" in *The Poems of Alice Meynell* (1923). Cf. *L* 585, which may be incorrectly dated.]

My dear Willie —

    Will you let me have your address? I have two books for you, — one my compilation 'The Wild Harp', to which you are so generous. The other my new little volume of poems, in which I know you will find something to like because you are so generous a critic & for the sake of old times.

    Mrs Meynell told me that you were not angry with me for using your letters in the Reminiscences. I was afraid to ask you lest you should say no. Any how I dont think I have committed any indiscretions, and I am glad to see the people recognize you as one of the heroes of the book. It is like Mrs Meynell's sonnet, — do you remember? —

    Your own fair youth, you care so little for it.

    If you are ever within easy reach of me do come to see us.

                                        Yours ever affectionately
                                        K.T.H.

From ELIZABETH RADCLIFFE

                                        London
MS Yeats   19 December [1913]

[Yeats answered that he did not know who the woman was, but wondered if she were "Isabella", one of the spirits who had been appearing.]

Dear Mr. Yeats.

I had no chance to speak to you this afternoon or I would have told you that yesterday at Mrs. Shakespear's house, I saw, standing behind you a tall woman with rather a long thin face — very bright eyes & thick eyebrows. She had dark hair plainly parted & just a little grey. She wore a cloak, dark green turned back with dull red, & was rather taller than the average woman, or else she was standing on the ground. I could not see which because of the hats in front of me. I wonder if you know who she could be? I should so like to know. Here is a copy of the scripts you wanted, I hope these are the right ones.

Yours sincerely,
BESSIE RADCLIFFE

From ST JOHN ERVINE

TS Berg Collection,   London
New York Public Library   12 January 1914

[Already popular at the Abbey (three of his plays having been produced prior to this date), Ervine was to become, briefly, the manager (1916); later he was an original member of the Irish Academy of Letters. The play Yeats returned may have been *The Orangeman* (produced 13 March 1914). The tragedy with which Ervine was preoccupied was most likely *John Ferguson* (produced 30 November 1915).]

Dear Yeats,

Your letter is a humiliating one, but I begin already to feel that it is a purge. Every writer needs some sore thing to happen to him — and I know well that I needed a humiliation more than most men; for I was catching the journalist's trick of writing easily: I was in that state when I was inclined to fill up the gaps in my imagination with jokes. Please do not think that I knew that when I sent the play to the Abbey: it was your letter which had the effect of clarifying my sight. If I had known what I now know I should not have sent the play to you. I will put it away for a while and perhaps I shall be able to do something with it later. At the moment I am too preoccupied by a tragedy for the Abbey to think of anything else. There must not be any humour in a tragedy, even when it is natural humour. The danger of writing in natural style, as I do, is that the humourous things follow on the heels of bitter and terrible things, and make laughter where there should only be silence. I suppose a comedy is like a tree in foliage, while a tragedy is as bare as the branches in winter. I have been in the country for a short while this winter and I know now, as I never knew before, that bare branches are very beautiful. I suppose I was unaware of their beauty because I had always before seen only the foliage.

I hope you are very well. I am sorry that I was unable to help Lady Gregory more effectually in finding a new manager for the Abbey.

Sincerely,
ST JOHN G. ERVINE

From EVERARD FEILDING

Kolozsvar, Hungary

MS Yeats   22 January 1914

[Already good friends as associates in the SPR, Yeats and Feilding (the Earl of Denbigh) had in all probability attended many seances together. Thomas Anstey Guthrie, who published under the pseudonym of F. Anstey, and Sir Henry Rider Haggard wrote many popular romances. Feilding calls his host a jokester (*blagueur*) and rake (*viveur*). The Ouija board, on which the alphabet and various signs are written, is used to obtain mediumistic messages. The papers Yeats referred to were probably the automatic writing of Elizabeth Radcliffe.]

Private
My dear Yeats,

Your letter reached me here today. I don't expect to be back till some time after Feb 8th. I am at the present moment in the middle of the most fantastic romance I have ever heard of. Imagine a mixture of Anstey & Haggard & the Arabian Nights & you will get the situation in which I now find myself. I am staying, in short, with a Jinn. My host, a Hungarian lawyer, an intelligent, reckless, frivolous, goodhearted man, blagueur & viveur & spendthrift, has one of his own, a merry friendly imp, late a Roumanian of the name of Vassilika, & now as companionable & entertaining a hobgoblin as one could wish for. When my lawyer, 2½ years ago, was at his wit's end for money & contemplated suicide, Vassilika made, so to speak, his first bow, intervening with gulden, cigarettes & pears dropped out of the air, & eggs slung from the hook of the chandelier on the roof of a very high room. And ever since then he has gone on, throwing into the room, at any hour of the day or night, objects of all sorts & sizes, from a bromide tabloid to a large marble slab, & from an ancient pair of pincers to a very respectable sized pump. I have stayed with him now a week, & have seen many of these things, sometimes under non evidential conditions & sometimes under excellent ones, as for example when a glass lands softly at my feet with no one within more of 12 ft. of me; or when a 4 or 5 ft. pole jumps out at me from a corner when I am the first to enter the room. Vassilika, who communicates by ouija, is good enough to say he likes me & is going to produce a really good programme. If he goes on as well as he has begun I shall be quite pleased. The whole thing is complicated up with an elaborate story of previous incarnations, family details being given in profusion, also topographical features which are confirmed by ordnance maps of distant or unknown places, involving buried treasure which we're probably going off to hunt for! I shd. very much like to see the papers you speak of, if I am allowed. I don't guarantee much intellect (after my present adventures) but I will certainly have loads of sympathy for even the most flagrantly impossible phenomena.

Hoping to see you after my return

Yours very sincerely
E. FEILDING

From ARTHUR EDWARD WAITE

MS Yeats   31 January 1914

[Still concerned with the communications of spirits through Elizabeth Radcliffe, Yeats sought information from Waite (Sacramentum Regis), prolific historian of occultism and a colleague in the Golden Dawn until the split in 1903. The Astral Light is said to proceed from bodies of spirits as perceived by clairvoyant sight. Éliphas Lévi Zahed, pseudonym for Alphonse Louis Constant, and Louis Claude de Saint-Martin were well-known French occultists and authors about whom Waite had written. Waite refers to an essay in Saint-Martin's "The Crocodile" (1798) entitled "Influence of Signs upon Ideas", issued as a pamphlet in 1799. Jacob Boehme and Paracelsus (i.e. Theophrastus Bombastus von Hohenheim) were

influential alchemical philosophers and authors. For Dr Rudolph
Steiner see letter for 15 September 1912. Charles W. Leadbeater
became Secretary of the London Lodge of the Theosophical Society
in 1889 and was the author (with Annie Besant) of numerous occult
books. The Akasic records, sometimes described as pictures or
reflections, are "the conscious memory of the Logos of our
system".]

Dear Yeats:

So far as my studies can tell you, the theory of the Astral Light
as a receptacle of forms, and having therefore "pictures" therein, was
first originated by Éliphas Lévi, after the year 1860. Some of the
Parisian occultists pretend that the doctrine of the Astral Light is to
be found in a cumbrous and rather ridiculous allegory of L. C. de
Saint-Martin, called "The Crocodile," which would put the idea back
into the late 18th century. I have not found it and believe that it has
been "read in." It has been said to be in Jacob Böhme, but this is
untrue also. Finally, it is not in Paracelsus, though he speaks of
Astral Science in his book "Concerning the Nature of Things" and, in
his "Hermetic Astronomy," of Astral or Sidereal Spirits, who may be
compelled to serve men like slaves.

I looked up this question long ago. Of course Eliphas Levi
writes as if his favourite idea were in all the eminent philosophers.
There may be something in the East, but about this I do not know.
Dr Steiner and Leadbeater claim to read what they call "the Akasic
records" and come to opposite conclusions on the faith of what they
see. I would help you if I could over this side of the question, but it
is one for a reliable eastern student, on the understanding that he is
not a theosophist.

Yours sincerely
A. E. WAITE

From HARRIET MONROE

Chicago
TS University of Chicago Library   3 February 1914

[In the address of thanks for the dinner (on 1 March) Yeats observed
that "nearly all the great influences in art and literature, from the
time of Chaucer until now" have come from Paris. He praised Pound
and read two of his poems.]

My dear Mr. Yeats:

I was delighted to receive your letter saying that you would give us the pleasure of entertaining you as our guest, should you come to Chicago. And still more to learn from your lecture agent in New York that you will be in Chicago for at least a week.

I am now writing to ask a great favor. We, of the editorial staff of POETRY feel that you would honor us very highly if you would permit us to give you an informal dinner while you are here, to which we may invite our guarantors and contributors. We are not insensible of the fact that this would be conferring greater honor upon us than upon the guest of honor; but it is probably for just that reason that we are bold enough to ask it of you. We hope that you will confer this recognition upon our attempt, not unlike your effort for the Irish Theater, to create and perpetuate beauty among us. Chicago has many endowed institutions, and all, except ours, offer some chance of social contact. This will be the first thing of its kind that we have attempted, and should you once get us on the high plane of your approval, we should be compelled ever after to live up to it.

At this present writing I am not quite sure that it is within our means to ask you on this occasion to give us a brief talk upon contemporary poetry, as we should like to do. If, however, you will gratify us by accepting this invitation to honor POETRY we shall enter into communication with your agent. We should particularly like you to say something to our guarantors of the most recent tendencies of poetry — not of the Nineties, but of the 'Teens.

From what we have heard from New York, either Sunday Night, Feb. 22nd, or Sunday Night, March 1st, would be possible occasions for the supper. We have to say Sunday Night as that is the night when we may have possession of the Cliff Dwellers, which is an informal and rather pleasant place, we feel, for the dinner, or supper. Will you be kind enough, in the event of your accepting, to let us know which of these two dates would be most convenient for you? If it does not crowd you unduly, it would seem to us that February 22nd would be the better of the two. But that is, I believe, the date of your arrival here.

I am looking forward to your visit to us with great pleasure, and I am, my dear Mr. Yeats,

Yours very sincerely,
HARRIET MONROE

From JOHN QUINN
TS Manuscript Division,   New York
New York Public Library   9 February 1914

[Quinn had charged Yeats with gossip about his relationship with
Dorothy Coates in August 1909.]

My dear Yeats:
    I wonder whether you will be surprised to receive this note
from me. A good deal of water has flowed under the bridges since
you and I parted. The lady to whom you talked has been very ill for
months — almost at the point of death — and has been and is now
away in the mountains making a brave fight for life and health, and
from there she has written to me about you and hoped that you and
I would be friends again.
    I have always felt that apart from intellect you were always
generous in your sympathies and full of humanity and that your
heart was in the right place.
    So if the suggestion appeals to you, I should be glad to shake
hands with you and let by-gones be by-gones.

Sincerely yours,
JOHN QUINN

From JOHN BUTLER YEATS

                                           New York
MS Yeats   10 February 1914

[Yeats was in America on a lecture tour when this letter was written.
Since the summer of 1909 JBY had been living at a boarding house
run by three Breton sisters named Petitpas. George Harvey was
editor of *Harper's Weekly*, 1901–13, Norman Hapgood, 1913–16.
General John O'Regan, which had a short run on Broadway, was
written by "George A. Birmingham" (Canon James Owen Hannay),
author of many popular novels. Miss Ann Squire, an interior
decorator, dined frequently at Petitpas.]

My dear Willie,
    I am ashamed to say I owe the Petitpas 537 dollars. Could you
let me have 250 dollars? The rest I can manage with commissions &c
that I have in hand, one a portrait of myself for which by express
agreement I am to ask my own price. John Quinn is the man.

Last year I had many strokes of ill luck. The sale of *Harpers Weekly* cancelled commissions for three articles, and threw back on my hands an article received and accepted by the Editor. (The Editor himself admitted that they were legally liable, but added that in America no one cares for law.) The editor of the new *Harpers Weekly* saw me by appointment and asked me to do for him four articles on certain artists. The first was the article on John Sloan. It was all settled as far as words went, and I was to get 100 dollars for each article. As yet I have heard nothing further. Had *General John O'Regan* been a commercial success I should have asked 250 or perhaps 500 dollars, and I have received nothing, though now suing them for 175.

In preparation for those articles on the four artists I read several books. I intended them to be *manifestos*. The artists themselves were eager for my articles. A certain professor, a stranger to me, sent a year's subscription to Harpers because of my article on Sloan. The magazine printed his letter.

The result of my reading and thinking so much is that I now have several articles in my mind, and partly in writing. And they are wanted by a literary agency.

Yrs affectly
J. B. YEATS

Last night over the 'phone I was promised two tickets for the Wednesday lecture. I hope they will come in good time, as I have promised to give one of them to Miss Squire.

From EVA FOWLER

Rock, Worcestershire

MS Yeats   13 April [1914]

["B" is Elizabeth Radcliffe. For the Hungarian poltergeist see Feilding's letter of 22 January 1914. Baron Albert von Schrenck-Notzing recorded four years of experiments with a famous medium known as "Eva C." in *Materialisations Phénomène* (1914). Yeats participated in experiments with her in Paris on 19, 22, and 26 May 1914. G. R. S. Mead was (with Annie Besant) joint-secretary of the Esoteric Section of the Theosophical Society while Yeats was a member. Dr Robert Isaac Eisler was a German writer and occultist. Mrs Fowler refers to the engagement of Dorothy Shakespear and Ezra Pound; they were married on 20 April 1914.]

Dear Mr. Yeats —

    Your letter has found us here, but starting off again on Wednesday. It's a pity — else I should have sent you a wire to come and join us. Taffy and George Clerk have had an orgy of golf and go back to London to-morrow night. We have the car and are going across Dartmoor and then up the coast & through the New Forest and on to Daisy Meadow for Friday night — home Saturday & B. stays there with me till Monday. Would you like to come to dinner Saturday 7-30? My sister will be out & Taffy away so B. & I alone, and we could have a talk. I can't give you any address except D.M. & if you write there put "await arrival." If you like I will send you a telegram as soon as I know what time we get to D.M. and you could come down too — but there are no servants there, and I warn you that we are going to picnic on eggs & tea only. And you'd have to help scrape potatoes & B says "if necessary kill a pig." Also I've no idea what time we should get there. There has been very little writing but I've got the bits for you. B. has been ill practically all the time you have been away except for the fortnight in Oxford and then she was sickening with what came after. She is apparently all right now — and we spend the days on the sands & rocks & in the car. I wonder what you will hear from Mr Feilding. I heard his Hungarians were frauds. Also Dr. von Schrenck Notzing has found out his medium wasn't straight. Mr. Mead told me he heard it from Dr. Eisler. It is hopeless to get at all this. Dorothy, when she wrote me of her engagement said "Mother says you'll go up in a flame when you hear my news." I did — but I've recovered! and I think Ezra the luckiest of mortals.

    Our greetings to you and we are glad you are back.

                                 E.F.

From JOHN QUINN

TS Manuscript Division,
New York Public Library

New York
28 April and
3 June 1914

[*Nine Poems*, privately printed by Mitchell Kennerley, was prepared at Quinn's direction for a farewell dinner for Yeats on 1 April. The references to Yeats and Moore appeared in "The Seven Arts", Huneker's regular column in *Puck*. *Nine Poems* contained a photograph of Yeats by Arnold Genthe. When Liebler and Company, theatrical agents, refused to accept the portrait of Maire O'Neill

(Molly Allgood), Quinn purchased the painting. The book collector in California was Henry E. Huntington. Quinn had purchased *La Rivière* and *Le Vendage* by Puvis de Chavannes in 1913. W. Bourke Cockran was a New York congressman. Mrs Leonard M. Thomas ("Michael Strange") was a minor poet.]

My dear Yeats:

I am sending you under separate cover to the Woburn Buildings six copies of the Kennerley print of the nine poems. I am sending one to Lady Gregory, one to each of your sisters and one to Madame Gonne, making four in all, and with these six making ten in all that have gone to your side. They are rather interesting, and the photograph is a good one, and although they do not rise to the dignity of an edition, I thought you would like to have these copies.

I am sending you two copies of "Puck" for April 25th, which contains a reference to George Moore as well as to yourself. I am sending a copy of it to Lady Gregory, one copy to Madame Gonne, one to each of your sisters and one to Jack.

Wednesday, June 3, 1914

My dear Yeats:

You will see I started to dictate this letter to you on April 28th, and a month has gone by, but I haven't had time to continue. I have been out of town a great deal; been to Washington three or four times — a day or two each week; out to Ohio; and last Saturday up to the Adirondacks to see Miss Coates. It is a hard, all-night trip, from seven o'clock at night till seven the next morning, and then back again the next night.

I received on May 22d yours of May 14th from Paris.

I hope that you got rested from your work by this time, but one doesn't recover in a day or two from two months' hard work

I enjoyed that part of your letter in which you tell about the Catholic miracle. If Feilding, the man you write about, knows his business and knows how to take blood slides or good specimens of the blood, an examination by a competent chemist will be able to give him the blood count and will show whether it is human blood or fake blood, and if it is real saint's blood a real discovery will have been made in the anatomy of the saints, for science will then for the first time be able to tell the relative number of red and white blood corpuscles in the saint's blood. The examination of the blood is of course the key to the whole thing. If you hear from Feilding what the result of the blood examination is, I shall be glad to have you let me know how it came out.

I got from Arnold Genthe a few days ago three sets of prints: the print of yourself and myself; a few of the full-face view of yourself alone, with the same pose as the small one that was the frontispiece to the selection of poems, and some of another view, a three-quarters view, which is not so good as the full-face view, but is interesting.

I have sent one of the pictures of you and myself to Maud Gonne; one to Lady Gregory, and two to your sisters, one for each of them. I am sending to you in a separate parcel at the Woburn Buildings the following: three copies of the picture of yourself; two copies of the large full-face picture of the same or almost the same pose as the one that was the frontispiece to the little brochure (and I am sending one of these to your sisters in Dublin); and three copies of the three-quarter head.

I paid your father thirty pounds for his painting of Miss O'Neill, and it is in my apartment. I think I shall keep it. The hands are not quite finished, but otherwise it is a very good painting. The background is especially good. They paid him five pounds for the pencil drawing. So that gives him thirty-five pounds. That, together with what you gave him, has I think paid him out of debt with the Petitpas. I haven't seen him for a couple of weeks, but the last time I saw him he was quite cheerful and looked well.

I am in a Congressional matter that will take me to Washington perhaps several times before the adjournment of Congress, and Congress may not adjourn until the middle of July or the beginning of August. The Republicans are likely to win the Lower House this autumn. Our Lower House is the House of Representatives. That is elected for two years. Hence this autumn we elect the members of the Lower House of Congress. If the Republicans capture that, we will then have the Democrats in control of the Senate and the Republicans in control of the House, and Wilson will have difficulty in getting his program through. So that he is anxious to get through all the legislation he can before the adjournment of the present Congress. Businesmen are getting tired. A great many of them are saying that the Democrats aren't businessmen; that the backbone of the Democratic Party is from the South, and that the Democrats aren't capable of being trusted with the administration of the affairs of the national government. The Democrats are almost certain to lose this state, including the Governor, the State Legislature (both Senate and Assembly), the United States Senator, and at least half their present representation in Congress.

Roosevelt of course wants to run in 1916 for President. He has a certain nuisance value and a large following, but it is doubtful whether he can be elected again. If the Republicans go back in to power this autumn they are likely to become so cock-sure that they will pick out some new man and nominate him to run against Wilson in 1916, for there is a good deal of bitterness towards Roosevelt because he bolted the Republican ticket in 1912. If he had only stayed out in 1912, or stayed out of the country, Taft would have been defeated, and then the Republicans all over the country would have turned to Roosevelt for 1916. But as it is a great many Republicans blame him for Taft's defeat and will feel that in 1916 they can give him a dose of his own medicine, if he attempts to run.

I am not certain about going abroad this summer, and the chances are that I shall not be able to go abroad. If I went abroad I should like to do some motoring, and to look at some paintings for a few days in London, and to see some artists and their works for a week or so in Paris. But the chances are all against my being able to get away. If I don't go, I should like to get some little place out in the country, either on the north shore of Long Island, where it is woody, or up in the hills somewhere, where I can go before regular vacation time from Friday till Monday, and where I can have some friends and get some exercise, either riding or golf.

I think you know that I collect manuscripts, but only the manuscripts of men whose work I like. I disposed of most of my Meredith and Morris and Swinburne and Hardy manuscripts to a man who is founding a big library in Los Angeles, California, and put the money in the two big Puvis paintings. But I still like the manuscripts of certain living men. So I should like to make an arrangement with you, if you care to do it, to have you assemble your manuscripts, and pay you so much a year for them, depending upon the quantity and the different things, taking articles as they are or poems as they are. I could put them in separate cases, and I will pay you a reasonable price for them, more perhaps than you would get of any dealer, who would pay you only a small price, and then shop them around at a high price. I could either make an arrangement for an annual amount with you, or for each article or essay or group of poems, after you had had them typewritten from your manuscript, depending upon the length and their importance. How does this suggestion strike you?

I should like to be on the other side for a little while now, but I fear it is out of the question this summer.

Do let me know how the saint's blood examination comes out.

Oh, I nearly forgot something important: You perhaps will recall that very handsome young woman who was at Mr. and Mrs. Cockran's lunch to you at the St. Regis that Mrs. Astor attended, before we went to that matinee. Her name is Mrs. Leonard Thomas. She is a beautiful young woman and very clever. She writes poetry and composes music. She wants very much to meet Bernard Shaw. She wrote to Mrs. Cockran and asked Mrs. Cockran whether she would not ask you to send to her (Mrs. Thomas) a personal letter of introduction to Shaw. Her address is:

> Mrs. Leonard Thomas,
> c/o Morgan, Grenfell & Co.
> 65 Old Broad Street,
> London, E.C.

She is young and is a beauty and is a very interesting woman. Cockran lunched with me today and asked me to write to you as a special favor at once. And here I nearly forgot it. I told him that I would write to you and ask you to send to Mrs. Leonard Thomas (care of Morgan, Grenfell & Co., 65 Old Broad Street, London, E.C.) a letter of introduction to Shaw, and also to send a personal note to Shaw to ask Shaw to see her; in short, to give a letter that would count and not, as is often done, a mere letter of introduction, which is not meant to be honored. I wouldn't ask you to do this, even at Cockran's request or at Mrs. Cockran's request, if the girl wasn't a beauty and young and interesting; and she is all of these. She is going to be in London only a few days longer, and therefore if you send the letter to Shaw to her, the sooner you do it the better; and if you write a separate note to Shaw telling him that she is young and beautiful and interesting and that she wouldn't bore him, that might make him more willing to see her with your letter.

I received ten or twelve letters after the dinner to you from those who were there, telling me how much they enjoyed it, and many others whom I have met have spoken in the same way.

With kind regards, I am, Sincerely yours,

JOHN QUINN

P.S. As to the manuscripts: What I mean is that I should be willing to pay you a certain amount yearly on condition that I get your manuscripts, say seventy-five or eighty pounds; or else, if you don't wish to make such an arrangement, that I buy the manuscripts of your poems, of course not single poems, but when they are grouped or re-written, and of your essays and articles, paying you per group of poems or by the essay or article.

This of course is confidential to you, and if you care to make the arrangement it would be personal between you and me.

From JOHN BUTLER YEATS

New York

MS Yeats   12 May 1914

[Reviewing *Responsibilities* in *Poetry* (May 1914), Pound wrote: ". . . it is impossible to take any interest in a poem like *The Two Kings* — one might as well read the *Idylls* of another." JBY refers to a lavish dinner in honour of Yeats on 1 April, the night before he sailed for home. Richard Le Gallienne, living in Connecticut by this time, attended the dinner.]

My dear Willie

I am *inundating* you with letters. I sometimes wonder if you read them. But what the devil does Ezra Pound mean by comparing "The Two Kings" with Tennyson's *Idylls*? *The Two Kings* is immortal, and immortal because of its *intensity* and *concentration*.* It is so full of the "tears of things" that I could not read it aloud. And yet Ezra Pound is the best of critics and writes with such lucid force, and I am only an amateur. But I have this advantage, I am longer in the world and have travelled further, and concentration and intensity are not Tennysonian.

I am writing not to say this, but that a friend of mine met Le Gallienne, and found him greatly pleased with your spirit at the dinner and at the way in which you brought his name into your discourse.

I have no more to say, except that it is again winter — curse it.

Yours affectly

J. B. YEATS

What a curiously wistful thing is that Japanese play. I find it fascinating — though I wish someone would supply a key.

*In *The Two Kings* there is another quality often sought for by Tennyson, but never attained, and that is *splendor of imagination,* a *liberating splendor,* cold as sunrise. I don't agree with Ezra Pound.

From EVA FOWLER

London

MS Yeats 23 May [1914]

[The book for Miss Radcliffe was *Responsibilities*, published in May. Olivia is Mrs Shakespear. Possibly Mrs Fowler is speaking of Ignaz Jastrow, a German economist and historian, a prolific writer.]

Dear Mr. Yeats —

I went to see Mr. King at the Museum yeaterday. He says Ishtar of Arbela & I of N. are one and the same and as far as he knows there were no marked differences in the ceremony and worship. I insisted there must be. He told me to get Jastrow's book — which I shall do from the London Library. That he would look it up too and if he came across anything interesting he would write me. Of course he had heard about the other paper.

The book came for B. and I will send it on. Her address is 45 Kensington Square.

Olivia was here this morning — a pleasant oasis in the desert of trotting the "Portuganders", it's Sargent's phrase, not mine, about London.

When you come back we must have a meeting in the drawing-room. The three of us. B. can write there — and perhaps more may come.

I think perhaps we have to help one another on — though I marvel at the odd conjunction of the three of us. Thank you for what you said.

E.F.

Enclosed is a copy, as accurate as B. can make it, of the hieroglyphic.

From MAUD GONNE

Paris

MS Yeats 9 July [1914]

[Diva Brat Mukerjea, who had studied in Calcutta, Exeter, and Cambridge, was applying to the Indian Educational Service for a professorship. Helena Moloney had played numerous roles at the Abbey during 1913. Maud had promised Everard Feilding that she would return to Mirebeau to investigate the bleeding oleograph (see ltr. dated 10 July 1914). The "Medium's account" probably refers to the automatic writing of Elizabeth Radcliffe. Yeats's "new poems" (*Responsibilities*) had been published on 25 May. John Quinn had arranged Yeats's lecture tour of America in the first three months of 1914.]

My dear Willie

forgive me for not writing all this time, I have been & still am very much worried over business affairs & over Iseults health – & hadnt the courage to answer even your letters – We are starting for the mountains on the 14th which I feel sure will do Iseult good – I am going to try & forget all worries for the present –

Mukerjea arrived in Paris a day or so after your first letter – I sifted the mystery down – It was after all as you supposed when here, a literary invention of Iseults, complicated by her having told it with wonderful amplifications to Christianne Chirfil who in her turn repeated it in half confidence & much excitement & it came round again to me, but I believe the whole thing originated with Iseults imagination – & poor Mukerjea had never even heard of it –

The Bengali lessons have been going on ever since his return & they are really working very hard. Mukerjea has given up the bar & wants a professorship – In the mean time he is very hard up & has with great difficulty at last consented to receiving a very small remuneration for the lessons – He is coming to Arrens with us but will not consent to be my guest entirely – He insists on paying his lodging but consents to take his meals with us. He is extraordinarily delicate about money matters, & but for old Mr. Chirfils intervention I dont think he would have ever consented to take money for the lessons. They hope to do a good deal of translations this summer. Mukerjea is also going to let them teach him French which will certainly be of use to him – The Chirfils are coming to Arrens also so my duties of chaperone will be lightened.

Mukerjea just applied for a professorship of literature & history. I took down the enclosed particulars & send them to you, in case you might be able to recommend him usefully – I believe recommendations tell a great deal in such appointments. I would be very glad indeed if you could help him. Lady Gregory knows so many powerful people it is possible you or she could recommend him –

Helen Molony is with us. She is looking ever so much stronger & better & from what the Doctor writes here I believe the cure is complete. She is also coming to Arrens & I hope I shall be able to tell you that she is really quite recovered & able for steady work again in the Autumn — I hope I shall be able to see Abbe Vacher some time during the summer. I have promised to go & stay with my old friend Dr. Fabre at Poitier later on.

It was quite interesting your Mediums account, but as you say she may have got it from your mind. Iseult alarmed us very much by getting one or two faint fits last week — & several very severe nose bleedings. The Dr is rather anxious about her, says her heart is weak. He orders her to give up smoking, to eat meat & keep her windows open — all of which she refuses to do. I think the country will do her good & she will find it harder to get the cigarettes she likes there.

I suppose you will soon be going to Ireland. How I envy you — be charitable, return good for evil & write to me soon in spite of my long silence.

Always your friend
MAUD GONNE

When shall we see your new poems? Quinn sent me a photo of you & of himself taken last time you were in America. Quinn has come out better than you have in it, some how you never photograph well.

From EVERARD FEILDING

London
TS Yeats   10 July 1914

[Yeats, Feilding, and Maud Gonne had been to Mirebeau, France, in May to investigate a bleeding oleograph in the possession of Abbé Vachère, who allowed them to dip their handkerchiefs in the "blood". Rev. Monsignor Robert Hugh Benson, a writer of religious fiction, was appointed Private Chamberlain to Pope Pius X in 1911. Cardinal Merry Del Val was Pontifical Secretary of State (1903—14) and then Secretary of the Holy Office (1914—30). Yeats wrote an essay about the Mirebeau experience.]

Dear Yeats,

The Lister Institute writes: "An extract from the handkerchief gave no precipitate with anti-human serum which therefore excluded the possibility of its being human blood. I have also tried anti-horse, -sheep, and -ox sera, but they gave no reaction. There are no other tests of the same delicacy as the precipitin tests for blood. I have also made a spectroscopic test but the colour is too faint to decide one way or the other. If you care to obtain another sample I will make the test again, but it should be taken on clean filter paper such as I am enclosing and sent here immediately. Perhaps the fact that it is not human blood is sufficient."

I have written to Madame Gonne in hopes that she may be able to pay another visit to Mirebeau and to get further samples of the blood. If you have any influence over her do try and persuade her. I have received another letter from Mlle Fontaine who says that another picture, this time under glass, in the Abbé's sacristy has begun to bleed. It appears that the lady who was paying for the erection of the Stations had doubts after the decree of the Holy Office and wanted a sign as to whether she should continue. This was the sign. Whether she saw the beginning of it I am not sure, but have written to ask. Meanwhile I have sent to Rome to an inquisitor to make further investigations through Monsignor Benson, and through another priest friend who knows Cardinal Merry del Val extremely intimately I am making further enquiries.

Yours sincerely,
E. FEILDING

From MAUD GONNE

Arren, Pyrenees
25 July [1914]

MS Yeats

[*The Gardener*, translated by the author, was published by Macmillan in 1913. James D. Anderson was University Lecturer on Bengali at Cambridge. André Gide's translation of *Gitanjali* was published in Paris in 1914. The International Eucharistic Congress was held in Lourdes, 22–23 July. Feilding had asked Maud to investigate the bleeding oleograph at Mirebeau. Mrs Kathleen Pilcher was Maud's sister. King George V called a conference on 21 July to consider whether or not Ulster should be excluded from a pending home rule bill. At the outbreak of war on 4 August, Asquith, the Prime Minister, persuaded the Irish leaders to accept his decision to postpone home rule. Miss Moloney returned to the Abbey for two productions in 1915.]

My dear Willie

We are in these wonderful mountains. How I wish you were here with us. You would love this country & the life here! Mr

Mukerjea is with us. He & Iseult are working hard at the translations. They have already translated a good many poems of Tagores direct from the Bengali — some from the Gardner — some that have not been translated into English, some of them are very beautiful & I think their translations are very good. They have tried to translate as literally as possible & they have obtained wonderful beauty & freshness of expression. I think you will think their work very good. I cant tell you how glad I am to find Iseult really working & interested in the work.

Now we want you to write to Mr. Tagore as soon as possible saying what you think of Iseults style, & asking permission for them to bring the poems out as a book if they can find a publisher in France — This is rather urgent, as we have heard of a Jewess, a Mlle Carpetis, who has been in India & who knows the Tagores (especially the artist) & who wants to get the right of translating Mr. Tagores work in French. She is trying to make a speciality of translating Indian things, but Mr Mukerjea says she is quite incapable of doing it well. She does not know as much Bengalee as Iseult & I doubt her having much literary ability or style but she is very intelligent & very pushing. She tried hard to get hold of Mr Mukerjea & get him to work for her & help her translate, but she said some very cruel & false things about Madame Cama who Mukerjea reveres as an Indian nationalist & Mukerjea said he would not go to her house again. She than turned her anger against Mukerjea & abuses him to every one, among others Iseult who she hardly knows.

She has now gone to Cambridge to work Bengalee with Mr. Anderson professor of Indian Language, but who Mukerjea says does not know very much Bengali. She may of course pick up some Bengali student who would translate for her & there is danger that she may get from Mr Tagore, permission to translate his works before Iseult does.

Your recommendation of Iseult would carry real weight with Mr Tagore. I hear that Tagore, or Tagore's agent, has quarreled with Gide about the financial arrangements of the translation of Gitanjali so he is not likely to want to do any more. Iseult is sending by next mail some specimens of her translations to Mr Tagore, but I fear he doesnt know French well enough to really appreciate the style.

Your opinion would weigh a great deal with him, I think. I will tell Iseult to copy out some of her translations for you, so you can say you have seen them. I think it is important you should write to Tagore soon, on account of the activity of Mlle Carpetis.

We went to Lourdes for two days to the Eucharistic Congress. It was a most wonderful sight & most impressive. Cardinals & Bishops from all countries in their crimson & purple robes & the heads of most of the great religious orders & thousands of priests & thousands & thousands of people of all classes & all countries all met together at Lourdes to affirm their belief in the supernatural & in the highest form of manifestation of spiritual life.

It was wonderful & very beautiful. I & Helen Molony as Catholics were deeply moved, & Mr Mukerjea who is a Brahmin was equally so — I wish you had been there. It was an extraordinary & very inspiring sight —

I have a long letter from Mr Feilding which I must answer soon. I may be able to go to Poitier on my way back to Paris. Dr Fabre who lives near Poitier has asked us to stay. I will probably be able to get much information about Mirebeau there.

When are you going to Ireland? Kathleen wrote me you dined with her & greatly interested everyone with your talk. I am longing for the papers to know the result of the conference. Have you much inside news. From the French papers it looks as if a split in the liberal party was inevitable. It seems strange to an outsider that Asquith should have allowed the kings speech. Is he playing straight, or does he want an election before Home Rule?

Helen Molony is here. She seems *perfectly well & strong again*. I am going to make her practice her voice. I hope she will be able to join the Abby again in the Autumn. She is a charming companion. We are all fond of her —

> Write soon
> With love from Iseult I remain
> Always your friend
> MAUD GONNE

Did you get the letter I wrote before leaving Paris asking if you could get Mukerjea recommended for an appointment as professor in India.

From WILLIAM THOMAS HORTON

London

MS Yeats   25 July 1914

[Yeats gathered much of the material for "Swedenborg, Mediums and the Desolate Places" in the summer of 1914, and he finished revising "Preliminary Examination of the Script of ER" on 7 June. Horton alludes to Rossetti's translation of a famous line from Villon: "Where are the snows of yester year?" The Beloved is the inspired friend (Horton, in this instance) who represents "the perfect communion of the good" in Plato's *Phaedrus* (sections 255–6), which Horton clearly refers to in his note of 20 July. After his signature Horton drew a sketch of a triangle with a flame issuing from the upper angle.]

Private
My dear Yeats
    Ever since I saw you on Monday evening I have been troubled about you.
    I pray God you will take to heart the warning I gave you.
    It makes me absolutely sick to see & hear you so devoted to Spiritualism & its investigation. Dear old friend, forgive me but I have known you for nearly 20 years & because of my affection & respect for you as a man & my admiration for your beatiful work I feel I must be honest & frank with you & speak out to you face to face what others say behind your back. You know that I am only actuated by deep & sincere friendship – forgive me or scoff at me as you will – I must be true to the Light within come what may.
    All this Spiritism & Spiritistic investigation leads to nothing. It is just turning round & round in a circle & is never a spiral. Spiritists do not want to be convinced they are that already. Unbelievers scoff at the whole thing & Scientists will accept nothing but strictly Scientific demonstration. Telepathy, the vast powers of the hidden self, suggestion, hypnotism & self hypnotism account for nearly everything in the way of automatism. It wants a peculiarly hard, precise & unimaginative mind to sum up the for and against of all these matters. You may say or write what you will in all sincerity but the very nature & quality of your own beautiful imagination & dear poetry, so well known to thousands, will stand in your way. They will say "this is one of Yeats' imaginations," they will read it for its beauty & poetry but as a thesis or scientific argument they will pass it by. There are no proofs that can stand against all argument. Words can prove anything but they cannot make an unreal thing real or an untruth a truth. Of course it is easy to prove the reality of an assertion to a mind less capable than one's own – hence the sheep who follow any shepherd if he but call loud enough – but to get at as solid a basis as one can, in a matter incapable of demonstration by

any of the five senses, one must appeal to Caesar & prove it to his satisfaction & therefore to the keenest minds of the day.

What is the use of it all, no new light or knowledge comes, nothing that is not already known, in fact as a rule what does come is on a low level. What of your own wonderful poetry in the meantime. Are we not all of us waiting for more of the Singer's songs, the exquisite music of your verse, the whispering of unseen beauty that melts us to tears with emotion

> *"Where are the songs of yesteryear."*

To see you on the floor among those papers searching for an automatic script, where one man finds a misquotation among them, while round you sit your guests, shocked me for it stood out as a terrible symbol. I saw you as the man with the muck rake in "The Pilgrim's Progress" while above you your Beloved held the dazzling crown of your own Poetic Genius. But you would not look up & you went on with your grovelling.

Rouse yourself & turn from all these things. Look up, look up, the Beloved is calling you to fresh & higher & yet nobler flights of songs. I have not come into your life for nothing. Hidden & unknown I walk among men but in the Spirit I am what I am & by the grace of God & the power He gives me I call upon you to arise & leave all these lower things, phantasmic & unreal, & ascend to the heights.

By the grace of God I am with you & through my mortal voice & pen I am allowed to do the work I have to do for you. Yeats, our way is not down here, our way is the upward one, from height to height beyond the stars to the very foot of God's throne upon whose steps we mount eternally, eternally.

Forgive me, dear Yeats, if I have said anything to wound or hurt or anything presumptuous or ridiculous; if I have it is quite unintentional, God forbid.

I am actuated by love for you & your work, & also loyalty to you & my own Self, so I hope you will take it in this spirit & not as an impertinence on my part. When the Spirit moves within me I must speak — I can no other.

I wish you all good now & ever.

Yours Fraternally
W. T. HORTON

From MAUD GONNE

MS Yeats   Arrens, Pyrenees
                                              30 July [1914]

[On 24 July the Irish Volunteers, who were ardent Unionists, landed arms at Howth in broad day. British troops sent to prevent the unloading opened fire on unarmed civilians, killing three. Maud's letter was not published in *The Freeman's Journal*. John Edward Redmond, leader of the Home Rule movement, was opposed to violence. Bal Gangadhar Tilak was widely known as "the father of Indian unrest". Bichon is apparently a term of endearment for Maud's son, Séan.]

My dear Willie

Once more I am going to bother you about Iseults work. M. Mukerjea has just received enclosed letter. He has written proposing that Iseult should do the work. He will help her with it — they will collaborate — he thinks your recommendation would again be most useful & if possible would like you to write & say you think Iseult competent.

He asked if you would write at once as here again there is a danger of Mlle Carpetis getting before them —

The Gardener is almost finished — they do not intend doing all the poems, only those that they have got written in Bengalee. Iseult is copying them & will forward some to you tomorrow —

When I read of the splendid coup of the Volunteers & of its tragic sequel I nearly rushed over to Dublin to be present at the funeral of the victims, but the difficulty of leaving Iseult & Bichon alone in France with the chance of war being declared which would probably make my return to them impossible stopped me.

How I love & *reverence* the Dublin crowd. They are always fearless & heroic when ever a national or religious idea is before them — They never fought like that all through the labor war last winter. They stood dejectedly listening to orators telling them to fight for themselves to better their conditions, there was no enthusiasm though they starved & suffered silently & bravely & stood to a blundering leader loyally as people of no other country would have done — I have written to the Freeman but I do not know if they will publish my letter — The war scare & the sarcifice of those poor Dublin men & women & children should make it possible for Redmond to obtain a great deal for Ireland. I am waiting for the paper with breathless anxiety & can hardly sleep for thinking of it all —

How are you, where are you & why dont you write to me? In spite of the condition appearing as promising for Ireland I had a haunting sort of vision yesterday of death & famine which put me in very low spirits, but today I try & explain it to myself by thinking I was desperately moved & excited by the thought of what had happened in Dublin, & by my powerlessness to help or to be with the people & this may have drawn to my mind thoughts & memories of scenes of famine & misery I have witnessed long ago. I think it must be that.

Write to me soon.

Always your friend
MAUD GONNE

What are you writing? You probably know about Balganadhar Tilak the great Indian scholar and nationalist leader who wrote the Age of the Vedas, the Origin of the Aryans & edited *Kasari* a paper written in English & in Marathi. Mukerjea says that apart from politics he has done wonderful work in rousing his countrymen to study their heroic literature & in teaching the value of spirituality.

The English put that man in prison for 7 years — he was only liberated last month. A meeting to celebrate his release is being organised by the Indians in London & probably they will ask you to raise your voice to welcome back to liberty the distinguished nationalist & scholar.

From HAMILTON MINCHIN ("KYMRY")

London

MS Yeats   4 August 1914

[Pound had married Dorothy Shakespear on 20 April. Yeats was acquainted with Mrs Asquith, wife of Herbert Henry Asquith, the Prime Minister (Lady Margot and Lord Oxford). Pamela Genevieve Adelaide Tennant, Baroness Glenconner, was the author of *Village Notes, and Some Other Papers* (1900). England declared war on the day this letter was written. Kymry predicts Home Rule for Ireland in 1917 when Jupiter is in the sign of Taurus. Mrs Ella Wheeler Wilcox was a popular American poet and journalist; Marie Corelli was a prolific writer of popular novels, including several with occult themes. In her letter to *The Saturday Review* (25 July) Mrs Wilcox censured the journal for not perceiving that her poems "mark a new order of verse".]

Dear Mr Yeats

   If you see yr friend or write to Mr Pound — tell him I have done
him a mathem[atical] horoscope —
6 hours work so far — also a sketch of horoscope of his wife & hope
to send soon — but have been unwell & am *weak* — want a change of
air — have the money — but am not sure I shall pluck up energy to
get away — the house at present quite empty till Saturday so am a
prisoner as my gold fish want water changed etc I have secured the
patronage of Lady Glenconner, sister in law of Mrs Asquith — a very
charming writer — Village Notes a really beautiful book but she has
not been pleasant to me — I hope she may be a stepping stone to
something better. I send you two copies of my latest predictions in
fact 3 — I hope you will send one to a friend in USA.

   This war is an abominable crime — The Russian coward & bully
is at the back of it — may God destroy him! Curiously enough I feel
rather sorry for the Germ[an] Emp[eror] — a brave strong man —
about to be defeated & slain. I dont *see* England in this war. You
remember I told you some years back Home Rule Ireland this year or
1917 when ♃ ♉. By the bye if you have no objection & I believe
that you will have none I wish you would give me yr leave to add yr
name to my list of predictions — preferably for a bad date — as more
likely to be known in 1917 with Home Rule. I recollect one but find
I have mislaid notes of predictions I did for you. This war should
shake every throne in Europe badly. When Socialism is the ruling
power in Europe any such crime will be impossible thank God!

                                          Yrs truly in the Ancient Wisdom
                                          KYMRY

PS
I hope you advertize me conversationally when you get the chance.
There was a comical letter in the Saturday Review the other week
from E. W. Wilcox who seems to have a prodigious opinion of her
own genius — in this quite equal to Marie Corelli. I wonder if a
popular ephemeral *rocket* ever realizes that it is not a comet.

From JOHN BUTLER YEATS
                                          New York
MS Yeats   14 August 1914

[Concerning Pound and "The Two Kings", see letter dated 12 May
1914.]

My dear Willie —

People everywhere (though not *all* people) are living the surface life, and Americans, led *by their women kind*, are leading the surface life with an absolute intensity. This is the gospel here and everywhere, and certain poets have taken it up and are also leading it though with nausea and a sense of its vacancy and futility. That I take to be the meaning of Ezra Pound's verses. In his work is no creation. To create means to follow desire and go *from* the surface life. Here is only criticism of the observed facts. In the hands of such poets, literature is only criticism, and Matthew Arnold is justified. With this proviso I admire very much Ezra Pound's verses — by broken meanings and broken music and plentiful use of the ellipse he gives a portentous importance and menacing significance to all the trivialities of the surface life. Yet there are people who *cannot* live the surface life — a mother or father anxious about their children, your own grandmother for instance, a man in love, *real love*, and patriotic soldiers as we see them this moment going to almost certain death. Among those who cannot live the surface life I would count *all* poets, Ezra Pound for instance. Yet their *effort to live this life shuts them out of the world of dream and desire*. Not for them the shaping power of imagination. They are exiles consoling themselves as they can, by saying things which are to convince themselves and others that they are superior beings, like poor devils in rags and out at elbows who would fain persuade you that they come of decent people, the only proof being that they are unhappy and speak with the accents of refinement and all the time professing to love their "method of existence."

So you see why I prefer your *Two Kings*, which I cannot read without tears, the intensity instantly assuaged by the rhythms of art, and the tears of sorrow mingling with the tears of beauty.

W Whitman is the exact opposite of poets like Ezra Pound. Both live the surface life, Whitman ennobling it by throwing over it every kind of glamor false and true. Ezra Pound degrades it, showing it to be unworthy and doing it with a concentration of cleverness. That excites our admiration.

Yrs affectly
J. B. YEATS

A pretty American woman said to me that she considered she had a perfect right to do what she liked providing she did not injure herself. Here you have the philosophy of the surface life. The man who would be himself lives the intense life and is neither a Walt Whitman nor an Ezra Pound.

From EVA FOWLER

                                        Brasted, Kent
MS Yeats   25 August [1914]

[When *From the Hills of Dream* (1896) was republished by Thomas B. Mosher in 1901, it included a section entitled "Foam of the Past" dedicated "To W. B. Yeats", from which Mrs Fowler quotes. Eva Focke, the girl with the whooping cough, was Mrs Fowler's niece; Yeats preserved a letter from her containing information about an occult friend of Goethe.]

Dear Mr Yeats

You will think I am cracked — but the other day I picked up "From the Hills of Dream" and was reading some of the things over again including the little dedication to Foam of the Past, to you. Perhaps you remember a bit "You have heard The Rune of the Winds, the blowing of the four white winds and the three dark winds; perhaps if you have not seen, or heard, my little Moon-Child, you remember her from long ago. . . . etc etc." My mind jumped to an odd sentence B. & I got at White Cottage last year, the night before you came. We thought it was quite mad and could not make head or tail of it. I know we showed you the paper because it had further on "J.S. W.B.Y. In Kedar's tents five years to the sea," and a drawing of an island.

The sentence I refer to — and I looked up the paper as soon as I came on Sharpe's words — is "Willie I have seen the Moon-Child." It's very odd isn't it? I don't know if it has any meaning for you but I thought I'd better tell you.

B. was coming here last week again but was prevented. We've missed you but I'm glad you are at the work.

Eva has whooping cough so I had to put off the Pounds and the Dulacs who were coming this month. There has been nothing of any particular interest. Mrs Rendel thinks she knows what that 7th Division of Three may mean. It came three times.

                                        All greetings to you
                                        EVA FOWLER